INSIDERS' GUIDE® TO
RALEIGH, DURHAM & CHAPEL HILL

HELP US KEEP THIS GUIDE UP-TO-DATE

We would love to hear from you concerning your experiences with this guide and how you feel it could be improved and kept up-to-date. Please send your comments and suggestions to:

editorial@GlobePequot.com

Thanks for your input, and happy travels!

INSIDERS' GUIDE® SERIES

INSIDERS' GUIDE® TO

RALEIGH, DURHAM & CHAPEL HILL

FIRST EDITION

AMBER NIMOCKS

INSIDERS' GUIDE

GUILFORD, CONNECTICUT
AN IMPRINT OF GLOBE PEQUOT PRESS

All the information in this guidebook is subject to change. We recommend that you call ahead to obtain current information before traveling.

To buy books in quantity for corporate use or incentives, call **(800) 962–0973** or e-mail **premiums@GlobePequot.com**.

INSIDERS' GUIDE ®

Editor: Amy Lyons
Project Editor: Lynn Zelem
Layout artist: Kevin Mak
Text design: Sheryl Kober
Maps by Nick Trotter © Morris Book Publishing, LLC

Library of Congress Cataloging-in-Publication Data is available on file.

ISBN 978-0-7627-5700-8

Printed in the United States of America
10 9 8 7 6 5 4 3 2 1

This book is dedicated to the generations of visionaries who have worked hard to make their dreams come true in central North Carolina. Explorers, patriots, civil rights leaders, intellectuals, entrepreneurs, artists, and dreamers have all helped shape the unique character of the Triangle. It's also for all the interesting people who took a chance and moved here, then stuck around.

CONTENTS

Directory of Maps

ABOUT THE AUTHOR

Amber Nimocks is a graduate of the University of North Carolina at Chapel Hill, where she fell in love first with shrimp and grits at Crook's Corner and then with journalism at *The Daily Tar Heel*. She holds a degree in religious studies. Her 15-year career in newspapers included stints at her hometown paper, *The Fayetteville Observer*, the *Wilmington Star-News*, the *Fort Worth Star-Telegram*, and *The News & Observer of Raleigh*, where she was food editor until 2008. She is the food editor for *The Independent Weekly* and serves as associate editor of *Edible Piedmont* magazine. She is also a contributing producer for "The State of Things" a public radio talk show on WUNC-FM. Her work has appeared in *Our State* magazine, *The Washington Post* and other major newspapers. Her favorite place outside of North Carolina, is the Dingle Peninsula of Ireland. She lives with her husband Josh, her son Sam, and her two dogs, Ava and Senora Wences, in downtown Raleigh.

ACKNOWLEDGMENTS

Thank you to the many friends and associates who shared their favorite Triangle places and things with me, both while I was writing this book and simply as a matter of friendship. One of the greatest things about this place is how much people love to pass on their secret finds and passions.

A special thank you to Sarah Lindenfeld-Hall and Illyse Lane, who put me in touch with my agent Julie Hill, whose support and enthusiasm have been invaluable, and to my editor Amy Lyons, who gave me the chance to write about my home, which has been a true pleasure.

Extra special thanks go to my mom and dad, Quincy and Debbie Nimocks, and my in-laws, Tom and Nancy Shaffer and Dave and Jo Gadsby, who helped keep Sammy happy and busy while Mommy wrote. And more gratitude and love than I can measure go to my husband Josh Shaffer, whose deep knowledge of and passion for our home delight me, and who had the bright idea to move here in the first place.

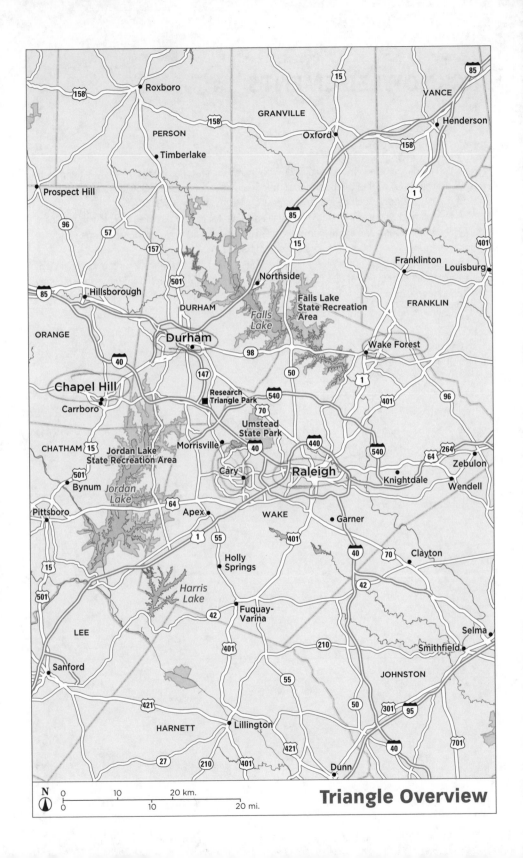

Triangle Overview

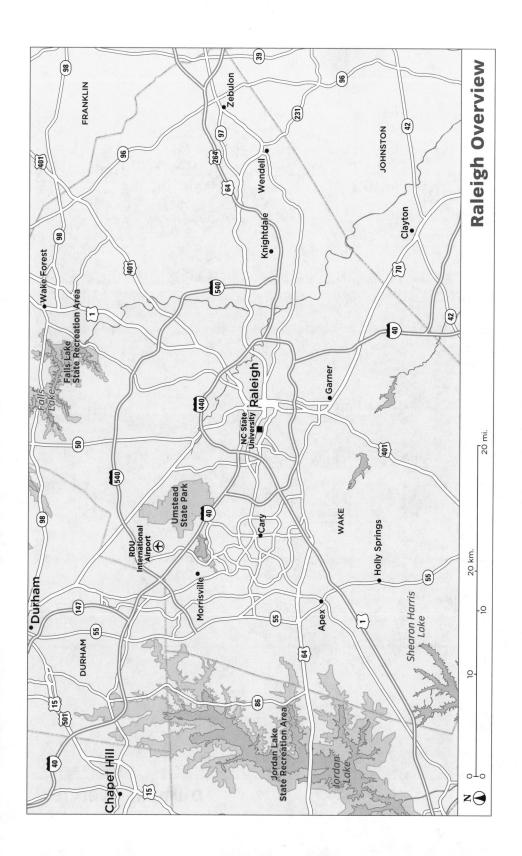

Raleigh Overview

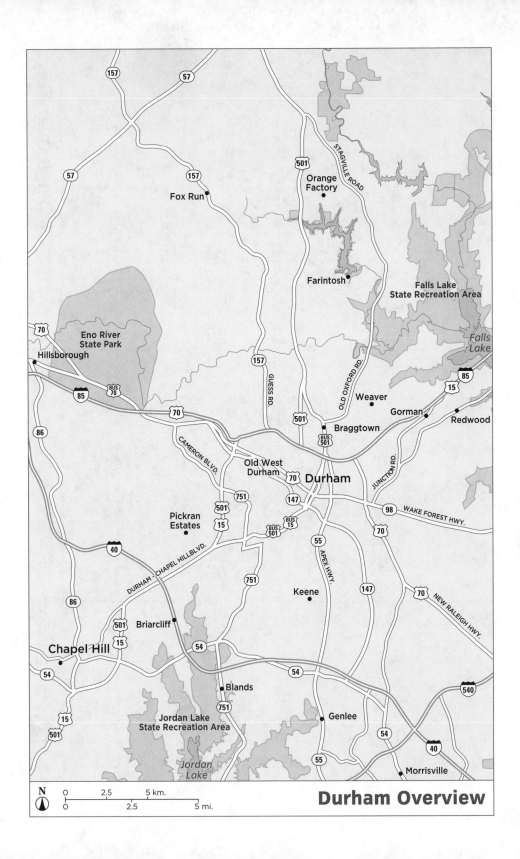

Durham Overview

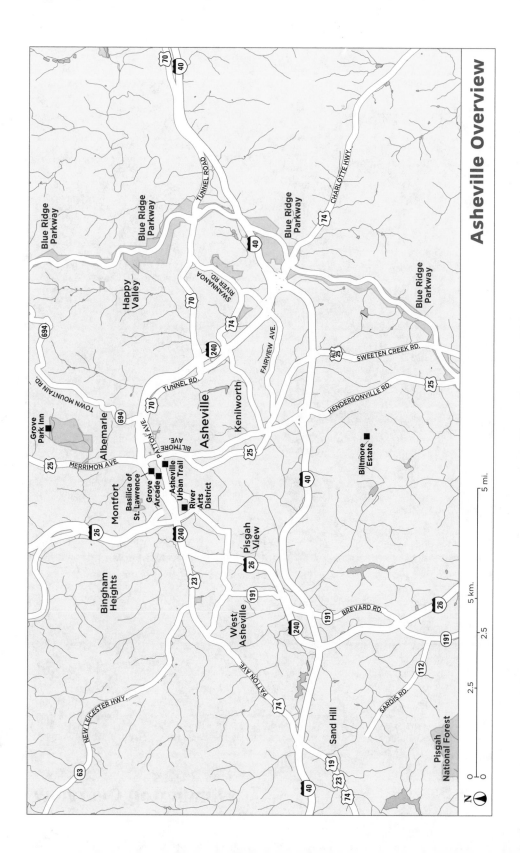

Asheville Overview

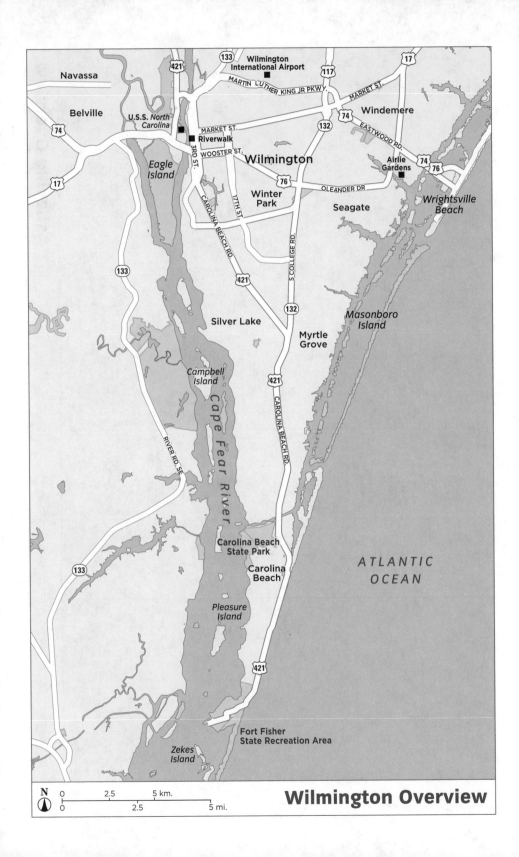

Navassa

Belville

U.S.S. *North Carolina*

Eagle Island

Wilmington International Airport

MARTIN LUTHER KING JR PKWY.

MARKET ST.

Windemere

EASTWOOD RD.

MARKET ST.

3RD ST.

Riverwalk

WOOSTER ST.

Wilmington

Winter Park

Airlie Gardens

Wrightsville Beach

OLEANDER DR

CAROLINA BEACH RD.

17TH ST.

Seagate

S COLLEGE RD.

Masonboro Island

Silver Lake

Myrtle Grove

Campbell Island

Cape Fear River

RIVER RD. SE

CAROLINA BEACH RD.

ATLANTIC OCEAN

Carolina Beach State Park

Carolina Beach

Pleasure Island

Fort Fisher State Recreation Area

Zekes Island

N

0   2.5   5 km.

0   2.5   5 mi.

Wilmington Overview

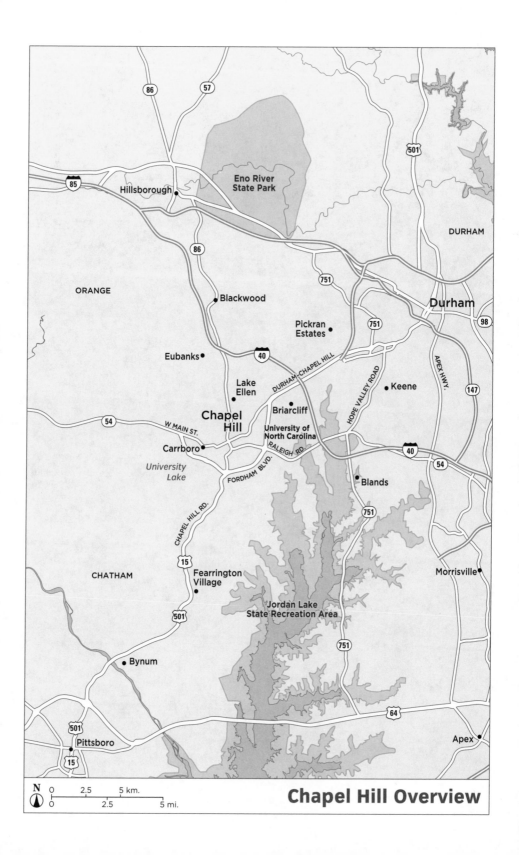

Chapel Hill Overview

PREFACE

When I first moved to the Triangle, I knew I belonged here. It was 1989, and I was a 17-year-old fresh-man at the University of North Carolina at Chapel Hill. Though I had spent most of my life in Fayetteville, just an hour south, my new home seemed a world away from where I had grown up. I spent hours walking beneath the shady, old hardwoods on campus, stumbling upon new monuments and histori-cal tidbits. One day I discovered a memorial to North Carolina–born author Thomas Wolfe, hidden in a forgotten nook near the old journalism school. A moss-covered bas-relief angel inscribed with the haunting phrase, "O lost, and by the wind grieved, ghost, come back again," it made me feel like the place had secrets to tell me.

A dozen or so years later, I returned to the Triangle, this time to Raleigh. We bought a house downtown, where we could walk to work. Again, I was enchanted by the place's understated beauty and the memorials I found along my walks: a pair of gargoyles salvaged from a razed high school, the enormous pot belly on the statue of Governor Zebulon B. Vance, the simple stone marking President Andrew Johnson's birthplace on Fayetteville Street. But I also discovered there is much more to Raleigh and Chapel Hill than historical markers and sleepy stories.

Long a magnet for intellectuals and progressives, the Triangle blossomed in recent decades into a mecca for business and groundbreaking technological and scientific research. The Research Triangle Park, dreamed up by 1950s visionaries looking to bring brain power to the region, does just that. Thousands of people from across the country and the globe have flocked to Raleigh, Durham, and Chapel Hill and the no-longer-tiny towns around them. The business climate, combined with the weather, affordable housing, and respected public schools keep landing the Triangle and its towns on the media's "best" lists—best place to start a business, best place to raise a family, best place to live.

What you'll discover is that the lists are right. While the Triangle will never compete with places like New York City for glamour, its rewards are many and its demands are few. In the Triangle, you can see world-class works of art, watch internationally renowned modern dance and ballet, and cheer on national champions without fighting the crowds and paying the prices that residents of many other larger cities do. Institutions like the Nasher Museum of Art at Duke University and the new North Caro-lina Museum of Art in Raleigh and organizations like the Carolina Ballet and the Carolina Hurricanes have boosted the Triangle's quality of life and helped forge its national reputation.

Likewise, you can eat a meal every night that would inspire envy in members of the national food press. A thriving farm-to-table scene, an influx of talented, ambitious chefs, and an increasingly adventurous eating public have made the Triangle one of the most respected dining areas in the country. Between these influences, and the melting pot of food cultures that new Triangle residents have brought with them from across the country and around the world, it has become a darn good place to eat.

Knowing that their good reputations are their golden geese, government leaders across the Tri-angle focus on making sound decisions and planning for growth. In general, municipal services are good, and policy making is progressive. Plus, voters are involved. When *The Daily Beast* ranked Raleigh-Durham the smartest city in America in 2009, it considered a number of factors. The area scored big on the education factor, since it has one of the highest rates of PhDs in the country, but it also racked up points for high voter participation.

Beyond the amenities, it really is the people that make the Triangle a great place to live. Between the homegrown Southern hospitality and the willingness of newcomers to make friends, people are welcoming here. The weather doesn't hurt either. Rarely does the mercury dip below 40°F in the winter, which means folks are out and about. Sure, August can be sweltering, but most people see that as a reason to ask friends over for a cold drink.

When we decided to have our child in Raleigh, I knew it was truly my home. I began to see it through new eyes, and fell in love all over again with all the ways the community cares for children. Fabulous museums like Marbles in Raleigh and the Museum of Life and Science in Durham, and parks like Raleigh's Pullen and Cary's Kids Together (aka "the Dragon Park") are part of the scene. But so are the approaches that so many institutions take in catering to little ones' needs, like the children's-only pediatric emergency room at WakeMed and the top-notch neonatal care available at UNC Hospital and Duke. These places make a real difference in children's lives.

Since returning to the Triangle, I've continued to explore attractions like its celebrated restaurants and art museums. I've also kept my eye out for discoveries in quiet nooks. On an early morning walk through UNC's campus recently I found that the Thomas Wolfe memorial I loved as a freshman had been moved from its moldy alcove to a more prominent place on campus. "How could they?" was my first thought. But my dismay quickly gave way to delight in knowing that more eyes would see the lovely statue and recall the writing of one of North Carolina's most famous native sons. Much like the Triangle, the monument has moved to its rightful place in the sun.

Insiders' Guide to Raleigh, Durham & Chapel Hill aims to help you discover the many wonderful aspects of spending time in our region, whether you're here for a weekend or for the rest of your life. Take your time and walk around a bit under the shade of the hardwoods. You might find you want to stay longer than you intended.

HOW TO USE THIS BOOK

If you are new to the Triangle or if this is your first visit, the best place to start is the book's Area Overview. This chapter provides a lay of the land, giving you sketches of the many communities and cities that make up the Triangle. After that, take a look at the Getting Here, Getting Around chapter. Once you are oriented, the rest of the information should fall into place.

Because you will no doubt be hungry before too long, move onto the Restaurants chapter. It is not a complete listing of every eatery in the Triangle, but aims to offer a range of options throughout the region. Because the Triangle has so many outstanding restaurants, it is the largest chapter. In most of the book, information is organized by categories and then by town. The Restaurant chapter is an exception. Restaurants are listed by category and then divided into the geographical designations "Chapel Hill–Durham" and "Raleigh-Cary." Chapel Hill and Durham are side by side in the western part of the Triangle, while Raleigh and Cary are adjacent to one another in the east. It's fairly common for residents of these pairs of cities to travel to their closest neighboring town for a meal.

While you're eating or after you've returned to your room, peruse the History section. It will tell you the origins of the names for the new places you're visiting. Why, for example, does everything in Durham seem to be named Duke or reference the tobacco industry—the American Tobacco Complex, Brightleaf Square, even the Durham Bulls? Did Sir Walter Raleigh found Raleigh? Where was Black Wall Street?

If you're looking for entertainment, check the Annual Events chapter to see what special happenings will be taking place during your stay. Warm months, especially spring and fall, bring a slate of weekend festivals and street parties to the Triangle.

Are you considering a move to the Triangle or do you already live here? Be sure to check out the blue-tabbed pages at the back of the book, where you will find the **Living Here** appendix that offers sections on relocation, real estate, education, health care, and media.

In compiling *Insiders' Guide to Raleigh, Durham & Chapel Hill*, the goal was to offer information that was as up to date and complete as possible. Nonetheless, the world changes rapidly. Even longstanding events and well-established institutions can vanish overnight. Please call numbers or visit Web sites before heading out on an adventure to avoid disappointment.

AREA OVERVIEW

The 1.5 million people who inhabit the patch of land covered in this book don't often refer to home as "the Triangle." And no such creature as a "Trianglite" or "Trianglian" exists. The Triangle came to be in 1959 when a group of business leaders and educators established the Research Triangle Park (RTP) with the goal of creating an economic synergy between North Carolina's three most prominent universities. So they drew three imaginary lines to create an imaginary scalene triangle with North Carolina State University in Raleigh as the east point, Duke University in Durham roughly in the center, and the University of North Carolina at Chapel Hill in the west. In the midst they planted RTP, an infrastructure dedicated to economic and intellectual growth and research. Thanks to the universities and the high-technology industry, the Triangle is today home to one of the highest concentrations of PhDs in the country.

People who live in the Triangle refer to themselves, often proudly, as residents of Durham or Chapel Hill or Raleigh or Cary or any of the other smaller but thriving communities within easy range of RTP. Dependent as they are upon their shared association as the Triangle, each community retains an individuality that helps strengthen the character and appeal of the region. If there's a bit of good-natured civic rivalry, it serves to spur progressive growth, as no one wants to be seen as the lagging corner.

The region covered in this book includes Wake, Durham, and Orange counties primarily, and parts of Johnston and Chatham counties. The focus is on the towns that are economically and socially tied to RTP and to the core communities of Raleigh, Durham, and Chapel Hill. Most of the outlying communities are former farm towns now morphing into bedroom communities as population growth and suburban development radiate from the center of the Triangle. Clayton, on the western edge of Johnston County, marks the southeastern edge of the region. Its residents can commute easily to the Triangle's core via U.S. 70. The small Wake County town of Holly Springs is the southwestern edge. Much of Chatham County to the west of the Triangle lies outside the Triangle's sphere of influence, but growth spreading southward from Chapel Hill is changing Pittsboro and the area to its north. To the north of Chapel Hill, Hillsborough is experiencing similar effects. The city of Durham marks the northwestern reach of the Triangle. In Wake County, Zebulon marks the eastern edge of the Triangle, and nearby towns like Wake Forest and Rolesville are growing at a steady clip.

With the exception of rush-hour slowdowns and gridlock caused by university sporting events or happenings at the RBC Center in Raleigh, traversing the Triangle is usually easy. Between downtown Chapel Hill, the western edge of the core, and downtown Raleigh, the core's eastern point, lies a distance of little more than 30 miles. Between the farthest reaches of the Triangle, Hillsborough in the northwest to Clayton in the southeast, is only 55 miles of asphalt, most of it interstate highway. These are factors to consider when deciding whether an activity or site is a feasible day trip. Conversely, population concentrations in areas like North Raleigh or Chapel Hill can turn what might have been a quick errand trip into an exercise in snarl navigation. Luckily, amenities are spread evenly throughout the region, so what you need is usually within easy reach. That the Triangle gives you the option of making life easy on yourself is among its virtues.

CHATHAM COUNTY

On the western edge of the Triangle, Chatham County's 682 square miles are home to about 63,000, most of whom live outside the county's incorporated areas. Scores of artists and craft makers live and work in studios sprinkled around the county's remote areas. The county is also fertile ground for farmers who employ sustainable methods, shunning the chemical pesticides and fertilizers of industrial farming in favor of biodynamic and organic practices. Strong support organizations promote the work of both farmers and artists in the county, including a sustainable agriculture program at Central Carolina Community College's Pittsboro campus. Proximity to urban centers provides markets for the products of these rural enterprises.

In the past two decades, residential and retail development has crept down from Chapel Hill in Orange County, just north of Chatham County, along U.S. 15-501. The challenges posed by growth pit the interests of those who prize the county's status as a rural haven against those who welcome the increased revenues of development. Political issues aside, a ride through the gentle hills of Chatham County's countryside provides a lovely escape from the more hectic pace in the busier parts of the Triangle.

Bynum

A former cotton mill village that grew up along the banks of the Haw River, Bynum is 8 miles south of Chapel Hill and 4 miles north of Pittsboro but feels a century removed from both. Founded in the late 19th century, the unincorporated community of a couple hundred declined after its mill closed in the 1970s. By the turn of the 21st century only the wooden Bynum General Store remained in business. That closed for business in 2006, but neighbors have since revived a popular Friday night music series that served as a social gathering before the store's demise. Neighbors organized a non-profit under the name Bynum Front Porch that stages a musical series on Friday nights May through October and other events throughout the year. Events in Bynum often draw

its most famous resident, folk artist Clyde Jones, who uses chainsaws to craft logs into "critters." It's worth a trip to take a look at Jones's critter-cluttered yard on Bynum Road and his creatures in neighbors' yards. Bynum Road is right off U.S. 15-501. As they say, blink and you'll miss it.

Fearrington Village

In sharp contrast to downtown Pittsboro's grass-roots, New-Age hippy vibe is Fearrington Village, 9 miles north on U.S. 15-501. A dairy farm stood on the property until the early 1970s when the Fearrington family that had owned the land for generations decided to sell. Developers R. B. and Jenny Fitch bought the 640 acres and created their ideal English village. Today, it is home to 1,800 or so residents who enjoy meticulously manicured English gardens, a croquet lawn, tennis courts, a bookstore, gift shops, a wellness center, and several eateries, among them the highly regarded Fearrington House Restaurant. It is housed in the charmingly restored 1927 farmhouse that the original owners built. The village's signature Belted Galloway cows—black with tidy white stripes around their middles—graze in the surrounding green pastures, completing the bucolic picture. The village is open to non-residents, and the property also includes the internationally recognized Fearrington House Inn, a lovely setting for a special weekend away. The village is a popular wedding site, and it offers start-to-finish packages. The annual Fearrington Folk Art Show fills the village's vast barn meeting space with interesting outsider works from across the Southeast. (For more on the Fearrington Folk Art Show, see the Annual Events chapter.)

Pittsboro

The seat of Chatham County, Pittsboro is on the eastern edge of the county less than 10 miles from Jordan Lake. North-south highway U.S. 15-501 and east-west highway U.S. 64 intersect at a traffic circle. In the middle of the circle sit the ruins of the county's 1881 courthouse. The courthouse was still in use until early 2010, when a fire gutted it. The county hopes to rebuild it.

Raleigh-Durham–Chapel Hill Vital Statistics

Important dates in history: Sir Walter Raleigh's "Lost Colony" disappears from North Carolina's Outer Banks, leaving behind just the word "Croatan" carved on a tree, 1590; Charles II of England grants charter to Lords Proprietors for the Carolinas, 1663; North Carolina is the first colony to officially authorize its Continental Congress delegates to vote for independence, April 1776; Raleigh named state capital, 1788; North Carolina secedes from the United States, 1861; Wright brothers achieve first manned flight at Kill Devil Hills, 1903; Research Triangle Park established, 1959.

Alcohol:

> **Drinking age:** 21
> **DUI:** 0.08 or higher for those 21 and older; 0 for those under 21; 0.04 for commercial drivers.
> **Sunday sales:** No alcoholic beverage sales are allowed between 2 a.m. and noon on Sunday.
> **Bar sales:** End daily at 2 a.m.
> **Sales locations:** Government-run ABC stores sell liquor. Private shops and supermarkets sell wine and beer. Local ordinances govern availability.

Capital of North Carolina: Raleigh

Major metropolitan area cities: Durham, Durham County; Chapel Hill, Orange County; Cary, Raleigh, Wake County.

Outlying counties: Durham, Johnston, Chatham, Orange.

Population:

> **City of Raleigh:** 385,000
> **Metro area:** 1.5 million
> **State of North Carolina:** 9.2 million

Average temperatures:

> **July:** 79 degrees
> **January:** 39 degrees

Major universities: Duke University, Meredith College, North Carolina State University, North Carolina Central University, Peace College, University of North Carolina at Chapel Hill, Shaw University, St. Augustine's College.

Major area employers: Cisco Systems, Duke University Health System, GlaxoSmithKline, IBM, Merck & Co., NetApp, Nortel Networks, Novo Nordisk, SAS Institute, University of North Carolina, UNC Hospitals, Wake County Public Schools, WakeMed.

Triangle Area's famous sons and daughters: Andrew Johnson, 17th president of the United States; Ava Gardner, mid-20th-century movie star; Michael C. Hall, actor; Emily Proctor, actor; Evan Rachel Wood, actor; Shirley Caesar, gospel singer; James Taylor, singer-songwriter; Clay Aiken, pop singer; Michael Malone, author; David Sedaris, humorist.

State holidays:

> **January:** New Year's Day, Martin Luther King Jr. Birthday
> **March or April:** Good Friday
> **May:** Memorial Day
> **July:** Independence Day
> **September:** Labor Day
> **November:** Veterans' Day, Thanksgiving
> **December:** Christmas

Major airports: Raleigh-Durham International

Major interstates: I-40, I-440, I-540, I-85

Driving laws:

> **Car seats:** required for children under 8 years old or weighing less than 80 pounds.
>
> **Right turn on red:** after a complete stop, unless posted otherwise.
>
> **Seat belts:** required for all passengers older than 8 years old.
>
> **Headlights:** required when operating windshield wipers during inclement weather.

Established in 1787, Pittsboro vied to be the state capital and the home of the University of North Carolina in the late 18th century but lost out to nearby Raleigh and Chapel Hill, respectively. The town was not connected to the rest of the state via railroad until relatively late, in 1885.

Today Pittsboro is home to around 3,000 people. Its profile has changed in the past two decades from a sleepy stop on the highway to a bastion of progressive businesses and locavore sensibilities. Piedmont Biofuels manufactures and sells alternative energy for diesel automobiles east of downtown at 220 Lorax Lane. The Pittsboro General Store Cafe serves a menu heavy with local and sustainable ingredients—including its famous green chili burrito—and welcomes local musicians, artists, and activists in a former Chevrolet dealership across from the courthouse. Chatham Marketplace co-op grocery and deli sells local produce and other foodstuffs. Antique shops, crafts galleries, and consignment stores dot the main streets. A dozen businesses in Pittsboro accept an alternative local currency, the NC Plenty.

DURHAM

Durham County's 290 square miles are home to more than 260,000 people. Its only incorporated area is Durham, where the majority of its residents live. American Indian tribes including the Eno and Occoneechee lived and established trading routes across the area for centuries before the first European explorers and settlers came to

the area in the 1700s. Revolutionaries were active in Durham County in the early 1770s, before the Declaration of Independence was signed. Most of the land outside the city of Durham has long been dedicated to agriculture, and in 1860, Durham County was home to Stagville, the largest plantation in the state. Today Durham County has one of the most racially diverse populations in the Triangle with 56 percent of its residents white, 37 percent black, 12 percent Hispanic, and 4 percent Asian.

The city of Durham is emerging from a 20th century largely defined by its relationship with big tobacco and the textile industry to make way for a more diversified future. The hulking warehouses that dot the city, former homes of cigarette manufacturing plants and cotton looms, are being transformed into airy loft apartments, art studios, restaurants, offices, and university space. The handsome red-brick home of the city's minor league baseball team, the Durham Bulls, and the new gleaming glass Durham Performing Arts Center help draw people downtown. Durham's revitalized areas manage to capture both the essence of the city's past and its hopes for this century.

Durham put itself on the map with a train station in 1853. Dr. Bartlett Durham donated the land for the station and lent his name to the town. The city incorporated in 1869. After the Civil War, soldiers who had passed through Durham and other parts of the tobacco-growing South retained a fondness for the light-tasting bright-leaf tobacco they had found there. Demand for bright-leaf came from all over the country. Sales took off, making Durham a tobacco market and a cigarette-manufacturing hub. By 1890, the family of Washington Duke owned the American Tobacco Company, the largest tobacco conglomerate in the world. Tobacco would remain the city's mainstay for a century. As late as the 1990s, the scent of stored tobacco wafting from the warehouses perfumed the summer air in the streets of downtown Durham. Industrialization begat industrialization at the turn of the 20th century, and Durham became home to large textile mills and the mill house villages that accompanied them.

The city owes much to higher education as well. Duke University, née Trinity College, moved to town in 1887 and adopted the family's name after a $40 million grant from James Buchanan Duke in 1924. In 1910, Dr. James E. Shepard founded the National Religious Training School and Chautauqua, the first public African-American liberal arts school in the country. Today it is North Carolina Central University, part of the University of North Carolina system. The African-American community in Durham has a long history of prosperity stemming from the early 20th-century founding of North Carolina Mutual Life Insurance Company and M&F Bank, which anchored a district of thriving African American–owned businesses known as Black Wall Street.

The departure of manufacturing and the decline of big tobacco took a toll on Durham in the 1980s and '90s. Violence marred its reputation. But today, the Bull City is North Carolina's fourth largest metropolitan area, boosted by nearby Research Triangle Park and the success of internationally renowned Duke University Medical Center, the county's largest employer. Affordable housing is drawing creative types to the city's core and helping it refashion its image. Durham's edgy vibe endears it to those who find other Triangle towns homogeneous. Among its more famous residents are jazz artists Branford Marsalis and Nnenna Freelon, hip-hop producer Ninth Wonder, and author Frances Mayes. It can also claim some of the best farm-to-table restaurants and chefs in the area. Those distinctions prompted *Bon Appetit* to name Durham-Chapel Hill "America's Foodiest Small Town" in 2008, an honor marred only by the fact that the magazine merged the two municipalities without their consent.

JOHNSTON COUNTY

Clayton

Growth from the Triangle is changing the western edges of Johnston County, most notice-

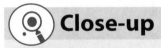

Close-up

Town Nicknames

A colorful nickname can lend a place cachet, especially if there's a good story behind it. In the Triangle, Durham wins the nickname game with "the Bull City," a reference to the town's past as a tobacco powerhouse that Hollywood immortalized with *Bull Durham*. The name comes from one of Durham's earliest tobacco purveyors, John Ruffin Green, who trademarked his product with a bull, inspired by the bull on British Colman's Mustard. The tobacco came to be known as Bull Durham. Today, an iconic bull decorates an exterior wall of the American Tobacco Historic Complex and another stands guard over left field of the Durham Athletic Park. Raleigh, meanwhile, is called the City of Oaks. Inspiration for the nickname is evident in the older parts of the city, where oaks tower over city parks and historic sites. The new light towers adorning City Plaza are decorated with oak leaves, and on New Year's Eve, the city drops a 1,250-pound acorn sculpture to mark a fresh calendar, an homage to the big ball drop in New York. The rest of the year, the giant acorn sits on its post in Moore Square, waiting for its chance to shine.

ably in and around the town of Clayton. The county's population grew by 34 percent in the past decade, to about 164,000 people, making it one of the fastest growing counties in the country. Around 9,000 of those people live in Clayton, which is about 20 miles from Raleigh and 35 miles from Research Triangle Park. Incorporated in 1869, Clayton's fortunes have ebbed and flowed with the tides of tobacco, cotton, and textiles like many small North Carolina towns. Today it has a stable economy based on its role as a bedroom community and a few key employers including Caterpillar, Talecris, and Novo Nordisk. The recently restored Clayton Center, formerly a schoolhouse, brings national and regional entertainers to town, and Clayton's historic downtown thrives with a variety of restaurants, a coffee shop, a couple of art galleries, and gift shops.

ORANGE COUNTY

Around 126,000 people live in Orange County, mainly in the towns of Chapel Hill, Carrboro, and Hillsborough. The county was founded in 1752. Its oldest community and the seat of county government is Hillsborough, which was settled by Quakers along the Haw River. For most of the past 200 years, Hillsborough stood fairly isolated from Chapel Hill, its neighbor a dozen miles to the south. But growth along the I-40 corridor is bringing the municipalities closer together. Just west of Hillsborough, I-40 merges with the north-south connector I-85, making the area convenient for commuters to Durham and to Burlington and the Triad to the west. The land is hillier in this northwestern corner of the Triangle as it climbs toward the North Carolina mountains. Farms dot Orange County's 400 square miles, many of them plots of 100 acres or fewer that supply the increasing number of farmers' markets in the population centers.

Carrboro

Next door to Chapel Hill, Carrboro relishes its reputation as the "Paris of the Piedmont." Spend an afternoon eating, listening to music, and people-watching on the lawn of the town's co-op grocery, Weaver Street Market, and it's easy to understand why. Populated by 19,000 or so residents, Carrboro is home to professors and academics as well as UNC grads and other professionals attracted by the university's liberal politics. Community involvement in civic matters and the arts is high. Coffee shops, locally owned restaurants, art and craft galleries, and the renowned Carrboro Farmers' Market are popular meeting places. Like Pittsboro, the town has many businesses that accept the local currency, the Plenty.

The community was settled in 1882 to serve as a railroad stop for the university. Incorporated in 1911, Carrboro was primarily a textile mill town and home for lower-paid university workers for the first half of the 20th century. The turn of the 21st century saw it experiencing rapid growth. Between 1960 and 2000, Carrboro's population had grown from 2,000 to more than 16,000. Prudent management of that growth earned the town a national reputation for good government. It has the highest population density in the state, which means parking spots are scarce. Fortunately, the town is compact and very walkable. It also has a free bus system and excellent bike paths.

Chapel Hill

Affectionately known as the "Southern Part of Heaven," the town of Chapel Hill is defined by its role as the home of the University of North Carolina. Chartered in 1793, UNC enrolled its first student, Hinton James, in 1795, making it the oldest public university in the country. Today, UNC enrolls more than 28,000 students and serves as the flagship of the 16-school University of North Carolina system. Students and faculty make up the bulk of Chapel Hill's population of more than 48,000. The school's 729-acre campus stretches from Franklin Street in the north to the Dean E. Smith Center in the south. The oldest part of the campus, bordered by Franklin, Raleigh, South, and Columbia streets, is its loveliest. Giant oaks and poplars shade a scattering of monuments that stand between the 19th- and early 20th-century buildings set along wide brick paths. The school's symbol, the Old Well, a small, columned rotunda, stands beside Cameron Avenue. Visitors to the town will notice the predominance of light blue, aka Carolina blue, both on the backs of students and on signs around town. The neighborhoods surrounding the university maintain the lovely wooded aesthetic of the campus and include three historic districts—the Franklin-Rosemary District, the Cameron-McCauley District and the Gimghoul District.

The early years of Chapel Hill were defined by UNC's development as a small, male-only classics-centered university. The scope of the school's mission changed during the 19th century to include more emphasis on scientific research. By the beginning of the Civil War, Chapel Hill was a thriving rural village. UNC remained open during the war and federal troops spared the town and the school when they occupied Chapel Hill beginning in 1865. But the university suffered during the bleak years of Reconstruction, closing from 1870 to 1875. Shortly after reopening, the university began offering medical courses, laying the groundwork for today's UNC Hospitals, the town's second largest employer after the university.

During the 20th century, the university and Chapel Hill developed a reputation for liberal politics beginning with the tenure of left-leaning UNC President Frank Porter Graham in the 1930s. Protests and sit-ins occurred regularly during the racial desegregation movement of the 1960s and '70s. The state legislature's 1963 speaker ban, which prohibited known Communists from speaking on state campuses, met with massive student opposition and a lawsuit that saw it overturned. It is said that North Carolina's longtime conservative senator Jesse Helms would not step foot in Chapel Hill.

In the past decade, the town's highly regarded public school system and rich quality of life have begun to draw transplants not necessarily affiliated with the university, spurring development on the town's south side and into Chatham County. Growth management is a key issue in town council and school board elections.

Hillsborough

Human settlement has thrived on the land near the headwaters of the Eno River for centuries, starting with American Indian settlements as early as A.D. 1,000 European settlers arrived in the mid-1700s and established Orange, which later became Hillsborough. In the 1760s and '70s, Hillsborough was a hotbed of anti-government sentiment known as the Regulator movement. Upland farmers angry at being taxed by what they viewed as a corrupt and indulgent ruling class on the coast staged a rebellion against the Colonial government. That rebellion was quelled, but Hillsborough remained politically active through the mid-19th century. More than 100 late 18th- and 19th-century buildings stand as reminders of the town's prominence in this period.

Today Hillsborough is a quaint but modern village of more than 5,000 residents. On Churton Street, the main drive through the historic district, are a number of art and craft galleries, a wine shop, a coffee shop, a branch of the Carrboro-based Weaver Street Grocery co-op, several eateries, and the Wooden Nickel, a true local watering hole. It is home to a number of writers, including bestselling authors Allan Gurganus, Michael Malone, and Lee Smith.

RESEARCH TRIANGLE PARK

The intersection of I-40 and N.C. 147 marks the approximate center of Research Triangle Park. Leaders in business, politics, and education spearheaded the formation of the park, which opened in 1959. It was a visionary attempt to steer the state's economy in the direction of emerging technologies that continues to fuel economic growth today. RTP's aim was to give research-oriented companies easy access to area universities and economic incentives to locate there. Included in the park's mission was a directive to maintain the land, which means trees and green space frame the corporate campuses.

RTP founders' efforts began to pay off in 1965, when IBM announced plans to build a

600,000-square-foot research facility in the park, necessitating the move of hundreds of technology workers to the area, especially from the Northeast. Fans of humorist David Sedaris will recall that the IBM move brought him and his family to Raleigh, where many of his biographical essays are set. Today, about 40,000 people work in RTP, bringing in more than $2.7 billion in salaries that help boost the local average salary to between 5 and 15 percent higher than the national average. The 7,000-square-foot park is home to close to 140 research and development facilities concentrated in chemicals, electronics, communications, engineering, and management services. RTP residents include IBM, Nortel, Glaxo-SmithKline, Cisco, BASF, and the National Institute of Environmental Health Sciences among many others. Projects undertaken at RTP have resulted in Nobel prizes and countless patents. The influx of intelligence has contributed to growth outside the park's borders as computer companies including Red Hat and SAS have thrived nearby.

WAKE COUNTY

Wake County is the most populous and fastest-growing county in the Triangle, with more than 860,000 residents in 830 square miles. In 2007–2008, the Raleigh-Cary metro area was one of the two fastest growing in the country, alongside Austin, Texas. The area has been racking up accolades for more than a decade, and every year another round of media mentions keeps Wake County and its cities in the news—one of the best places to start a small business, America's smartest city, best place to raise a family, best small town, etc.

Outside of its highly developed areas, Wake County's landscape quickly changes from urban to rural along the roads that lead to its smaller towns. Few corners of Wake County remain untouched by population growth. But if you drive east beyond the reach of Raleigh, amid the remaining tobacco farms and soybean fields, you get a sense of what most of the county and the state were like for much of the 20th century.

Created in 1771, the county is named for Margaret Wake, wife of William Tryon, North

Carolina's royal governor at the time. Lawmakers didn't name it the site of the new state capital until 1788. It wasn't until 1794 that state legislators met for the first time in Raleigh's statehouse.

Apex and Holly Springs

Just west of Cary along U.S. 1, Apex has grown from a former railroad town of 5,000 to a thriving suburb of more than 30,000 in the past 20 years. Its location at the intersection of U.S. 1 and N.C. 55 makes it easily accessible from Cary and RTP. The completion of the I-540 loop around Apex, expected for 2012, will no doubt continue its growth spurt. Apex takes it name from its former status as the highest point on the Chatham Railroad, which connected Richmond, Virginia, and Jacksonville, Florida, beginning in the mid-1800s. The town's motto is "Peak of Good Living," and Apex Peakway, not parkway, skirts its historic downtown. The downtown, a National Register of Historic Places district, is quaint and vibrant with shops and eateries in restored late 19th- and early 20th-century buildings.

Until the recent population surge, Holly Springs could have been described as Apex's skinny little sister. Lacking a railroad connection, the town languished for much of its 200-year history. Just south of Apex on N.C. 55, Holly Springs has seen similar growth. Its population of less than 1,000 in 1990 surpassed 17,000 by 2006. The many quiet subdivisions springing up around the two towns offer affordable housing options and a sense of retreat from the nearby hustle.

In addition to thousands of new residents, Holly Springs also became home to a brewery in recent years. Carolina Brewing Company, with its roaring lion logo, makes a range of beers at its Holly Springs facility. Its pale ale is easy to find at stores and restaurants throughout the Triangle. Tasting tours are offered every Saturday.

Cary

Just a few exits south of RTP on I-40, Cary was among the first communities to experience considerable growth related to the park, beginning in the late 1960s. A high population of transplants

Visitor Information Centers

Tourism and relocation are big business in North Carolina and the Triangle. A number of government agencies can help you find information on what you're interested in. In Raleigh, the Capital Area Visitors Center is where to start if you want to arrange tours of state government–owned sites such as the State Capitol or the Executive Mansion.

The N.C. Department of Commerce's Division of Tourism, Film and Sports Development
301 North Wilmington St., Raleigh
(919) 733-4151
www.visitnc.com

Chapel Hill and Orange County Visitors Bureau
501 West Franklin St., Chapel Hill
(888) 968-2060
www.visitchapelhill.org

Capital Area Visitors Center
N.C. Museum of History Lobby
5 East Edenton St., Raleigh
(919) 807-7950
(866) 724-8687
www.ncmuseumofhistory.org

Durham Convention and Visitors Bureau
101 East Morgan St., Durham
(800) 446-8604
(919) 687-0288
www.durham-nc.com

Johnston County Convention and Visitors Bureau
1535-A Booker Dairy Rd., Smithfield
(800) 441-7829
(919) 989-8687
www.johnstoncountync.org

Raleigh Convention and Visitors Bureau
421 Fayetteville St., Suite 1505, Raleigh
(800) 849-8499
(919) 834-5900
www.visitraleigh.com

Visitor Information Center
Raleigh City Museum
220 Fayetteville St., Raleigh
(919) 832-3775
www.raleighcitymuseum.org

Pittsboro–Siler City Convention and Visitors Bureau
118 West St. or 365 N.C. 87, Pittsboro
(919) 542-8296
www.visitchathamcounty.com

from the Northeast led to the joke that Cary was actually an acronym for the phrase "Containment Area for Relocated Yankees." Cary has been a leader in suburban growth management going on four decades, and it shows in the town's tidy parkways and well-tended shopping centers. Evidence also shows up on the national magazines' "best" lists, where Cary consistently ranks among the top places to live in the United States. Today the town is home to more than 137,000 people. It provides some of the best amenities in the Triangle through its parks and recreation department, libraries and top-ranked schools. It also has some of the strictest zoning laws and appearance codes in the area.

Cary has the Triangle's highest population of Asian and Indian residents, who have helped shape the town's culture in visible ways. The most striking example is a $3.4 million intricately carved Hindu temple that was completed in 2009. Indian-owned restaurants and businesses dot the Cary area. At the Galaxy Cinema you can see regular screenings of Bollywood films and buy samosas, an Indian specialty, at its snack bar.

Cary began as a railroad stop in 1854, and incorporated in 1871. It is named for Samuel Fenton Cary, a temperance leader and Union general from Ohio whom town founder Frank Page admired. Page's 1868 hotel, a rare example of French Second Empire architecture, today serves as home to the town's Page-Walker Arts & History Center.

Garner

Just south of Raleigh at the intersection of I-40 and U.S. 70, Garner is a growing town of more than 27,000 people. Settlers have been here since the mid-1700s, and the town began to pick up steam when it rated a stop on the Goldsboro-to-Charlotte railroad in the 1850s. Garner incorporated in 1901. Suburban growth drew residents to the outlying areas, leaving downtown to languish until recently. Efforts to revitalize the historic area, including the Garner Station Depot and the Garner Historic Auditorium, continue.

Knightdale

Knightdale sits just east of Raleigh, across the Neuse River. It was incorporated in 1927 after the Norfolk and Southern brought rail traffic to the town. For most of the 20th century it was a farm town that served the surrounding rural population. It has seen growth in the past 20 years, attaining a population of more than 7,000, up from 1,700 in 1990. I-540 was recently routed through Knightdale, and it is expected to boost development in the town.

Among Knightdale's more renowned historical figures was John Hinton, who settled near the Neuse River around 1730. He was a Revolutionary War soldier and politician. Homes built by Hinton's descendants still stand in Knightdale area. One of these plantation houses, Midway, was the subject of a recent well-reviewed documentary, *Moving Midway*. The film chronicles the move of the house to make way for a shopping center and the meeting of two men, one black and one white, both with roots at Midway.

Morrisville

If much of Morrisville looks like it was just built yesterday, that's because the town has experienced exponential growth since 1990. The population in that census was 1,022. Today, Morrisville is home to about 15,000 people. Sandwiched between RTP to its north and Cary to its south along I-40, the town is in the right place at the right time. Before 1990, Morrisville had seen the coming of the railroad in the mid-1800s, one of the last skirmishes of the Civil War in 1865, and mill openings in the late 19th and early 20th centuries. But the mass influx of people to the RTP area has been the town's defining event. Like that of its neighbor Cary, Morrisville's population includes a high percentage of residents of Indian and Pakistani descent. Its corporate residents include the U.S. headquarters of computer maker Lenovo, publishing company Lulu, and telecom company Tekelec.

Raleigh

Raleigh is a city of more than 380,000 people spread out over 142 square miles. It is defined in part by its proximity to RTP, the work of the state government headquartered there, the six institutions of higher learning within its city limits, the museums and fairgrounds, and its rapid pace of growth. Since 1990, the city has added more than 176,000 people and is the second largest city in the state behind Charlotte.

Raleigh's personality is ephemeral, changing from neighborhood to neighborhood. Around the Legislative Building, where the state's General Assembly meets, daytime sidewalks are crowded with office workers in dark suits or summer seersucker. A few blocks away on Glenwood South, twentysomethings in high heels clatter between clubs, restaurants, and art galleries until the wee hours of the morning. Miles away in the suburbs miniature soccer players spill out of minivans onto green playing fields. The influx of residents has changed Raleigh from a somewhat sleepy state government and university town into a more cosmopolitan metro area with highly regarded restaurants, arts, and schools.

Raleighites view I-440, the Beltline, as something of a cultural dividing line. ITB—inside the Beltline—is the home to older and more historically powerful neighborhoods. But plenty of influence resides outside the Beltline, especially in North Raleigh. As suburbs continue to spread

Woody the Lizard

If you happen to be driving N.C. 97 east of Zebulon, keep your eyes peeled for Woody. A giant lizard statue perched atop an ATM, he's not hard to miss. When you see him, you'll know you're in Lizard Lick. That's the name of the unincorporated community surrounding the crossroads of N.C. 97 and State Road 2329, aka Lizard Lick Road. The State Employees' Credit Union installed the giant lizard to celebrate the opening of its 1,000th ATM and to call attention to the quirky name. Legend holds that lizards lazing in the sun, attracted to a whiskey still near the crossroads, inspired the name.

Wake Forest

Wake Forest is home to an institution of higher learning, but it's not the one that shares its name. Wake Forest University is today in Winston-Salem, some 100 miles west. The North Carolina Baptist Convention chartered Wake Forest University and gave rise to Wake Forest in 1834. The town and school grew together for more than a century until the school's move in 1956. The old Wake Forest campus is now home to Southeastern Baptist Theological Seminary.

North of Raleigh on U.S. 1, Wake Forest has a charming historic district that looks much like it did 100 years ago. Its well-preserved main street draws patrons with restaurants, shops, and, during the growing season, a busy farmers' market that sets up every Saturday morning. Like other small Triangle towns, Wake Forest has grown in the past two decades, from almost 6,000 residents in 1990 to more than 26,000 today, giving rise to subdivisions and shopping centers.

Wendell and Zebulon

On the eastern edges of Wake County, Wendell and Zebulon are growing small towns that sit about 5 miles apart along U.S. 64. Wendell claims about 5,000 people while Zebulon is home to more than 4,700. Both have preserved historic downtowns and clutches of picturesque older homes. Zebulon, created as a railroad stop between two large farms, incorporated in 1907. It is named for Zebulon B. Vance, a charismatic politician who served as North Carolina's governor during the Civil War. Wendell came to be in the 1850s when the failure of a tobacco crop in Granville County to the north prompted a mass exodus of farmers. Some of them resettled in the community that became Wendell. It is named for Oliver Wendell Holmes, a favorite poet of the local schoolmaster, but is pronounced Wen-DEL, in the fashion of railroad porters who announced the stop to passengers. Zebulon's biggest employer is GlaxoSmithKline, which has a manufacturing and packaging plant in the town. Zebulon is also home to Five County Stadium, home turf for the Cincinnati Reds' AA-affiliate Carolina Mudcats.

and residents put down roots, they're turning their energies to restaurants, farmers' markets, and other locally owned projects that soften the generic edges of development. Driving past the strip malls, it's easy to assume life within is as generic as their facades but many are home to innovative eateries, and specialty shops.

Ragged in the 1980s and '90s, Raleigh's downtown is experiencing a revival marked by high-rise condos and gentrification of once-forgotten communities accompanied by restaurants and shops to serve new residents. The highlights of this renewal are a new $221 million convention center and the renovation of Fayetteville Street. Historically a busy shopping district and a celebration spot for events of statewide importance, the street was closed to traffic as a pedestrian mall for the past 30 years. Now reopened to vehicle traffic, Fayetteville Street is regaining its cultural significance as art galleries, restaurants, bars, and coffee shops open.

GETTING HERE, GETTING AROUND

If you're visiting the Triangle and want to explore its every corner, the most efficient means of transportation is a car. Because the Triangle is actually a circle of communities and towns that radiate from the core cities of Raleigh, Durham, and Chapel Hill, getting from one side of it to the other can be a matter of 60 miles or more. A well-developed network of federal and state highways makes this fairly easy for anyone in a driver's seat.

It is possible to take a bus to many places in and around the cities, but not always quick or convenient. Notable exceptions are students at Duke, UNC, and N.C. State, who often prefer using the bus systems to fighting for one of the scarce parking spaces on campus. Plenty of commuters, especially in Chapel Hill and Carrboro, can bike or even walk to work on an extensive greenway system that runs throughout the Triangle. More than 10 percent of Chapel Hill commuters hoof it to work every day, according to a Census Bureau study. This is less convenient for residents of the larger cities, which are much more spread out. Rail travel, unfortunately, is still in the planning stages, as it has been for decades. With close to 200,000 Triangle workers crossing county lines to get to work every day, collective frustration with rush hour slowdowns may foment public opinion in favor of a light rail eventually. But even bad traffic in the Triangle seldom comes close to the gridlock experienced in larger metro areas like Northern Virginia and Atlanta.

If you're visiting the Triangle and want to concentrate on one downtown area, walking or biking is probably your best bet. Raleigh, Durham, Chapel Hill, and Carrboro all boast areas that are easy to explore by foot, with sites, food, and shopping that would keep almost anyone busy for at least an afternoon.

ROADWAYS

One of the Triangle's selling points for businesses and residents is its accessibility. I-40 and I-85 intersect in the area, and I-95 is within an hour's drive. Originating in Wilmington on the North Carolina coast, I-40 runs through the Triangle from Johnston County in the east to Hillsborough in the west. There it joins I-85, which connects the Triangle with the Triad cities of Greensboro and Winston-Salem, then Charlotte. I-85 runs north from Hillsborough through Durham, continuing through Petersburg, Virginia. I-40 connects with I-95 about 30 miles southeast of Raleigh at Benson. Northbound travelers can take U.S. 64 from Raleigh to its connection with I-95 in Rocky Mount, about 60 miles east of Raleigh.

Within the Triangle, I-40 connects Raleigh, Durham, and Chapel Hill, traversing the Research Triangle Park. During morning and evening commute times, accidents or roadwork on the eight-lane highway can bring traffic to a crawl. An alternative east-west route is U.S. 70, which roughly parallels I-40 from Hillsborough through Durham and into Raleigh, where it becomes Glenwood Avenue until joining the I-440 loop.

I-440, called the Beltline, is an amoeba-shaped stretch of asphalt that runs around Raleigh. It takes some time to become familiar with the vagaries of the Beltline, so visitors shouldn't get discouraged. Perhaps the strangest quirk is that most signs along the Beltline advise drivers that they are traveling either the Inner (clockwise) or Outer (counterclockwise) loop. It's a confusing directive and trying to sort it out while an 18-wheeler is accelerating behind you can lead to panic. A useful navigation strategy is to consult the exit signs leading to the Beltline for the names of towns that lie in the direction the road runs. If you think of the Beltline as a clock, Creedmoor is at 12. Wake Forest is at 2. Knightdale and Rocky Mount are at the 3 position. Clayton is at 5. Apex and Sanford are at the 7 position. Cary is at 9. Durham and Chapel Hill are at 10. Once you orient yourself in relationship to the towns on the exit signs, it's easier to tell where on the Beltline you are.

I-540, a second loop connecting Raleigh's farther outlying areas, is partially complete. Currently it runs from U.S. 64 in Knightdale, east of Raleigh, to I-40 near Morrisville in the west. Along the way it intersects U.S. 401, U.S. 1, N.C. 50 (Creedmoor Road) and U.S. 70. Construction is underway to extend the road westward through RTP to Holly Springs. Part of that road, which will be called the Triangle Expressway, will become the area's first toll road.

I-440 provides access to Cary and the communities of Apex and Holly Springs from the east, where it intersects with U.S. 64/U.S. 1. From the north, N.C. 55 and N.C. 54 run from I-40 into Morrisville and Cary.

Durham, which sits to the north of I-40, is connected to the interstate via N.C. 147, aka Durham Freeway, and N.C. 55 and N.C. 751. N.C. 147 was built expressly to provide access the Research Triangle Park, which it intersects on its way to Durham. Major attractions in Durham, including the Durham Performing Arts Center and Duke University's campus, are accessible from N.C. 147.

Between Chapel Hill and Durham, the most direct route is U.S. 15-501, which is usually clogged during rush hours. An alternative is N.C. 54, which runs alongside U.S. 15-501 between Chapel Hill and Durham.

AROUND RALEIGH

Through town, U.S. 1 is called Capital Boulevard. It runs from the center of town past miles of shopping centers north to Wake Forest. When U.S. 70 crosses into Wake County northwest of RDU it becomes known as Glenwood Avenue. It runs

past residential and commercial development, including Crabtree Valley Mall, which sits at the intersection of Glenwood Avenue and Creedmoor Road, a north-south connector. Glenwood ends at Hillsborough Street, a few blocks from the State Capitol. The street's southernmost few blocks are known as Glenwood South, a popular dining and drinking district. Wade Avenue runs from Capitol Boulevard near downtown to I-40 in the west. It is one of Raleigh's prettiest thoroughfares, a hilly road that cuts through wooded neighborhoods.

The one-way streets of downtown Raleigh pose obstacles for newcomers at first. But the

---

Hillsborough Street Roundabouts

Hillsborough Street, which runs from the State Capitol through the oldest part of N.C. State University's campus and continues to the State Fairgrounds, has long been a slow-moving stretch of road. These days it's slower than ever. To encourage pedestrian traffic and give a boost to businesses along the stretch of Hillsborough Street across from campus, the city is installing roundabouts and brick medians. The renovations will narrow traffic to two lanes and reduce the vehicle speed from 35 mph to 25 mph or less. Disruptive construction work should continue through mid-2010. Meanwhile, the section of Hillsborough Street from Oberlin Road to Gorman/Faircloth Street is best avoided. Alternative routes for those leaving downtown Raleigh heading west are Wade Avenue, which runs parallel to Hillsborough to the north and Western Boulevard, which runs parallel to the south. Both connect to I-440.

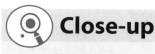

Close-up

Walk, Ride, or Glide with a Guide

A few groups offer tours of downtown Raleigh, Chapel Hill, and Hillsborough. The most striking of these is doubtless the Triangle Segway tours, which cover downtown Raleigh, the Oakwood Historic District, and Oakwood Cemetery. If you've never seen a line of tourists moving upright on motorized scooters through a graveyard, it will make you look twice. Triangle Segway is located at 327 Blake St. in City Market. Get details at (919) 828-1988 or www .trianglesegway.com.

Visitors can also see Raleigh by trolley on the narrated Historic Raleigh Trolley Tours, which run Saturdays from 11 a.m. to 2 p.m. March through December. Trolleys leave hourly from Mordecai Historic Park 1 mile south of downtown on Wake Forest Road. Passengers can get on at any stop on the route. For more information call (919) 857-4364.

A free one-hour walking tour of Fayetteville Street leaves the Raleigh City Museum every Thursday at 10 a.m. Call (919) 832-3775 ext. 11 for more information.

In Chapel Hill a guide leads a walking tour of downtown's historic sites on Wednesdays and Sundays at 2 p.m., starting from the Horace Williams House at 610 East Rosemary Street. Call (919) 942-7818 for more information.

Guides in Hillsborough lead tours organized around a number of themes from Revolutionary War and Civil War sites to ghost tours around Halloween. Check the Alliance for Historic Hillsborough for schedules: (919) 732-7741 or historichillsborough.org.

oldest part of the city is laid out in a neat grid, so it's easy to get a handle on it. At the heart of downtown is Fayetteville Street, which runs from Lenoir Street north to the State Capitol on Hillsborough Street. The state museums are north of the capital across Edenton Street, and the Legislative Building is across Jones Street from the museums. Once you arrive in downtown, it's advisable to park and walk.

AROUND DURHAM

Durham is tricky to navigate, especially downtown, where street names are apt to change abruptly. N.C. 147, aka Durham Freeway, is a useful orientation line. It runs from I-40 in the east to I-85 in the west. Along the way its exits provide access to RTP, downtown Durham, Duke's east and west campuses, Duke University Medical Center, and U.S. 15-501. Major north-south roads are U.S. 15-501 Business (Roxboro Street/University Drive), N.C. 751 (Hope Valley Road), and Fayetteville Street. North Carolina Central University sits between Fayetteville Street to the west and

Alston Avenue to the east, just south of Durham Freeway at exit 12A.

Once in downtown Durham, drivers may find themselves going in a circle—specifically the Downtown Loop. The 1-mile, one-way loop joins stretches of four streets—Roxboro, Morgan, Great Jones, and Ramseur—and is also labeled U.S. 70 Business. Within the loop are the Durham Civic Center, the Carolina Theatre, and the Marriott hotel. It runs alongside the American Tobacco Historic District and the Durham Performing Arts Center. The good thing about the loop is that you can stay on it until you figure out where you need to get off. Just keep circling until you get oriented. City officials are studying ways to do away with the loop, but no plans are definite.

AIRPORTS

Raleigh-Durham International Airport

Nine major airlines and six regional carriers serve Raleigh-Durham International Airport, abbreviated RDU. Nonstop and direct commercial flights provide access to 35 destinations including London and Cancun. Airlines with service at RDU include AirTran, Continental, Continental Express, JetBlue, Southwest, US Air, US Airways Express, Air Canada, American Airlines, American Eagle, Delta, Delta Connection, Delta Northwest, United, and United Express. RDU flights offer direct service to Philadelphia, Atlanta, New York, Chicago, Orlando, Dallas–Fort Worth, Newark, Boston, Las Vegas, and Tampa. A general aviation terminal provides fueling and hospitality services for non-airline pilots and crew.

Dining

The airport has two terminals. Both are home to restaurants, shops, bars, and coffee shops. At Terminal 1, passengers can wait for their flights at the Carolina Varsity Bar & Grill, a sports bar with big-screen TVs, or at AJ's Tavern, a casual menu spot named for two presidents North Carolina claims as natives, Andrew Johnson and Andrew Jackson. (Most historians locate Jackson's birthplace in South Carolina, but the boundary was murky so North Carolina disputes it.) Also at Terminal 1 are standard airport purveyors Cinnabon, Starbucks, Freshens yogurt, and a Godfather's Pizza. Terminal 2 has an outpost of Raleigh's longtime hangout for politicos, 42nd Street Oyster Bar, and a Brookwood Farms BBQ, which serves Eastern Carolina-style pulled pork. California Pizza Kitchen, A&W All-American Food, and Starbucks are also represented.

Shopping

Travelers who have waited until the last minute to buy souvenirs can stop in Terminal 1 at Taste!, an outpost of Chapel Hill's famed gourmet store A Southern Season, to pick up North Carolina specialties, such as Moravian sugar cookies or cheese straws, or a cookbook by a local chef. PGA Tour Shop sells gifts for golfers, and Brooks Brothers has a store in the terminal as well. In Terminal 2 is University Marketplace, which carries T-shirts and hats with Triangle-area team logos, a duty-free store, a Taxco Silver jewelry store, and a couple of newsstands.

Other Amenities

RDU has a 24-hour nonsectarian chapel in Terminal 1 near the baggage claim area. A USO lounge is open 24 hours a day on the second floor of Terminal 2 for members of the military and their families. Wi-Fi is available throughout the airport, and Internet kiosks are available in Terminal 1. Terminal 2 has a pay e-mail station. Travelex Currency Exchange operates two stations in Terminal 2. If you have extra time, you can watch the planes taking off from RDU's longest runway from an outdoor observation deck near Terminal 2. A park with playground equipment sits below the deck, and there is a snack bar on site. Observation Park is free and open to passengers and the general public. (See the Kidstuff chapter for more on the Observation Park.)

Transportation from the Airport

Depending on traffic, it is 20- to 25-minute car trip from RDU to downtown Raleigh, Durham, or Chapel Hill. A one-way taxi ride from the airport should cost about $38 to Chapel Hill, about $20 to Cary, and about $30 to Durham or Raleigh.

Eight rental car companies serve the airport. They are Alamo (919) 840-0132, (800) 327-9633; Avis (919) 840-4750, (800) 331-1212; Budget (919) 840-4781, (800) 527-0700; Dollar (866) 434-2226, (800) 800-4000; Enterprise (919) 840-9555, (800) 736-8222; Hertz (919) 840-4875, (800) 654-3131; National (919) 840-4350, (800) 227-7368; and Thrifty (919) 832-9381, (800) 847-4389. Car companies run shuttles from the terminals to the rental car area about every 15 minutes.

SuperShuttle vans offer shared rides to all parts of the Triangle. Reserve a shuttle at the Web site www.supershuttle.com or at one of their three airport counters. Shared rides are generally cheaper than taxi service.

Bus service is available every half hour from the Triangle Transit Authority's transit center near RDU to locations throughout the Triangle. A shuttle moves passengers between the transit center and the airport terminals. Other TTA bus line transfer centers are in Raleigh, Cary, Chapel Hill, and Durham. A one-way trip is $2 and a regional day pass accepted by TTA and other public trans-

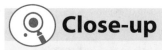 **Close-up**

Raleigh Rickshaws

No, those healthy-looking cyclists pulling what look like adult-size strollers around downtown Raleigh are not fraternity pledges trying to earn their letters. They're rickshaw drivers, and they love their jobs, even though they work for tips only. Raleigh Rickshaw has been operating in and around downtown for about three years and has a fleet of 16 pedal-powered taxis. While it may seem silly, it's a fun way to get from one side of downtown to the other. The service ranges from Moore Square to Glenwood South and includes the warehouse district, Progress Energy Performing Arts Center, and Seaboard Station. Sure, it's possible to walk from one side of downtown to the other, but it's a mile-long trek from, for example, an art gallery on Glenwood to a bar on Fayetteville Street. Taking a rickshaw will save your stilettos and keep you from having to park your car every time you hop to a different bar. Rickshaw drivers say their busiest times are late weekend nights, and that some repeat customers keep their cell numbers on speed dial. Passengers can call the rickshaw dispatch line at (919) 623-5555 or, Thursday through Sunday nights, e-mail for pick up via www.raleighrickshaw.com. Raleigh Rickshaw drivers also conduct historical tours of the city between 10 a.m. and 4 p.m. for $30 per rickshaw. The service does not run on Mondays.

So what's a fair tip for someone who just worked up a sweat giving you and a friend a ride? It's up to you, but any cyclist who pulls a pair of full-grown adults up the steepest stretch of Glenwood Avenue to Peace Street deserves an extra five bucks, don't you think?

portation systems in the Triangle is $4. For more information on Triangle Transit Authority or a map of routes, call (919) 485-7433 or go to www.triangletransit.org or www.gotriangle.org. TTA buses do not run on Sundays.

Other Airfields

The University of North Carolina at Chapel Hill operates the Horace Williams Airport north of campus at the intersection of Martin Luther King Jr. Boulevard and Estes Drive Extension. It serves as a base for the school's Area Health Education Center, which helps provide doctors and other medical personnel to remote parts of the state, and for other university purposes. It is open to private aircraft. Call (919) 962-1337 or go to www.airport.unc.edu for more information.

The Johnston County Airport (JNX) is open to private flyers, sells fuel, rents corporate jet storage, and offers flying lessons. It is about 30 miles west of Raleigh, just north of Smithfield at 3149 Swift Creek Rd. For more information, call (919) 934-0992 or go to www.johnstonnc.com and click the Business Resources tab.

Several small, private airfields operate around the area: Lake Ridge Aero Park is in northern Durham County off I-85 adjacent to Falls Lake Recreation Area. Near Apex are Deck Airpark, off U.S. 64 west of town, and Cox Airport off U.S. 64 east of town. North of Zebulon off N.C. 96 is Field of Dreams. Raleigh East Airport is between Knightdale and Wendell on U.S. 64/264. Near Fuquay-Varina, south of Garner off U.S. 401, is Triple W Airport.

BUSES

Greyhound serves Raleigh and Durham with stations in each city's downtown. The Raleigh Greyhound Station is at 314 West Jones St. between the legislative office district and the Glenwood South entertainment district. Call (919) 834-8275. In Durham, Greyhound shares space in the city's shiny new $17 million, glass-and-metal Durham Station Transportation Center at 515 West Pettigrew St. The station is next to the American Tobacco Historic District and within walking distance of many downtown sites. Call (919) 687-4800.

Capital Area Transit (CAT) buses serve Raleigh from the downtown station at Moore Square to the edges of the city limits. A one-way fare is $1, and transfers between CAT buses are free. A regional day pass accepted by all bus systems in the Triangle is $4. Buy passes at the Moore Square station, the CAT operations office at 1430 South Blount St., Mechanics and Farmers Bank locations at 13 East Hargett St. and 1824 Rock Quarry Rd., and some Harris-Teeter grocery stores. CAT buses generally run from 5:30 a.m. to 11:30 p.m. weekdays, 6 a.m. to 7 p.m. on Saturdays. Limited service runs 8 a.m. to 7 p.m. Sundays. Exceptions include the downtown R-Line. For route and service details go to www.gotriangle.com or call (919) 485-7433.

Wolfline buses connect North Carolina State University's three campuses as well as neighborhoods to the west and south of the campuses and downtown Raleigh. Buses are free and open to the general public as well as students. Special service runs on football Saturdays and on weekends between campus and downtown. Go to www.ncsu.transloc.com for a map with real-time bus locations.

Cary's C-Tran buses run throughout Cary and into part of west Raleigh. The buses operate Monday through Saturday from 6 a.m. to 8 p.m. The fare is $1 for a one-way trip. The town also offers personal transportation service for Cary residents who are 60 or older or disabled. One-way fares range from $2 to $6. Call (919) 481-2020 for reservations. For more information on C-Tran service, call (919) 469-4086 or go to www.gotriangle.com.

DATA buses operate within Durham. Day passes are $2 and can be purchased on the bus or at the transit station at 515 West Pettigrew St. Durham buses run Monday through Saturday 5:30 a.m. to 12:30 a.m. and Sunday 6:30 a.m. to 7:30 p.m. For details on routes, go to www.data.durhamnc.gov or call (919) 485-7433.

Chapel Hill Transit buses serve Chapel Hill, Carrboro, and the University of North Carolina. Buses run 5:30 a.m. to 11:30 a.m. when classes are in session. Service is reduced when campus is closed. The bus service is free. For details on routes, call (919) 969-4900 or go to chtransit.org, where you can also get real-time information on specific routes.

The Triangle Transit Authority routes link the Triangle's largest cities, Research Triangle Park, and RDU International and extend to smaller communities including Zebulon and Wake Forest. Fares are $1 for a one-way trip, and a day-pass good for transit on any bus system in the Triangle is $4. For routes and other information, call (919) 485-7433 or go to www.gotriangle.com.

i The R-Line is a free city bus that circulates around downtown Raleigh. The R-Line makes 20 stops on its route, which reaches from Seaboard Station on Peace Street to the Progress Energy Center for the Performing Arts, and includes Glenwood South, the warehouse district, Moore Square, and Wilmington Street. Buses run every 10 to 15 minutes, Monday through Wednesday from 7 a.m. to 11 p.m., Thursday through Saturday from 7 to 2:15 a.m., and Sunday from 1 to 8 p.m.

TRAINS

Amtrak stops at stations in downtown Cary, Raleigh, and Durham. The Silver Star stops daily in Raleigh and Cary on its run between New York City and Miami. The Carolinian makes daily trips between Charlotte and New York with stops in Raleigh, Cary, and Durham. The Piedmont runs a daily three-hour roundtrip between Raleigh and Charlotte, stopping at nine North Carolina cities, including Cary and Durham. The Raleigh-to-Charlotte trip is in the morning. The return trip is in the evening. A second mid-day roundtrip is planned to begin in 2010.

The Cary Amtrak station is at 211 North Academy St. The Raleigh Amtrak station is at 320 West Cabarrus St. in the warehouse arts and club district. A new Amtrak station opened in Durham in 2009 at 601 West Main St. in a restored tobacco warehouse between Brightleaf Square and the American Tobacco Historic District.

HISTORY

Long before Europeans landed on North Carolina's barrier islands, American Indians made their homes in what is today the Triangle. Historians know that two tribes, the Eno and the Occaneechi, settled and farmed in what are today Durham and Orange counties. The Great Indian Trading Path passed through the area and continued to offer explorers a way through the land for generations. You need travel only as far as Eno River State Park or Occoneechee Mountain State Natural Area, a few miles north of the heavily populated cities of Durham and Chapel Hill, to imagine what the land was like during the American Indians' time. Longtime Raleigh residents who remember the construction of the I-440 loop around the city in the 1960s can recall sifting through upturned earth to find arrowheads and other relics of the age.

After European settlement began in North Carolina, it took a couple hundred years for it to reach inland to the eastern Piedmont. Sir Walter Raleigh sent colonists to the Outer Banks in the late 16th century, but never set foot in North Carolina himself. The Roanoke Colony was the first English settlement in America, before Plymouth and Jamestown, and it was the birthplace of the first white child born in the New World, Virginia Dare. But it didn't last. Members of the colony returned to England for supplies, leaving a small band of settlers behind. When they returned the colonists had vanished, the only clue to their disappearance the word "Croatoan" carved on a tree. History remembers them as the Lost Colony, and an outdoor drama penned by North Carolina playwright Paul Greene brings their story to life during the summer on Roanoke Island.

COLONIAL PERIOD

It wasn't until 1752 that Hillsborough was laid out in Orange County at the intersection of the Great Indian Trading Path and the Eno River. The town became a nexus of political activity and was an important player in the War of Regulation during the late 1760s, something of a precursor to the American Revolution. North Carolina's Colonial power was concentrated around its coast, where its more established towns thrived. Sheriffs and other local officials, the Colonial governor's emissaries in the inland counties, were given free rein to administer rules and collect taxes, and often these local officials were corrupt. The poor and middle classes banded together to put an end to their thieving practices, becoming known as Regulators. The group committed a series of violent acts in protest, including breaking up court proceedings in Hillsborough in 1768. Royal Governor William Tryon eventually crushed the insurrection, and six Regulators were hanged in Hillsborough in 1771.

Despite the turmoil, Hillsborough continued to grow and prosper, and several Colonial and post-Revolution governors lived there. North Carolina did not have a fixed capital city until the founding of Raleigh in the 1790s so government sessions often convened in Hillsborough. Among these was the state's Constitutional Convention of 1778, where delegates demanded a Bill of Rights be added to the document. Hillsborough harbors the area's best-preserved architectural landmarks of the late 18th century, including the home of William Hooper, a signer of the Declaration of Independence.

Another historical figure to leave his mark on Hillsborough was Daniel Boone. Legend holds that the frontiersman came through and led a group of settlers west from King Street in 1778.

Historians do not always concede the story, commemorated by a marker erected in the 1930s, as fact. But that didn't stop a Hillsborough shopping center developer from capitalizing on the legend's resurgence in popularity in the 1950s. A giant Daniel Boone statue, depicting the pioneer wearing a beard and floppy hat, welcomes customers to what are today called The Shops at Daniel Boone.

A CAPITAL AND A UNIVERSITY

After the Revolutionary War, state leaders turned their attention to the stabilization of a capital city. New Bern, where Royal Governor William Tryon had built his palace, Hillsborough, Tarboro, Fayetteville, and several other towns and settlements vied for the honor. No agreement could be reached, and legislators wound up wandering from place to place for more than a decade. The General Assembly tasked the state's Constitutional Convention with deciding on a suitable site for the permanent location of state government. After much wrangling, the delegates decided that the capital should be located within 10 miles of Isaac Hunter's Tavern, a well-known and hospitable spot a few miles north of where the capital stands today. Legend holds that more than a few tankards of cherry bounce, served by a popular landowner named Joel Lane, played a role in the proceedings. Cherry bounce, a version of which appears on at least one downtown Raleigh cocktail menu, is an infusion of brandy, cherries, and sugar. Joel Lane, who is remembered as the Father of Raleigh, wound up selling the state the 1,000 acres where the core of Raleigh sits today. His house is today an historic site. A marker near an I-440 overpass recalls Isaac Hunter's Tavern.

The new capital city was named for the courtier who sponsored the doomed settlement of the Carolinas. A bronze statue of Sir Walter Raleigh, in court dress complete with the cloak he surely used to toss over Queen Elizabeth's puddle, greets visitors to the Raleigh Convention Center. A surveyor and legislator named William Christmas laid out the traditional grid pattern.

While the conventioneers were picking out a site for the capital, 30 miles away at a crossroads in southern Orange County educational leaders were setting up a university. An Anglican chapel that stood at the site, New Hope Chapel, lent part of its name to the town, which came to be Chapel Hill. The first building, Old East, was under construction by 1793, and the first student, Hinton James, enrolled in 1795.

i North Carolina claims to have the oldest public university in the country, but the University of Georgia disputes it. The controversy turns on the definition of "old." UNC was chartered in 1789 and enrolled its first students in 1795, graduating them in 1799. UGA was chartered in 1785 and graduated its first students in 1804.

THE "RIP VAN WINKLE" STATE

The first half of the 19th century was a period of dormancy for North Carolina, as state leaders failed to raise taxes to build schools and roads or lead agricultural reforms. Mass emigration to the frontier beyond the Appalachians caused a drain of intellectual power from the state. Among those who loaded into wagons and headed for the frontier were the families of Andrew Jackson, the seventh president of the United States, born near the South Carolina line in western North Carolina; James K. Polk, the 11th president of the United States, born near Charlotte; and Andrew Johnson, the 17th president. Johnson's father worked at a boarding house on Fayetteville Street. The young Johnson headed west when he was a teenager. The stagnancy of the state prompted newspaper editorialists to hang the "Rip Van Winkle" name on North Carolina, recalling Washington Irving's fabled sleeper whom time passed by. Political reform began bringing North Carolina up to date in the 1840s, when the state established its first public schools and sponsored railroad and plank road construction.

Though educational opportunities were few, some bright spots existed in and around the area that would become the Triangle. In the early 1800s,

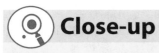

Close-up

What Is a Tar Heel?

North Carolina's most popular nickname is the Tar Heel State. Since that's also the name of the University of North Carolina's athletic teams, you won't hear too many N.C. State or Duke fans refer to their home state as such. Several versions of the story explain the nickname. The most popular one holds that a group of North Carolina soldiers held fast during a Civil War battle while their counterparts from Virginia retreated. Virginians had been known to look down their noses at their neighbors to the south for being less landed gentry. A Virginia soldier asked a North Carolinian condescendingly after the battle if there was any more tar left in North Carolina. The North Carolinian told him there was, and that he intended to stick it to the Virginians' heels before the next battle lest they retreat again. Some storytellers add that when General Robert E. Lee heard the story he said, "God bless the Tar Heel boys." Other versions recall that the name stems from a Revolutionary War battle. Whichever version you choose, note that the moniker is always two words—Tar Heel.

John Chavis, a free African American, opened a school in Raleigh where he taught black and white students side by side. The integrated school didn't last long, and eventually Chavis relented to the segregationists, teaching white children during the day and black children at night.

NORTH CAROLINA IN THE CIVIL WAR

By 1860, North Carolina was awakening from its dormancy and making strides in education and industry. Among the most prolific industries in the state was the production of naval stores—tar, turpentine, and pitch. Two-thirds of the nation's turpentine came from North Carolina by the middle of the 19th century. Cotton and wool mills were also important economic engines, but the massive industrialization experienced in northern cities had not occurred in North Carolina. The state remained primarily rural. It's most impressive urban area was Wilmington, a coastal port with little more than 9,000 residents. Raleigh was comparatively smaller, with 4,780 residents, but it had made strides. A railroad had been in operation since the 1840s, when the stately domed State Capitol was built. Public schools were more numerous than earlier in the century, and more whites could read and write than in previous decades.

When the tide of secession rose in the South, North Carolina was one of the last two states to vote to leave the union. Its population was not as economically dependant upon the plantation system and slavery as those of neighboring states. Nonetheless, about 42,000 North Carolinians died in the Civil War, more than any other state. When the fighting was all but over, the largest surrender of troops occurred in Durham at the Bennet farmhouse, where Confederate General Joseph E. Johnston negotiated the terms with Union General William T. Sherman.

RECONSTRUCTION AND INDUSTRIALIZATION

Sherman spared most of North Carolina the wrath that he inflicted on nearby Southern states, but Reconstruction was scarcely less dire for North Carolina. Among the bright spots were the beginnings of education and economic independence for African Americans and the rise of the tobacco and textile industries, which brought great wealth to a few and employment to many.

In Raleigh in 1865, Dr. Henry M. Tupper began Raleigh Institute, today Shaw University, by teaching theological classes to freedmen. It was the first coed college for African Americans in the country. Two years later, Episcopal clergy opened St. Augustine's College, a teacher training school for African Americans on the far side of Oakwood Cemetery in Raleigh. Perhaps the most famous of St. Aug's graduates were the Delany sisters, Sadie and Bessie, who authored the best-selling book *Having our Say* when they were both more than 100 years old. The book also spawned a Broadway play and television movie.

Settlements of Raleigh freedmen began to form new communities, including a clutch of slab houses in west Raleigh near what is today Meredith College. The community became known as Method, and it stood as a proud middle-class black township for almost a century. Raleigh annexed the area in the 1960s.

Raleigh grew steadily in the post-war years with the establishment of what was to become North Carolina State University in 1889 and the opening of Rex Hospital, which had the state's first nursing school, in 1894. Meanwhile, Durham boomed. Named for Dr. Bartlett Durham, the landowner who donated a site for the railroad station in 1849, Durham became renowned for the quality of its bright-leaf tobacco after the Civil War. Soldiers who had chewed or smoked it while stationed near or passing through the area sought more after they headed home. The demand for bright-leaf gave rise to fortunes such as that of the Duke family, the region's most dramatic example of the Industrial Age. Without train fare in his pocket, Washington Duke walked home from his service in the Civil War to his farm near Durham. Duke had switched from cotton to tobacco before the war, and he and his six children continued growing and processing bright-leaf into smoking tobacco. He began peddling his tobacco around the eastern part of the state, and found a lot of takers.

Other tobacco entrepreneurs had also set up shop near Durham. By 1880, North Carolina was home to 126 tobacco factories that manufactured $2.3 million worth of chewing and smoking tobacco. Durham was a hub for the industry, aided in part by the marketing of John Ruffin Green. He labeled his product "Genuine Durham Smoking Tobacco," added the image of a bull, and the Bull Durham brand was born. In 1884, the Dukes began using a Bonsack machine to roll

cigarettes at their Durham factory, boosting production to 120,000 cigarettes a day. In 1890, after more than two decades of staggering growth, the Duke family merged its company with four others to become the American Tobacco Company, the largest tobacco conglomerate in the world.

BLACK WALL STREET

The Dukes weren't the only businessmen prospering in the post–Civil War era. In 1898, a former slave named John Merrick joined with Dr. Aaron Moore and C. C. Spaulding to open the North Carolina Mutual Life Insurance Company. Today it is the oldest and largest African-American life insurance company in the country. During its early years, it served as a pillar in the black business community in Durham. The community was so prosperous it earned the black business district on Parrish Street the nickname Black Wall Street. Along with N.C. Mutual, the Mechanics and Farmers Bank was a driving economic force in the community. Today, M&F has assets of more than $250 million. Scores of other black-owned businesses kept African Americans employed and thriving during the segregated years of the early 20th century. Community leaders such as Booker T. Washington and W. E. B. DuBois pointed to the black middle class in Durham as a beacon for the black population across the country. In addition to businesses on Parrish Street, the black community built the Hayti community, and its grandest symbols of achievement, St. Joseph's African Methodist Episcopal Church and White Rock Baptist Church. St. Joseph's is now the Hayti Heritage Center. White Rock Baptist and much of Hayti were leveled to make way for N.C. 147 in the 1970s.

THE 20TH CENTURY

During the first half of the 20th century, the towns that would come to make up the Triangle grew steadily. Villages like Chapel Hill, which had population of 1,623 in 1900 and claimed 7,995 in 1940, became towns. Modern amenities like paved roads, sewers, and street lights became standard. Events of worldwide scale took their toll. The world wars cost thousands of North Carolinian lives, and the Great Depression between them stagnated growth. During the First World War, the United States Army ran its only tank training operation at Camp Polk, at the N.C. State Fairgrounds in Raleigh. During the Depression, the Civil Conservation Corp worked in the Crabtree Creek area between Raleigh and Durham, where Umstead State Park would later be. During the Second World War, the U.S. Army operated an airfield between the two cities, which become Raleigh-Durham International.

The G.I. Bill and the return of fighting troops from war in the late 1940s prompted a population boom in Chapel Hill and Raleigh as veterans enrolled in the universities. As the schools expanded their visions and their services for this new class of students, community leaders began to consider the possibilities that a research-based economy could offer. In 1959, the Research Triangle was created to synergize the intellectual capital of the area's universities and to lure prospective employers with a highly educated workforce.

Social change made its mark on Triangle communities in the 1950s and '60s as well, as African-American leaders and progressive whites began to question the bonds of segregation. The Triangle saw the founding of the Student Nonviolent Coordinating Committee during a conference at Shaw University and was host to one of Martin Luther King's most famous speeches. Dr. King delivered a speech at Durham's White Rock Baptist Church on the heels of the Greensboro Woolworth lunch counter sit-in in 1960. He implored his brethren to "fill up the jails" and be arrested for their nonviolent protests if they needed.

By the 1980s, the Triangle had begun to distinguish itself as a place conducive to business, and soon after, as a great place to live. Since 1990, the area has been transformed, as the population of its small towns and cities has exploded, presenting leaders with the challenge of managing and encouraging growth without stifling the factors that gave rise to it. If current predictions for continued population growth are correct, that will remain the challenge for decades to come.

ACCOMMODATIONS

Keeping pace with the Triangle's population explosion of the past two decades, the number of places to stay and the range of experiences a traveler will encounter have grown as well. If economy and convenient location are your priorities, you'll find them at one of the area's many chain motels. If you're seeking a luxurious getaway or a little pampering to make your business trip less stressful, you'll find that, too, sometimes for less than you might expect. And the Triangle's many bed-and-breakfasts offer everything from getaways on the farm to in-town escapes within walking distance of the attractions you came to see.

Finding a place to lay your head in the Triangle is usually easy, though the tide of visitors does ebb and flow with the seasons. Football season, which draws crowds to stadiums in Raleigh, Durham, and Chapel Hill, tends to fill hotels, as do spring graduation weekends. It's a good idea to look into reservations for graduation weekends as soon as a year to six months before the date, as coveted rooms go fast. Because Raleigh is a larger city with more lodging options, the problem is less acute. Chapel Hill and Durham are smaller towns so demand for accommodations on these weekends outstrips supply more quickly.

Price Code

The rates listed are what a pair of travelers should expect to pay for one room. Prices for suites will be greater. Occupancy taxes, which vary from 3 percent to 6 percent depending on the county, are not included in the listed rate.

$	Under $75
$$	$75 to $125
$$$	$126 to $200
$$$$	Over $200

This list aims to provide a thorough picture of the kinds of accommodations available in the Triangle, but is by no means comprehensive. It's safe to assume that all the listed accommodations accept major credit cards. Hotels are smoke-free and wheelchair accessible unless otherwise indicated. Those that accept pets are indicated.

Because innkeepers offer more personalized service than owners of most large hotels, it's a good idea to call and see what accommodations they are willing to make for travelers. The inns included in this chapter are smoke-free, unless noted, but some innkeepers allow smoking on decks and patios. Many of the historic inns are not wheelchair accessible due to the physical restrictions of their properties. Likewise, it's good to call and check on whether you can bring along your own furry friend.

HOTELS AND MOTELS

Cary and Western Wake County

BEST WESTERN CARY INN AND EXTENDED STAY SUITES $$
1722 Walnut St., Cary
(919) 481-1200
www.cmchotels.com
The Best Western in Cary is 3 miles from the State Fairgrounds and the RBC Center in Raleigh and the Koka Booth Amphitheater in Cary. The hotel has 140 rooms including 42 suites and two suites with kitchenettes. All rooms have HBO and high-speed wireless Internet. On-site amenities include a fitness center and pool and free continental breakfast. Pets are allowed, with some restrictions, and smoking rooms are available.

**CAMBRIA SUITES RALEIGH–
DURHAM AIRPORT** $$
300 Airgate Blvd., Morrisville
(919) 361-3311
www.cambriasuites.com
Just a mile from RDU in Morrisville, the Cambria
Suites is a great deal for business travelers work-
ing in RTP or western Wake County. Comfortable
common rooms are decorated with details like
drop lights and stonework walls. Its on-site facili-
ties include a coffee bar, indoor pool, whirlpool,
fitness center, a bar, and a restaurant that serves
breakfast and dinner. Wireless Internet access and
printing are available throughout the hotel.

CANDLEWOOD SUITES RALEIGH/CARY $
1020 Buck Jones Rd., Raleigh
(919) 468-4222
www.ichotelsgroup.com
Convenient to southeast and downtown Raleigh
and Cary, Candlewood Suites is a good buy for
travelers who want to be in the thick of things.
The hotel is located near the I-40/440 intersection
and the plethora of shops at Cary's Crossroads
Plaza. Every suite has a kitchen with a refrigerator,
microwave, stove, and dishwasher. Free high-
speed Internet access is available in-room. On-
site amenities include a convenience store and
fitness center. Candlewood Suites allows pets
and has smoking rooms.

HOTEL SIERRA $$
10962 Chapel Hill Rd., Morrisville
(919) 388-5355
www.hotel-sierra.com
A small chain of about a dozen boutique properties, Hotel Sierra offers more posh amenities
than most national chains for a reasonable rate.
Bathrobes, flat-screen TVs, iPod docking stations,
sound machines, and high-thread-count linens
come with every room. On-site perks include free
breakfast with custom-made omelets, a business
center with high-speed Internet, and a fitness
center where the towels are kept chilled. The
hotel's Lax Lounge serves gourmet pizza and
other light bites, and shuttle service is available to
nearby restaurants and the airport. The patio area

includes an outdoor pool, whirlpool, and fire pit.
Hotel Sierra is just off I-540, two exits from RDU.

THE UMSTEAD HOTEL AND SPA $$$$
100 Woodland Pond Rd., Cary
(866) 877-4141
www.theumstead.com
The Umstead raised the bar for lodging in the
Triangle when it opened in 2007. Just off I-40
at the edge of the SAS corporate campus, the
hotel is set in a stand of pines that perfectly
complements its modern design, inside and out.
Floor-to-ceiling windows help meld the wooded
aesthetic with the sleek lines of the lobby. Large
pottery pieces and paintings, mostly by North
Carolina artists, adorn the common areas. One
notable exception is the dramatic glass sculpture
by Dale Chihuly that dominates the entryway.
The rooms are replete with luxurious touches like
flat-screen plasma TVs, DVD players, limestone
and granite bathroom details, and 330-count
linens. Balcony rooms overlook the three-acre
lake and vanishing-edge pool. The spa is open
to guests, who can relax in the whirlpool, sauna,
and steam room or by the gas-log fire in the
comfortable lounge. The fitness center is fully
equipped, but guests can also work up a sweat
on the wooded nature trail that surrounds the
lake. Heron's, the in-house restaurant, is a dining
destination in its own right. The Umstead is one
of two AAA Five-Diamond award winners in the
state.

Chapel Hill

THE CAROLINA INN $$$$
211 Pittsboro St., Chapel Hill
(800) 962-8519
www.carolinainn.com
The Carolina Inn is a charming historic hotel that
puts guests in the middle of campus life at UNC.
Built in 1924, the inn's arches and columns are
typical flourishes of the neoclassical style popular
in the era. Rooms are appointed with traditional
florals and plaids, and Audubon-style sketches
of pheasants and hounds dot the walls. Recently
renovated, the inn is comfortable and up to date.

Its 184 rooms and seven suites have data ports and coffeemakers. Top-floor rooms are smaller and feature slanted ceilings, so ask for a lower floor if you want the extra space. On-site amenities include a fitness center, dry cleaning service, a restaurant, and a bar. Parking is available at the inn. The inn is a short walk from Memorial Hall, Kenan Stadium, and the shops and restaurants of West Franklin Street.

Fridays On The Front Porch At The Carolina Inn

From late April through mid-October, the Carolina Inn's lawn and patio become a bluegrass concert space with the series "Fridays on the Front Porch." Performances, which run from 5 to 8 p.m., are free and open to the public. Attendees can order from the inn's picnic menu and its full bar. It's a comfortable way to wind up the week and kick off the weekend in the heart of Chapel Hill.

THE FRANKLIN $$$–$$$$
311 W. Franklin St., Chapel Hill
(866) 831-5999
www.franklinhotelnc.com

Opened in 2007, The Franklin brings a stylish urban vibe to the west end of Chapel Hill's Franklin Street. In-room touches include marble bathrooms, iPod docks, and a pillow menu. The balconies are lovely spots from which to gaze at downtown while soaking in the sounds of foot traffic and chatter below. The hotel is two blocks from UNC's campus and about a mile from downtown Carrboro. A third-floor interior courtyard offers fireside sofas and reading nooks. Downstairs is Roberts, a cozy street-front piano bar and sidewalk patio that serves cocktails and gourmet munchies and dessert, a sweet last stop after an evening out. The Franklin's on-site restaurant, Windows, serves breakfast and provides an elegant setting for weddings and reunions. Some of the best restaurants in the Triangle are within walking distance. The Franklin has a business center and a fitness center and arranges in-room spa services. Rooms include free high-speed wireless Internet access, on-site and valet parking, and nightly turndown service.

HAMPTON INN CHAPEL HILL $$
1740 Fordham Blvd./U.S. 15-501, Chapel Hill
(919) 968-3000
www.hamptoninn.com

This is a convenient and affordable option for visitors to Chapel Hill and Carrboro. The Hampton Inn is on U.S. 15-501, about 4 miles from the Dean E. Smith Center and UNC Hospitals. The hotel offers 122 rooms all with free high-speed Internet access. A fitness room, outdoor pool, and business center are on site. Smoking rooms are available.

THE SHERATON CHAPEL HILL $$$–$$$$
One Europa Dr., Chapel Hill
(919) 968-4900
www.starwoodhotels.com

Sheraton renovated the 168 rooms and two suites at this Chapel Hill property in 2008. The remade rooms feature flat-screen TVs, 300-count sheets, and wireless Internet connections. The hotel has a restaurant, Shula's 347 Grill, on site as well as a large outdoor pool and fitness center. The Sheraton is just off U.S. 15-501 about 3 miles from the UNC campus and the hotel offers a free shuttle to downtown Chapel Hill and Carrboro.

THE SIENA $$$–$$$$
1505 E. Franklin St., Chapel Hill
(919) 929-4000
www.sienahotel.com

The Siena embraces the luxurious vibe of the European hotels that inspired it. Marble floors and gilt mirrors greet guests entering the lobby. The 67 rooms and 12 suites are large and classically appointed. On-site amenities include Il Palio, a well-regarded Italian restaurant with an

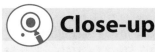

Close-up

"What It Was Was Football"....

One of North Carolina's most famous favorite sons, Andy Griffith, launched his career with a comedy routine first performed in the ballroom of the Carolina Inn. Griffith was a UNC student in the late 1940s and '50s, during the golden age of UNC's football program when a room at the Carolina Inn during football season was the most coveted reservation in town. Inn managers arranged entertainment to cater to returning alumni passions during the era. Mount Airy native Griffith made the most of his mountain accent with a country-come-to-town stand-up routine that featured a backwoods preacher marveling at the spectacle of a Carolina football Saturday, and two groups of men fighting over "a funny little pumpkin." A promoter heard Griffith's rendition of "What It Was Was Football" and had him record it for Capitol Records, bringing him national attention. Griffith went on to star in the 1950s movie hits *A Face in the Crowd* and *No Time for Sergeants*, as well as the television series *The Andy Griffith Show* and *Matlock*.

extensive wine list. Turndown service, a hot buffet breakfast, and wireless Internet come with all rooms. The Siena also has a business center and is pet-friendly. The hotel is on Franklin Street about a mile and a half from campus and directly across from the shops and restaurants at University Mall.

Durham

AMERICA'S BEST VALUE
CAROLINA DUKE INN $
2517 Guess Rd., Durham
(919) 286-0771

This is a budget traveler's best bet—complimentary breakfast, mini-fridge, outdoor pool, and some of the best rates in the Triangle. It's not shiny, but it's cheap. The hotel is close to Duke's campus, and offers a shuttle to Duke University Hospital. The more expensive rooms have high-speed Internet connections. Pets are welcome.

i Because so many visitors to Durham are in town for medical treatment, many of the hotels close to Duke University and its affiliated hospitals offer complimentary shuttle service. This service is noted in the individual listings here, but make sure you inquire of any property close to the school.

COMFORT INN MEDICAL PARK $$
1816 Hillandale Rd., Durham
(919) 471-6100
www.comfortinn.com

Location and value are the biggest draws for this Comfort Inn, which is about a mile and half from Duke. The hotel offers free shuttle service to the campus, hospitals, and downtown on weekdays, 8 a.m. to 4 p.m. In-room amenities include free high-speed wireless Internet and, in some rooms, sofa beds. The hotel has an exercise room, a guest laundry facilities, and an outdoor pool. Pets smaller than 50 pounds are allowed and some smoking rooms are available.

DUKE TOWER HOTEL &
CONDOMINIUMS $–$$
807 W. Trinity Ave., Durham
(866) 385-3869
www.duketower.com

Duke Tower is a hotel of condominiums that offers short-term and long-term rates. It's a frequent choice for people moving to the area, patients at the nearby Duke Campus for Living diet centers, and for entertainers or scholars in town working on projects. Stars including James Earl Jones and Lauren Hutton have put up here. The architectural centerpiece is the redbrick fire tower that once stood guard over the grounds of the 19th-century Pearl Mill, a Duke-family cotton operation that stood where the hotel is. A cafe in the tower serves continental breakfast and offers views of west Durham.

A central landscaped courtyard has a large pool, cabana, and shuffleboard court. Rates begin at $85 per night and decline with the length of stay, resulting in $60 per night after 70 days. Pets are welcome, and smoking rooms are available. The hotel runs a free 24-hour shuttle to Duke University, Duke Medical Center, and Durham VA Hospital.

DURHAM MARRIOTT AT THE CONVENTION CENTER $$
201 Foster St., Durham
(919) 768-6000
www.marriott.com

The downtown Marriott is in the middle of Durham's revitalizing urban scene. From here, it's an easy walk to the American Tobacco Historic District and the Durham Performing Arts Center as well as some of the best restaurants in the Triangle. Its 185 rooms and two suites are tidy. The airy ground-floor restaurant includes several water features. Guests can use the on-site fitness room or the YMCA across the street.

THE WASHINGTON DUKE INN AND GOLF CLUB $$$–$$$$
3001 Cameron Blvd., Durham
(919) 490-0999
www.washingtondukeinn.com

Old-school elegance befitting the Duke name rules here. Built to mimic grand English inns, the Washington Duke opened in 1988. The inn is named for the family's patriarch, and Duke family artifacts and photographs adorn the hallways. It is set beside the Duke University Golf Course, and rooms offer views of the fairways or of the landscaped grounds. The inn has 271 guest rooms and suites, fitness center, and pool. The Fairview Dining Room serves sophisticated cuisine and afternoon tea while the Bull Durham Bar offers more casual fare. Free transportation is available by appointment to Duke campuses, the Duke University Medical Center, and Ninth Street daily from 6 a.m. to 6 p.m. The hotel is pet friendly.

Raleigh
Downtown and Inside the Beltline
CLARION HOTEL STATE CAPITAL $$
320 Hillsborough St., Raleigh
(919) 832-0501
www.clarionhotel.com

The Clarion's distinctive cylindrical design makes it easy to find in downtown Raleigh. It has 202 rooms with king, queen, and double beds and amenities like in-room coffeemakers, hair dryers, and computer hookups. High-speed Internet access is available for a fee. The Top of the Tower restaurant on the 20th floor offers panoramic views of the city.

DAYS INN DOWNTOWN RALEIGH $$
300 N. Dawson St., Raleigh
(919) 828-9081
www.daysinn.com

The Days Inn is at the edge of downtown, a couple of blocks from the Legislative Building. It has 72 rooms with microwaves and mini-fridges. High-speed Internet is available in the business center. Continental breakfast is included with the room. Smoking rooms are available.

HOLIDAY INN BROWNSTONE RALEIGH DOWNTOWN $$
1707 Hillsborough St., Raleigh
(919) 828-0811
www.brownstonehotel.com

On Hillsborough Street near the N.C. State campus, the Brownstone is also less than a mile from the State Capitol and downtown. The hotel has 187 rooms with free high-speed Internet, coffeemakers, hair dryers, irons, and balconies. The executive level rooms are a bit swankier, with granite and marble decor, and the hotel has five small suites. The hotel has a 24-hour fitness center and outdoor pool, and offers access to the recently renovated YMCA next door. The on-site bar is Ledo Pizza and Pasta, and guests can easily walk to Hillsborough Street dining or to Irregardless Cafe around the corner on Morgan Street.

**RALEIGH MARRIOTT CITY
CENTER** $$$–$$$$
500 Fayetteville St., Raleigh
(919) 833-1120
www.marriott.com
Completed in 2008 to serve the new Raleigh Convention Center, the Marriott recalls the grandeur of classic hotels. A wide lobby with sumptuous couches welcomes guests, and an airy bar beckons beyond. The hotel has 400 guest rooms and 10 suites, a fitness center with a pool, and a business center. Rooms include iPod docks and plasma televisions. On the ground floor are both a Starbucks and Posta Tuscan Grill, an independently run restaurant that features authentic regional Italian cuisine. The hotel provides transportation to RDU. It sits just a block from the Progress Energy Performing Arts Center and is an easy walk to the State Capitol and museums.

Outside the Beltline

COMFORT SUITES ARENA $$
1200 Hurricane Alley Way, Raleigh
(919) 854-0502
www.comfortsuitesarena.com
The Comfort Suites Arena is a good bet for travelers who need quick access to the RBC Center, Carter Finley Stadium, or the State Fairgrounds. Its 87 rooms offer free high-speed Internet access, coffeemakers, and sleeper sofas with pull-out queen beds. The hotel has a fitness center and outdoor pool and offers free breakfast and airport shuttles.

HILTON NORTH RALEIGH $$
3415 Wake Forest Rd., Raleigh
(919) 872-2323
www1.hilton.com
Just off the I-440 Beltline, the Hilton North Raleigh renovated its 189 rooms in 2008. It is convenient to North Raleigh neighborhoods and shopping at North Hills mall, just a few exits away. Rooms include high-speed Internet and coffeemakers. Dining is available at the on-site sports bar, the Skybox Grill and Bar, and at Lofton's Corner, which serves breakfast and Starbucks coffee. Also on site are an indoor pool and whirlpool

and a fitness center. A few of the rooms allow smoking and some are open to guests traveling with pets. The hotel offers free transportation to RDU Airport.

RALEIGH MARRIOTT CRABTREE VALLEY $$
4500 Marriott Dr., Raleigh
(800) 909-8289
www.marriott.com
Just across from Crabtree Valley Mall at the busiest intersection on Glenwood Avenue, the Raleigh Marriott Crabtree Valley is set off by beautifully landscaped grounds hidden from the passing traffic. The hotel has 375 rooms including five suites with high-speed Internet access, flat-screen TVs, and lush beds with 300-count linens. On site are two restaurants—Crabtree Grille and Quinn's Sports Bar—a fitness room, and an outdoor pool. Transportation to and from the airport is free.

BED-AND-BREAKFASTS

Chatham

THE FEARRINGTON HOUSE INN $$$$
2000 Fearrington Village Center, Pittsboro
(919) 542-2121
www.fearrington.com
At the heart of Fearrington Village, between Chapel Hill and Pittsboro, the Fearrington House Inn is a member of the prestigious Relais & Chateaux group. Its 35 rooms and eight suites overlook well-tended gardens and greens of the village. Decor runs to English country, with flourishes like marble accents in the bathrooms and heated towel racks. Included with the room rate are breakfast and afternoon tea in the Fearrington House Restaurant, a nightly turndown with port wine and truffles, and high-speed wireless Internet access. Guests may use the village's Duke Center for Living fitness facility, and the inn arranges in-room massage services. The inn is wheelchair accessible and allows pets. Shopping in the village includes McIntyre's bookstore, Dovecote garden shop, and the Belted Goat gift shop, which sells merchandise featuring Fear-

rington's trademark "Oreo" cows, including miniature stuffed replicas. Squeeze them, and they moo. The Fearrington House is one of two AAA Five-Diamond award winners in the state.

INN AT CELEBRITY DAIRY $$
2106 Mount Vernon-Hickory Mountain Rd., Siler City
(919) 742-5176
www.celebritydairy.com
About 20 minutes west of Pittsboro, the Inn at Celebrity Dairy was one of the first B&Bs in Chatham County, having been in operation for more than 20 years. The inn is on the site of a 300-acre dairy goat farm, and guests are welcome to visit the herd or sit on the porch and watch the chickens peck. Breakfast includes farm-made chevre, omelets, and pastries. The inn's seven cozy rooms are in the modern, Greek revival farmhouse, and one suite is in the refurbished 19th-century log cabin kitchen that adjoins the house. On the third Sunday of the month, innkeepers serve a Sunday dinner featuring local produce, meat, and cheese, followed by a tour of the barn and cheese room. The inn can accommodate guests in wheelchairs.

ROSEMARY HOUSE B&B $$
76 W. St., Pittsboro
(888) 643-2017
www.rosemary-bb.com
A block from Pittsboro's downtown traffic circle, the 1912 Colonial Revival inn sits on a quiet yard under towering sugar maples. The house is listed on the National Register of Historic Places. Its long-time second owners rented rooms to patients who came for treatment at the hospital that stood across the street. The current owners renovated the house in 2000. The inn has five rooms, all with private bathrooms. Two are outfitted with two-person soaking tubs. Decor includes hand-painted furniture, claw-foot tubs, and antique bed frames. Breakfast, high-speed wireless Internet, television, ironing board, and hair dryer are included in the room. The Rosemary offers discounts for last-minute reservations and extended stays. An afternoon tea service is available for a separate fee.

Durham

ARROWHEAD INN $$$
106 Mason Rd., Durham
(800) 528-2207
www.arrowheadinn.com
Built in 1775, the inn sits on six acres of gardens and lawns about 15 minutes north of downtown Durham. Seven rooms are in the house, all have fireplaces, and many have whirlpool tubs. A separate log cabin with a sleeping loft offers a whirlpool, wood-burning fireplace, TV, and dining area. The owners can amend the layout of the log cabin to make it accessible to guests in wheelchairs. The garden cottage, housed in the former carriage house and surrounded by landscaped paths and flowers, features a whirlpool tub, gas-log fireplace, private dining area, and TV. Phil Teber, who owns and operates the inn with his wife Gloria, is a trained chef. He specializes in breakfast pastry treats, such as mango-orange scones, which he bakes fresh every morning.

BLOOMING GARDEN INN $$–$$$
513 Holloway St., Durham
(919) 687-0801
www.bloominggardeninn.com
Architectural details inside and out, including a wraparound porch, original fireplace mantels, and high, curved ceilings, lend charm to the 1890 Queen Anne style house. The four accommodations include the three-room Morning Glory suite, which has an intricately carved wooden bed and a whirlpool for two. Period antiques and a carefully landscaped yard complete the picture. The Blooming Garden offers extended-stay rates for guests staying more than a week. The inn is about a mile from downtown Durham in the Holloway Street Historic District in the Cleveland-Holloway neighborhood, which includes some of Durham's most architecturally significant homes.

GREYSTONE INN AND CONFERENCE CENTER $$$–$$$$
618 W. Morehead Ave., Durham
(919) 688-1227
www.greystoneinn.info

A striking dressed-limestone mansion in the middle of Durham, the Greystone's grand scale and architectural details recall the Bull City's tobacco heyday, when this house was considered a modest addition to the neighborhood. Finished in 1910, it was built for James Edward Stagg, great nephew of Washington Duke, and Mary Washington Lyon Stagg. It is a rare example of the period, having survived the urban renewal of the 1960s that leveled many of Durham's turn-of-the-20th-century mansions. The carpenters who worked on Duke Chapel also created the intricate interior woodwork at Greystone. Set on six acres, the house has six rooms, three with fireplaces and three that open onto the wide second-floor veranda. A separate carriage house apartment has two bedrooms, two bathrooms, a kitchen, and a dining area. It is wheelchair accessible. All rooms include a hot breakfast buffet, transportation service, high-speed Internet, and DVDs.

THE KING'S DAUGHTERS INN $$$-$$$$
204 N. Buchanan Blvd., Durham
(877) 534-8534
www.thekingsdaughtersinn.com
Newly renovated and opened in 2009, the King's Daughters Inn was formerly a dormitory for elderly single women started with a gift from the Duke family. The 1920s-era building sits on the edge of Duke campus in the stately Trinity Park neighborhood. The inn offers guests free bicycles to explore the area. Its 17 rooms each have private bathrooms and plasma TVs with digital cable, and breakfast is included in the rate. Turndown service includes gourmet locally made chocolates and port. The parlor includes a bar that serves nightcaps. The inn has an elevator and is wheelchair accessible. Its owners completed the recent renovation with an eye toward energy efficiency and conservation. The landscaping includes drought resistant plants and pervious concrete, which helps eliminate some of the rainwater runoff on the property.

OLD NORTH DURHAM INN $$-$$$
922 N. Mangum St., Durham
(919) 683-1885
www.bbonline.com/nc/oldnorth

In the middle of one of Durham's first streetcar suburbs, the Old North Durham Inn is surrounded by Victorian-era and Arts & Crafts homes. The inn itself is an early 1900s Colonial Revival with a deep wraparound porch that makes it easy to imagine the days when streetcars and bicycles were the primary modes of transportation to downtown, about a mile away. Its four second-floor guest rooms feature antique bed frames and floral motifs. Innkeepers Debbie and Jim Vickery are regarded as excellent guides to the area, including sites that were featured in the movie *Bull Durham*. Breakfast is part of the deal.

Orange County

INN AT BINGHAM SCHOOL $$$
6720 Mebane Oaks Rd., Chapel Hill
(800) 566-5583
www.chapel-hill-inn.com
The Inn at Bingham School offers three rooms and a small cottage set in a 208-year-old, National Register of Historic Places home. The 19th-century headmaster for the Bingham School, a prep school for UNC, lived here. Amenities include gas-log fireplaces, heart pine floors, claw-foot tubs, TVs, and wireless Internet. Wine and cheese are served in the evening, and homemade chocolate chip cookies are available throughout the day. The separate Milkhouse Cottage includes a sitting room and whirlpool tub. The breakfast menu changes to include seasonal ingredients, and ranges from baked German pancakes to huevos rancheros. The setting is pastoral, with acres of pecan trees surrounding the grounds and house. It is 5 miles north of UNC's campus.

**ROCK QUARRY FARM
BED & BREAKFAST** $$-$$$
1700 N.C. 54, Chapel Hill
(919) 929-1408
www.rockquarryfarm.com
The decor of the three rooms at Rock Quarry Farm echoes the rustic aesthetic of the 120-year-old farmhouse. Wood floors, stone fireplaces, and simple antiques make for cozy surroundings. The lawn is shaded by 200-year-old oaks and

magnolias, and outdoor dining is available in the covered pole barn. Bluegrass bands play on some Saturday nights on the cabin porch. Rates include breakfast and either afternoon tea or evening wine and cheese. The inn is about 3½ miles west of downtown Carrboro.

Wake County

B&B COUNTRY GARDEN INN $$–$$$
1041 Kelly Rd., Apex
(919) 303-8003
www.b-and-b-country-inn.com

The innkeepers at the B&B are Realtors inspired to open their inn to meet the needs of those moving to the area. The inn is on eight acres in western Wake County near some of the fastest growing communities in the Triangle, including Apex and Holly Springs. Surrounding the home are acres of ponds and gardens where guests can feed the resident swans and borrow a pole to fish or take out the paddleboat. Rooms include flat-screen TVs, wireless Internet access, breakfast, and use of the hot tub. Accommodations include a suite option that includes a child's room decorated in a Mickey Mouse theme. The inn also offers weddings packages.

CAMERON PARK INN B&B $$$
211 Groveland Ave., Raleigh
(919) 835-2171
www.cameronparkinn.com

Cameron Park was developed in the early 1900s as one of Raleigh's first suburbs. A leafy, hilly neighborhood with charming winding streets, it is less than 2 miles from downtown and next door to the N.C. State campus on Hillsborough Street. The Cameron Inn's three recently renovated rooms and two suites have private bathrooms, flat-screen TVs, DVD players, and wireless high-speed Internet access. The current owners of the inn are the third couple to run a B&B in the 1912 house, and they provide top-notch service. The owners get help in the hospitality department from a friendly gray kitty named Tyler.

OAKWOOD INN BED & BREAKFAST $$–$$$
411 N. Bloodworth St., Raleigh
(919) 832-9712
www.oakwoodinnbb.com

The beautifully restored 1871 Oakwood Inn was one of the first dozen homes built in the historic Oakwood neighborhood. It became Raleigh's first B&B in 1984. Its six rooms are done in bold colors and furnished with Victorian-era pieces. All rooms have working fireplaces, Internet access, cable television, DVD players, and private bathrooms, some with antique tubs. Snacks and beverages are available throughout the day, and the rate includes breakfast and a sweet evening treat. The inn offers packages for theater fans and couples looking for one-night getaways. Downtown is less than a mile away, and the inn is within walking distance of state government offices, the Legislative Building, and Krispy Kreme, which is why the air is often filled with the scent of doughnuts.

WOODBURN COTTAGE $$$
117 Woodburn Rd., Raleigh
(919) 828-2276
www.woodburncottage.com

The Woodburn Cottage is a 1920s Arts & Crafts bungalow in the Cameron Park neighborhood with two guest rooms. Among the home's many interesting former residents is Red Upshaw, the first husband of author Margaret Mitchell. He is widely believed to have been the inspiration for Rhett Butler, the leading man of Mitchell's *Gone With the Wind*. Room decor is simple and elegant, in keeping with the architectural style of the house. Breakfast, wireless Internet and off-street parking are included in the rate. The inn does not accept children younger than 12.

CAMPING

State parks and Natural Areas charge a fee of between $18 and $23 for single-site campers. The fees are more for group campgrounds.

BIRCHWOOD RV PARK
5901 Wilkins Dr., Durham
(919) 493-1557
www.birchwoodrv.com

The park is in northwest Durham between I-85 and I-40 in a wooded area near Duke Forest. It is about 5 miles to Duke Hospitals, which makes it a convenient spot for patients in long-term treatment and their families. Most sites include phone hookups and wireless Internet access. The park has public phones, a laundry room, a playground, vending machines, a propane refill station, a repair shop, and storage space. It is pet friendly and open year-round. Spots are $32 per day, with weekly and monthly rates available.

ENO RIVER STATE PARK
6101 Cole Mill Rd., Durham
(919) 383-1686
www.ncparks.gov

All of Eno River's campsites are hike-in. Five are at Fanny's Ford Campground, a mile from the Fews Ford parking lot, and five are at Piper Creek Campground, a little more than a mile from the Cole Mill parking lot. Both campgrounds are near the river, but neither has a source for potable water. The campsites have tent pads and pit toilets.

i It's a good idea to reserve sites at the state parks and recreation centers in advance, especially during the summer months. Reserve by calling (877) 722-6762 or reserve online at www.ncparks.gov.

FALLS LAKE RECREATION AREA
13304 Creedmoor Rd., Wake Forest
(919) 676-1027
www.ncparks.gov

Spreading across parts of eastern Durham County and northern Wake County, the 26,000 wooded acres surrounding the 12,000-acre Falls Lake are home to 300 campsites for tents and RVs. The Rollingview sites are open year-round. Most other sites are open mid-March through November, so be sure to check before heading out. The Holly Point area on the north shore of the lake

off N.C. 50 has 153 campsites. Of those, 89 have water and electric hookups. Showers, restrooms, and dump stations are located nearby. The Rollingview area on the south shore of the lake off N.C. 98 offers 80 campsites with water and electric hookups for RVs and 35 sites for tents and trailers. Backpackers can find 47 hike-in sites accessible via the Shinleaf area on the south shore of the lake east of Rollingview. The park also has group sites available by reservation.

JORDAN LAKE RECREATION AREA
280 State Park Rd., Apex
(919) 362-0586
www.ncparks.gov

In Chatham County east of Pittsboro, Jordan Lake has more than 1,000 campsites. Some are open year-round, but not all, so call ahead to check on seasonal closings in the late fall and winter. Each campground offers showers, restrooms, and a dump station. The Crosswinds Campground on the eastern shore of the lake off U.S. 64 has 182 sites, 134 with water and electrical hookups. Parker's Creek on the western shore of the lake off U.S. 64 has 250 sites, 120 with water and electric hookups. Poplar Point on the eastern shore has 579 sites, 363 sites with water and electric hookups. Backpackers can find 24 hike-in sites via the New Hope Overlook area on the eastern shore off U.S. 1. The campsites are between 100 yards and half a mile from the parking lot, and toilets and drinking water are available. Jordan Lake also has group sites for tent campers and RVs available by reservation.

UMSTEAD STATE PARK
8801 Glenwood Ave., Raleigh
(919) 571-4170
www.ncparks.gov

Just off I-40 between Raleigh and Durham, Umstead State Park has 28 sites for tent and trailer camping open March 15 through December 15. The sites include picnic tables and grills and community restrooms and showers. There are no RV hookups in the park. Several group campgrounds and a lodge for groups are also located in the park.

RESTAURANTS

The Triangle's dining scene is much more diverse and rewarding today than it was just a decade ago. That's due in part to the influx of transplants who have brought their culinary customs along with them, from northeastern states and eastern countries alike. It's also the result of a sustained interest in Southern culinary traditions and a growing passion for ingredients grown close to home.

In the 1980s, a Duke grad named Bill Neal helped change the way the country thought about Southern cooking when he served shrimp and grits to *New York Times* food critic, and native Southerner, Craig Claiborne. The late Neal was a self-taught culinary genius who made a name for himself as an inspired chef of French classics before he opened Crook's Corner in Chapel Hill. Shrimp and grits was a low country breakfast staple that Neal transformed into haute cuisine. Rave reviews in the national press helped food lovers begin to see Southern cooking as a valuable cultural legacy. Throughout the Triangle, a number of the highly regarded restaurants thriving today embrace this view of Southern cooking. Chefs take Southern ingredients such as okra, green tomatoes, and pig innards, and elevate them through creative treatments and presentation.

While Southern food was gaining cachet, a wave of independent-minded farmers were settling outside the Triangle's cities, growing food without industrialized methods and chemicals. They found an appetite for their produce and livestock, first at farmers' markets and then at a growing number of restaurants. Chefs came to see that the quality of these local farm ingredients surpassed what they could get from mass-market restaurant supply companies. Thus, the Triangle's celebrated farm-to-table movement thrived.

These factors, combined with the Triangle's changing population, which now includes a great many people born elsewhere and raised on a variety of cuisines, have created an interesting array of choices to explore. Detailing every worthy restaurant in the Triangle would require a book of its own, so this chapter aims to offer a thorough portrait of the region's diversity and a variety of options throughout the Triangle. Restaurants are divided into genres and listed within those genres by geography. For the purposes of this section, the Triangle is divided into "Chapel Hill-Durham" and "Raleigh-Cary." Durham isn't too far to travel for a good meal if you live or are staying in Chapel Hill or vice versa, and Raleigh and Cary are close enough to merit putting them together in this case. Of course, many of these restaurants are worth traveling from one end of the Triangle to the other, if not farther.

Price Code

All the listed restaurants take credit cards and are wheelchair accessible unless otherwise stated. Smoking is no longer allowed inside North Carolina restaurants. The price code indicates the average price for two dinner entrees. Lunch and breakfast are generally less expensive.

$	Under $15
$$	$15 to $30
$$$	$31 to $60
$$$$	Over $60

ASIAN

Chapel Hill–Durham

JUJUBE   **$$$**
1201-L Raleigh Rd. (N.C. 54)
Glen Lennox Shopping Center, Chapel Hill
(919) 960-0555
www.jujuberestaurant.com
In a little shopping center on N.C. 54 that you might miss if you're not looking for it, Jujube serves up Asian-fusion dishes in a relaxed, hip setting. Oversized black-and-white documentary photographs of Chinese street scenes look down from the walls in the main dining room, and a row of cozy booths bathed in soft light beckons beyond. Surprising combinations like sweet potato fritters with black vinegar sauce and Jujube Bolognese—rice noodles in a sauce of braised pork, hoisin, and ginger—make for a delicious and light-hearted dining experience.

LANTERN   **$$$**
423 W. Franklin St., Chapel Hill
(919) 969-8846
www.lanternrestaurant.com
Chef Andrea Reusing has gained national fame for her dedication to using local ingredients and her expert renderings of Asian cuisine. While most of the Triangle's farm-to-table restaurants concentrate on Southern-inspired dishes, Lantern offers Chinese dumplings made with local pasture-raised pork, tea-and-spice smoked local chicken, and fried whole North Carolina fish with local carrot salad. The menu changes with the seasons and the inspirations of the chef. The dining room is a study in warm elegance, and if you haven't made a reservation, the more casual bar is a fun place to grab a bite. Wash down dinner with a saketini—potato vodka, sake, and fresh cucumber.

THAI CAFE   **$$–$$$**
2501 University Dr., No. 10, Durham
(919) 493-9794
http://thaicafenc.com

Thai Cafe serves a wide variety of carefully prepared, authentic dishes using impeccably fresh ingredients in a cheery setting. Their drunken noodles and massaman curry are memorable, as are the wonderful basil rolls. Entrees can be ordered in three degrees of spiciness—"spicy," "hot," or "Thai hot"—and the kitchen faithfully follows that order. The menu includes just two desserts, crème brulée and coconut cake, and both are lovely, creamy sweet finishes to a flavorful meal.

Raleigh-Cary

DALAT ORIENTAL   **$$**
2109 Avent Ferry Rd., Raleigh
(919) 832-7449
www.dalatrestaurant.com
The dining room is comfortable and fairly nondescript, but the food is what you'll remember. The menu offers a vast array of Chinese and Vietnamese dishes, and the kitchen executes them with precision and care. Most selections lean toward traditional specialties—pho, glass noodle dishes, spring rolls—and everything comes out kissed with bright flavor. Tofu sautéed with Chinese tender greens is a treat for soy fans, and squid with pickled mustard greens and cashews will satisfy anyone looking for adventure.

DUCK & DUMPLING   **$$–$$$**
222 S. Blount St., Raleigh
(919) 838-0085
www.theduckanddumpling.com
The Duck & Dumpling is a sleek setting for wonderful lemongrass-infused soups, tender dumplings and a litany of other great Chinese, Vietnamese and Thai dishes. Dumplings come with a variety of fillings—pork, duck, edamame, and mushroom, to name a few. Entrees include several delicious fish dishes, including pan-seared sea bass and poached diver sea scallops with ginger sauce. The interior is airy and warm, illuminated by scores of tiny lights that make each table feel intimate.

SAWASDEE $$–$$$
3601 Capital Blvd., Suite 107, Raleigh
(919) 878-0049

6204 Glenwood Ave., Suite 120, Raleigh
(919) 781-7599

Sawasdee's dining rooms are less ornate than some of the Triangle's other popular Asian eateries, but its food is as good or better than most. The restaurant serves a menu of Thai favorites prepared with careful attention to the details of flavor and presentation. Chef's daily specials reflect the needs of the season—hearty soups and stews in the winter and cool, tangy salads in summer. With a wide selection of curries, pad Thai, spicy eggplant dishes, and fried tofu, the menu offers something for just about anyone, from those with tentative palates to more adventurous diners. Sawasdee is kid-friendly, and they serve their portions of jasmine rice in the shapes of farm animals to cheer young diners.

BAKERIES

Chapel Hill–Durham

GUGLHUPF $$
2760 Durham-Chapel Hill Blvd. (U.S. 15-501),
Durham
(919) 401-2600
www.guglhupf.com

With its airy, stone-and-light architecture, innovative salads and sandwiches, and delicately rendered pastries and cakes, Guglhupf feels like a mini vacation to a hip European city—not even the fact that you order at the counter takes away from the experience. The bakery turns out beautiful breads, cakes, cookies, and tarts. Their strudel is a flaky work of art, and their ethereal cream puffs put the stale imitations sold at grocery stores to shame. But before you even think about dessert, you will spend a while choosing from the cafe's entrees, sandwiches, and salads. It's a rare menu that offers you the choice of schnitzel or Niçoise salad, and the paninis are always a good bet.

Doughnut Daze

The Krispy Kreme doughnut store on Person Street is a community landmark that has inspired more than one Raleigh watercolorist to commit it to canvas. And in 2004, it inspired a group of N.C. State students to establish a stomach-churning tradition that now draws more than 5,000 participants every year in January or February. The Krispy Kreme Challenge begins at the N.C. State bell tower on Hillsborough Street. Participants run 2 miles to the Krispy Kreme, where they wolf down a dozen doughnuts, then turn around and run back to the bell tower. The goal is to keep breakfast down and finish the run in under an hour. Money raised from entry fees goes to UNC Children's Hospital. It's fun to stand on the corner and watch the runners at the midway point, as they spread out across the doughnut shop parking lot and try to get through a dozen glazed. You might want to eat your own doughnut before the race, though. The sight can be less than appetizing. Find out more at www.krispykremechallenge.com.

NINTH STREET BAKERY $
136 E. Chapel Hill St., Durham
(919) 688-5606
www.ninthstreetbakery.com

You can find Ninth Street bread in grocery stores and restaurants around the Triangle, but if you want it just-out-of-the-oven fresh, stop by the bakery in downtown Durham for a cinnamon roll and a cup of coffee, or a sandwich and bowl of fresh gazpacho. Ninth Street specializes in organic breads, pastries, and cookies. It's cheap, too. All sandwiches are $5 and come with chips or baby carrots. Ninth Street is open for lunch only.

ℹ️ Inspired by the Krispy Kreme Challenge, a group of Duke grad students devised the Doughman, a more complicated relay race that involves teams of four athletes running and biking between a number of Durham restaurants, eating a variety of foods in a hurry, and an aquatic challenge as well. The route changes from year to year but always involves locally owned restaurants that embrace the slow foods ethos. Find out more at http://doughman .pratt.duke.edu.

Raleigh-Cary

HEREGHTY $
2603 Glenwood Ave., Suite 123, Raleigh
(919) 781-5850
www.hereghty.com
Tucked away in a shopping strip at the corner of Glenwood Avenue and Oberlin Road, Hereghty is a quiet European bakery that turns out beautiful tarts, cakes, and desserts. Specialties include the Prag cake, a hazelnut ganache sponge cake drizzled with rum, and the eye-popping mixed berry tart. It's a lovely place for a coffee and a treat.

LA FARM $
4248 Cary Parkway, Cary
(919) 657-0657
www.lafarmbakery.com
Master baker Lionel Vatinet turns out the kind of yeasty perfection at La Farm that most bakers spend their lives trying to achieve. Breads come in a number of incarnations, including anything-but-basic French, kalamata olive, and challah. Pastries include lemon bars, tarts, croissants, and an unforgettable pain au chocolate. The cafe serves soups, sandwiches, and salads for lunch and dinner. Breakfast selections include croque madame and homemade granola. Vatinet also offers baking lessons at La Farm.

BARBECUE

Chapel Hill–Durham

ALLEN & SON BARBEQUE $
6203 Millhouse Rd., Chapel Hill
(919) 942-7576
Allen & Son has set the standard for barbecue in the Triangle for almost four decades. Keith Allen smokes the pork the old-fashioned way, getting up at 3 a.m. to start the wood fires, smoking the hogs for eight or nine hours, and chopping the roasted meat himself. The pork is succulent and tangy, swimming in vinegar-based sauce. The restaurant itself is unassuming, with cinder block walls and plastic tablecloths, but the barbecue is legendary, as are the crispy coleslaw, crunchy hush puppies, and homemade desserts like peanut butter pie and peach cobbler. Allen & Son is between Chapel Hill and Hillsborough just off N.C. 86. It's worth seeking out even if you're not going in that direction.

THE ORIGINAL Q SHACK $$
2510 University Dr., Durham
(919) 402-4227
www.theqshackoriginal.com
This democratic restaurant cooks up as much beef and chicken as it does pork, which pleases transplants unfamiliar with North Carolina's preference for pig. Choose from smoked pork butt, chile-rubbed beef brisket, smoked chicken and turkey, St. Louis cut pork ribs, and smoked sausage. Sauces come on the side in two versions, a tomato-base spiked with chipotle and a vinegar-base with a hint of tomato and chiles. Sides like macaroni and cheese and fried okra are as good as the meat, and no one can resist adding a jalapeño deviled egg to their plate for 35 cents.

Raleigh-Cary

CLYDE COOPER'S BARBECUE $
109 E. Davie St., Raleigh
(919) 832-7614
www.clydecooperbbq.com
It's been there since 1938, which is why Cooper's squat little building looks like a relic from another

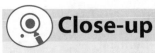 **Close-up**

B is for BBQ

In North Carolina, barbecue is a noun. In its most traditional sense, barbecue means pork, pulled from a whole pig that has been slow-cooked over hickory coals. Nowadays, a lot of folks cook their pigs on gas cookers, which can still render some pretty juicy barbecue but doesn't impart the subtle smokiness that wood-cooking does. So, if you find a barbecue place that still cooks over wood, you're in for a real treat. (See the listing for Allen & Son in Chapel Hill.)

No pit master in North Carolina would say he "barbecues" hogs. He "cooks a pig" and then it is barbecue. "Barbecue" is also used to describe an event at which barbecue is served. But, if you're going to fire up the grill at home, have some friends over, and roast hot dogs and hamburgers, what you're having is a "cook-out."

In the eastern part of the state, cooks douse their cooked pigs in a vinegar-based sauce spiked with red peppers and other secret ingredients. In the western part of the state, cooks ladle on a thicker tomato sauce that is generally sweeter than the eastern style. You won't find much of that western North Carolina barbecue in the Triangle, as it sits well east of the state's barbecue dividing line, which is Lexington. Most North Carolinians are loyal to whichever style of barbecue they grew up with, and many are fiercely so. If you are a newcomer, though, you don't necessarily have to declare a preference. Feel free to enjoy either, just don't expect to find both styles at the same place, because they rarely coexist peacefully. The rivalry is not quite as contentious as Duke vs. UNC, but close.

If you go to a traditional barbecue restaurant in the Triangle, don't try to order beef. There's not likely to be any. That's not to say that there is no beef barbecue in the state. Some newer restaurants and chains offer up all kinds of cooked meat and call it barbecue—ribs, beef brisket, etc. Much of it is very tasty. But to a North Carolinian, it's not really barbecue.

A traditional eastern North Carolina barbecue sandwich will come served on a hamburger bun and topped with creamy coleslaw. If you order the barbecue plate, you'll likely get the slaw on the side. In either case, it's good to eat the 'cue and the slaw together because the creamy coolness of the slaw complements the tang of the vinegar-based sauce. Trust us on this one. We've been eating it this way for a long, long time. If you would like even more zing on your 'cue, look on the table for a bottle of red pepper sauce labeled TEXAS PETE, which is made in Winston-Salem and cannot be found at all in the Lone Star State. Shake on a few drops and dig in.

time beside the sleek skyscraper looming over it. Generations of regulars keep coming back, and Cooper's reputation keeps winning new fans, including the members of U2. The band ordered Cooper's 'cue delivered to their jet after their Carter-Finley Stadium show in 2009. Pork barbecue (chopped or sliced), chicken (barbecued or fried), and ribs are the staples. Get them with a number of traditional sides, including collard greens, corn and butter beans, and Brunswick stew, a long-simmered mélange of vegetables and chicken. Hush puppies, of course, come with everything.

THE PIT $$
328 W. Davie St., Raleigh
(919) 890-4500
www.thepit-raleigh.com

Barbecue and white tablecloths rarely go together, but the pairing works at this popular warehouse-district spot. The pit master is national barbecue star Ed Mitchell, and he delivers juicy tender pulled pork, pit-cooked over oak or hickory in back of the restaurant. The menu draws from the traditions of North Carolina barbecue joints, but also includes Texas-style brisket, smoked turkey, fried chicken, fresh fish, and a barbecue tofu dish. Paired with sides like sweet potato fries and appetizers like fried green tomatoes, meals are an update of the classic Southern plate. While the setting is much sleeker than your average 'cue shack, it stops short of being pretentious. The carefully restored 1930s meatpacking warehouse is bright and warm, and the central bar has a great feel. The wine and beer list was designed with the smoky flavors of barbecue in mind, and includes a sweet and light sangria made with North Carolina native scuppernong wine.

BREAKFAST AND BRUNCH

Chapel Hill–Durham

ELMO'S DINER $
200 N. Greensboro St., Carr Mill Mall
Carrboro
(919) 929-2909

776 Ninth St., Durham
(919) 416-3823
Cozy and cacophonous at the same time, both Elmo's locations offer food to fill the belly and a welcoming atmosphere. The custom-made omelets are fun to create, with ingredients including kalamata olives, sprouts, turkey sausage, and broccoli. Waffles include a bacon-infused model and the French toast is made with sunflower bread. You can pore over the menu while the kids color with the crayons the waitress brings with the coffee.

Raleigh-Cary

BIG ED'S AT CITY MARKET $$
220 Wolfe St. in City Market, Raleigh
(919) 836-9909
Big Ed's looks like the kind of place where you're going to get real Southern cooking, and it is. It's a big, noisy room and every available inch of wall space is covered in antique farm equipment, old advertisements, and pictures of politicians and actors who've dined there. Service is prompt and friendly, and the portions are huge. The pancakes, omelets, and sausage gravy are spot-on, but it's the biscuits that make a trip to Big Ed's the best

part of your day. Warm from the oven, they are so light and airy that you hardly have to pick them up off the plate. Eat them with jam or smothered in creamy, savory sausage gravy. Big Ed's is closed on Sunday.

BRIGS $$
Brigs at the Crossing
1225 NorthW. Maynard Rd., Cary
(919) 481-9300

Brigs at the Park
4900 N.C. 55, Suite 520, Park W. Crossing
(919) 544-7473

Brigs Great Beginnings
8111-169 Creedmoor Rd.
(919) 870-0994

Brigs at Wake Forest
12338 Wake Union Church Rd.
(919) 556-8422
At Brigs, brunch service lasts all day long. Have one of the Royal Skillets and brunch will be the only meal you need that day. It's a mélange of home fries mixed with meats and veggies, coated in cheese, and topped with eggs cooked your way. The cooks are always coming up with new dishes and switching out the omelet of the week and the Benedict of the month. The first one opened in 1988, and Brigs now has four locations around the Triangle.

COFFEE SHOPS

Chapel Hill–Durham

BLUE COFFEE CAFE $
202 N. Corcoran St., Durham
(919) 688-2233
In downtown Durham, Blue Coffee is a roomy space with comfy couches, coffee drinks fueled by beans from local roasters Broad Street, and pastries from Ninth Street and Sweet Jane. There's plenty of room to spread out, and kids are welcome to play at a table their size. The crowd is an interesting mix of suits, moms, and downtown hipsters.

THE OPEN EYE CAFE $
101 S. Greensboro St., Carrboro
(919) 968-9410
www.openeyecafe.com
At Open Eye, you can get coffee made from 10 different kinds of beans from Carrboro Coffee Company. You can also see the work of local artists on the wall, listen to open mic poetry or local musicians, and stay up on community events. It's a hub of activity in downtown Carrboro.

i In North Carolina, as in much of the South, when you order tea, you will receive a tall, icy glass or Styrofoam cup full of liquid so intensely sweet that your teeth may begin to ache if you even contemplate its sugar content. This is sweet tea, and yes, the cook intended for it to taste just like that. If you find it overpowering, you can order the unsweet, or try half-sweet/half-unsweet. Of course, there are many restaurants in the Triangle that serve hot tea, especially Asian and Indian varieties. Most often you add your own sugar for those drinks.

Raleigh-Cary

HELIOS $
413 S. Glenwood Ave., Raleigh
(919) 838-5177
www.cafehelios.com
Glenwood South's favorite place to caffeinate, Helios is sleek inside with an airy, roomy sitting area. The coffee is good, the lattes and cappuccinos are well-made, and the menu options include bagels, cupcakes, and soy bars. The roomy patio is a great place to soak in the sun or sit in the shade of one of the wide umbrellas and watch the foot traffic on Glenwood.

THE MORNING TIMES $
10 E. Hargett St., Raleigh
(919) 836-1204
www.themorningtimes-raleigh.com
Next door to The Raleigh Times Bar in downtown Raleigh, the Morning Times brews powerful lattes and serves fresh sandwiches and bagels. The downstairs has great windows for people-watching, and upstairs is a roomy, cozy lounge with couches and tables where laptops are always glowing. Local artists' work dots the walls, and Morning Times is always a stop on the monthly First Friday gallery walk.

CONTEMPORARY AMERICAN

Chapel Hill–Durham

FOUR SQUARE $$$–$$$$
2701 Chapel Hill Rd., Durham
(919) 401-9877
www.foursquarerestaurant.com
Four Square's beautifully renovated Victorian mansion is home to an eclectic menu. Start with pretzel-crusted oysters with green apple and endive sauerkraut or country ham–cured sea scallops, and move on to local barbecued pork belly with steamed buns and Asian pear relish or dolmas made with local collard greens and butternut squash. Finish things off with fig and coriander cheesecake or caramel corn and apple crepe. The by-the-glass wine list is extensive with a worldly scope that echoes the international inspiration of the menu. The setting is at once elegant and understated.

NANA'S $$$–$$$$
2514 University Dr., Durham
(919) 493-8545
www.nanasdurham.com
Owner and chef Scott Howell studied at the Culinary Institute of America and cooked with renowned chefs around the world before returning to his native North Carolina. His menu is infused with his love of Southern food and his passion for French and Italian culinary traditions. Dishes could include venison carpaccio in a fennel crust and a grilled chicken over ratatouille and fried green tomatoes finished with red wine–thyme jus. It's Southern fusion cooking at its highest level that puts the spotlight on locally grown produce and North Carolina's coastal catches. The atmosphere is as invigorating as the menu,

with walls painted in bright, warm reds and yellows and adorned with the works of local artists.

PIEDMONT $$$
401 Foster St., Durham
(919) 683-1213
www.piedmontrestaurant.com
House-made charcuterie has put Piedmont on the national map as a destination for inventive food. The chefs use just about every part of the locally raised pigs they buy, rendering them into luscious pâtés, pork belly raviolini, and the like. The daily changing menu also includes dishes made with North Carolina fish, locally made cheese, and vegetables. A little cheaper than some of the more formal of the Triangle's farm-to-table temples, Piedmont is a good place to sink your teeth into the area's local-oriented food scene. The setting is an urban-chic renovation of a downtown Durham warehouse, comfortable but spare. Piedmont is also a popular brunch spot.

Raleigh-Cary
IRREGARDLESS $$$
901 W. Morgan St., Raleigh
(919) 833-8898
www.irregardless.com
The Irregardless led the Triangle's farm-to-table movement before there was a name for it. Open since 1975 around the corner from N.C. State's main campus, the Irregardless serves an interesting menu of vegetarian and omnivore entrees. Cheery landscapes and street scenes by local artists adorn the walls, and on Saturday nights the dining room's parquet floor makes way for dancing to the sounds of local jazz musicians. The menu is diverse, with everything from vegan grilled vegetable biryani to paella to buffalo chicken macaroni and cheese. Small plates are available for those who want just a nibble.

POOLE'S $$$
426 S. McDowell St., Raleigh
(919) 832-4477
www.poolesdowntowndiner.com
Oh-so-hip and truly delicious, Poole's combines a restored vintage setting with the inventive genius of one of the Triangle's beloved chefs, Ashley Christensen. The space began its life as a restaurant when Poole's Pie Shop opened there in 1945. The central double horseshoe-shaped bar, pressed tin ceiling, and red leather banquettes recall this first heyday. The small space at the edge of downtown Raleigh has been many things since the 1940s. Today it wears the Poole's name again, but instead of pies, Christensen serves a menu of farm-fresh food that changes several times a week if not every day. North Carolina clams with late summer squash go fast when they're in season, while duck hearts with sherry and bacon tempt those with adventurous palates. The menu is written on chalkboards above the bar, saving the earth a few sheets of paper every day.

ZELY & RITZ $$$
301 Glenwood Ave., Suite 100, Raleigh
(919) 828-0018
www.zelyandritz.com
A farmer is a partner in this Glenwood South restaurant, so the menu is shaped by what's fresh from the field. Coon Rock Farm, a family-owned farm in Hillsborough, grows much of the produce and livestock that Chef Sarig Agasi works with at this hip Glenwood South spot. The menu changes every week or so to reflect the new harvest. If you want to know just how many of the ingredients are locally sourced, pay attention to the green type on the menu, which indicates a raw material is from nearby. The sweet potato gnocchi with roasted squash in sweet potato sauce is a fall favorite, and in warmer months, the crab cake served with watermelon salsa is the essence of North Carolina summer. Wines are well chosen, and the setting is conducive to intimate date dinners or large groups that can gather around the dining room's long table.

COUNTRY COOKING
Chapel Hill–Durham
BULLOCK'S BARBEQUE $$
3330 Quebec Dr., Durham
(919) 383-3211

If you're looking to sample a wide range of down-home Southern cooking, all of it prepared as if you were visiting family, Bullock's Barbeque is the place to go. It's a low-slung brick building that has all the ambience of a church fellowship hall decorated by scrapbookers. The food comes piled on the plate, and it's clear that presentation is not a priority. What comes first is taste. Barbecue sandwiches, fried chicken, country ham, macaroni and cheese, turnip greens, and fried flounder sandwiches all come out just right. If you want to know what banana pudding is supposed to taste like—vanilla wafers soggy-crunchy from the creamy custard combining with slightly overripe bananas to create a wave of mild comfort—you'll find it here.

MAMA DIP'S $$
408 W. Rosemary St., Chapel Hill
(919) 942-5837
www.mamadips.com

Mama Dip, aka Mildred Edna Cotton Council, has built a life on cooking traditional Southern comfort food and serving it with a side of hospitality. She opened her first restaurant in Chapel Hill in 1976. Today she is the author of three cookbooks and a nationally renowned culinary treasure. Mama Dip's serves three meals a day, and is an excellent place to get a taste of fried green tomatoes, fried chicken, Brunswick stew, chicken and dumplings, or maybe even chitlins, which come plain or pan fried. Whatever you do, get the biscuits.

Raleigh-Cary

MECCA $$
13 E. Martin St., Raleigh
(919) 832-5714

One of the oldest restaurants in Raleigh, the Mecca has been filling the bellies of politicos and regular Joes for more than six decades. The place is small and dark inside, with wooden booths and lots of noisy chatter. Have the biscuits and gravy for breakfast or the daily special for lunch, which is usually meat—baked chicken, barbecue, hamburger steak, etc.—with Southern-style vegetables—slow-cooked collard greens, mashed

potatoes, macaroni and cheese (yes, that's a vegetable in the South). Mecca takes cash only, because the vintage register up front isn't set up for electronic cards. If you want to see what eating in Raleigh was like in the mid-20th century, this is a pretty good picture.

CUBAN

HAVANA GRILL $$
404 W. Chatham St., Cary
(919) 460-8662
www.thehavanagrill.com

Don't let the cafeteria-style layout turn you off. Havana Grill aims to replicate the experience of Cuban eateries popular in Miami. It's one of the only places in the Triangle to find tostones, maduros, ropa vieja, and picadillo. On Saturdays, the grill hosts dancing on the patio. The place is easy to find—just look out front for the palm trees that the owner had shipped in from Florida.

DELIS AND SANDWICH SHOPS

Chapel Hill–Durham

NEAL'S DELI $-$$
100 E. Main St., Carrboro
(919) 967-2185
www.nealsdeli.com

From the buttermilk biscuits that serve as the base for the morning's egg-and-meat sandwiches to sides like locally grown marinated green beans and roasted squash, Neal's does deli with a local, Southern ethos. The house-made pastrami will keep meat lovers coming back, but vegetarians don't need to feel left out because the veggie—an inventive blend of pureed Tuscan-style white beans with roasted carrots, wilted spinach, and pickled red onion on rye—is just as good. All the desserts are house made, so save room for the banana pudding or dark chocolate brownies.

SANDWHICH $$
407 W. Franklin St.
(919) 929-2114
http://sandwhich.biz/blog

The chef behind the culinary creations at Sandwich is a graduate of New York's French Culinary Institute, and he applies the same level of perfection toward his sandwich board that most other chefs direct toward elaborate French menus. Veggies and meat come from local farmers, and the combinations are inspired. Try Lex's Favorite, which mimics a classic country French salad—sunny-side-up farmers' market eggs, roasted tomatoes, crispy bacon, and local, organic greens on wheat—or the Paratha—spiced chickpeas, fried eggplant, fennel, spices, and fresh cilantro. Don't go in and try to micromanage the chef's vision. Just accept that he has created amazing sandwiches and trust his judgment. You'll be glad you did.

TOAST $

345 W. Main St., Durham

(919) 683-2183

www.toast-fivepoints.com

Everything Toast touches turns to sandwich gold, and the soup is nothing short of miraculous. Locally grown produce and meats go into the creative sandwiches that offer combinations of kale, ricotta, and sausage or mortadella, provolone, and pickled red onion. One of the homemade soups is always vegetarian, and they are anointed with top-quality olive oil. The cooler is full of specialty sodas and local beers, and Italian wines are available by the glass. It's a small, popular downtown space that gets packed at lunch time. Large tables are scant, so be prepared to split up if you come with a group of more than five.

Raleigh-Cary

SUNFLOWER'S $$

8 W. Peace St., Raleigh

(919) 833-4676

www.sunflowersraleigh.com

An equal-opportunity eatery, Sunflower's offers as many vegetarian options as it does meat-heavy sandwiches. Delicious combinations loaded with sprouts, cukes, carrot slivers, and half a dozen varieties of cheese populate the veggie side

of the menu. Carnivores should try the Mighty Quinn, roast beef with horseradish sauce. Next door to Peace College and within walking distance of downtown's state offices, the small dining room fills up quickly at lunchtime. It's a bright and airy spot for a nosh, but if you're in a hurry call ahead and pick up your sandwiches from the drive-through window. Sunflower's takes only cash or checks during the lunch service.

i In addition to the delis and sandwich shops listed here, the Triangle has a number of groceries and gourmet markets that serve prepared foods and have dining areas. These include Weaver Street Grocery in Carrboro, Foster's Markets in Durham and Chapel Hill, and Parker and Otis in Durham. See the Shopping chapter for details on these destinations.

DESSERTS

Chapel Hill–Durham

LOCOPOPS $

2600 Hillsborough Rd., Durham

231 S. Elliott Rd., Chapel Hill

1908 Hillsborough St., Raleigh

(919) 286-3500

www.ilovelocopops.com

The Triangle's favorite popsicle stand, Locopops' creative flavors are inspired and ever changing. Mojito, chocolate-wasabi, mango-chili, watermelon-cilantro—the combinations are always surprising. The environment is spare and cheery, with children's drawings and paintings on the wall and brightly colored Adirondack chairs. The popsicles are $2 apiece, which makes meeting a friend for Locopops a fun and cheap alternative to grabbing a latte. Locopops takes cash only.

SUGARLAND $$

140 E. Franklin St., Chapel Hill

(919) 929-2100

www.sugarlandchapelhill.com

Sugarland satisfies every craving, from scones for breakfast to lemon-drop martinis and cupcakes to cap off the night. The bakery makes everything from scratch using local organic eggs and dairy products and no high-fructose corn syrup. The lunch menu includes sandwiches on house-made croissants and soups. It's on Franklin Street, close to UNC campus.

Raleigh-Cary

THE CUPCAKE SHOPPE $
104 Glenwood Ave., Raleigh
(919) 821-4223
www.thecupcakeshopperaleigh.com
The cutest little stop on Glenwood South, the Cupcake Shoppe draws the afternoon stroller-pushers out for a snack as well as the nighttime noshers who opt for sweets in lieu of cocktails. Cupcakes come in a baker's dozen of flavors, from Plain Jane vanilla with vanilla buttercream frosting to You Mocha Me Crazy dark chocolate cake with espresso buttercream. They look as good as they taste, and the only complaint that resonates is that they lay the frosting on too thick. It's a good problem to have.

HAYES-BARTON CAFE $$$
2000 Fairview Rd., Raleigh
(919) 856-8551
www.hayesbartoncafe.com
Hayes-Barton Pharmacy still fills prescriptions, as it has done for more than 75 years, and behind this Five Points' landmark, the Hayes-Barton Cafe satisfies sweet tooths. The impossibly tall desserts—carrot, coconut, white chocolate-banana mousse pie, and lemon meringue pie—come in giant slices large enough to share. The warm red walls and 1940s-era decor set the mood for indulgence. The cafe serves lunch weekdays and Saturday and dinner Wednesday through Saturday. The Hayes-Barton takes cash only.

FRENCH

Chapel Hill–Durham

BONNE SOIREE $$$–$$$$
431 W. Franklin St., Suite 10, Chapel Hill
(919) 928-8388

A small place with amazing French food, Bonne Soiree is a reward for diners patient enough to score a reservation. The 10-table room is intimate, making it ideal for a romantic evening. The French-country dishes are crafted with a deft touch and include near-perfect renditions of pâté and Caesar salad as well as more complex creations like truffled pasta with fried egg served with a vegetable tart in puff pastry. Vegetarians will find their needs catered to with prescribed menu selections or the chef's modified versions of other dishes on the menu. The service is gracious without being fawning, and the sommelier makes choosing wine a joy rather than a dreaded encounter.

RUE CLER $$$
401 E. Chapel Hill St., Durham
(919) 682-8844
www.ruecler-durham.com
In downtown Durham beside the post office, Rue Cler is the kind of place that somehow makes you feel chic just sitting there. It's a spare space in a renovated office building with 18-foot ceilings and wide plate glass windows that bring the urban setting indoors. The food is simple Parisian bistro fare prepared expertly. The toasted sandwiches and omelet selections change daily for lunch and often include wonderful goat cheese and asparagus combinations. Dinner is a three-course prix fixe affair that provides an excellent portrait of the kitchen's talents. The short list of French wines by the glass is well chosen to complement the food. Bread from the adjoining bakery comes to the table with fresh creamery butter, and the chefs use local cheese and greens when possible. Finish things off with fresh beignets.

VIN ROUGE $$$–$$$$
2010 Hillsborough Rd., Durham
(919) 416-0406
www.ghgrestaurants.com/vinrouge
A short walk from Ninth Street, Vin Rouge offers a dinner menu that is a study in French classics. Poisson du jour, bouillabaisse rouille, and trout amandine are all can't-miss choices. Two prix

fixe menus—a three-course and a four-course—offer choices of house-made sausage du jour, salad Niçoise, and croque madame. The wine list provides a good variety of selections from throughout France, and the beer list includes several Belgians that suit the hearty fare. White tablecloths, red walls, and warm lights create a comfortable but elegant setting.

Raleigh-Cary

BLOOMSBURY BISTRO $$$
509 W. Whitaker Mill Rd., Suite 101, Raleigh
(919) 834-9011
www.bloomsburybistro.com

A favorite of its neighbors in Five Points, Bloomsbury's reputation draws regulars from all parts of the Triangle as well. Inspired by seasonal ingredients, the menu changes every six weeks to offer a new lineup of French dishes with global influences. Options could include sautéed Carolina mountain trout over acorn squash bisque and fresh Miki noodles in coconut curry with tropical fruit. Fans count the service as some of the best in town.

COQUETTE BRASSERIE $$$
4351 The Circle at N. Hills
N. Hills Shopping Center, Raleigh
(919) 789-0606
www.coquetteraleigh.com

The black and white tile floors, bentwood cafe chairs, and distinctive globe-light chandeliers offer a comfortable backdrop for Coquette's warming menu of French bistro food. The bread is baked in house, and you'll need lots of it to sop up the flavorful fennel-scented broth that accompanies the moules frites. Fish lovers can find a great variety of dishes prepared in creative ways—pistachio-crusted salmon, crispy trout with haricots verts, and grilled squid in arugula salad. Those seeking simply "Le Hamburger" will be pleased as well. The wines are all French, and the beverage director paid equal attention to the excellent selection of beers.

GERMAN AND POLISH

J. BETSKI'S $$$
10 W. Franklin St., Suite 120
Seaboard Station, Raleigh
(919) 833-7999
www.jbetskis.com

If your idea of German and Polish cuisine is limited to sausage and sauerkraut, J. Betski's will be a delightful surprise. It's a small place with dark wood, glowing lights, and a small patio that fills up quickly in the warmer months. Expected dishes like schnitzel arrive light and artfully rendered, as do sides like lacy spaetzle and dill cucumber salads scattered with lingonberries. Pierogies come filled with smoked pork and cambozola and covered with apple-curry sauce. Apple strudel makes a good choice for dessert but Chocolate-Hazelnut Torte with Sea Salt, Caramel, and Crispy Bacon would be far more exciting. Some ingredients are sourced from local farms, and the wine list is a revelation of German and Austrian selections that go far beyond the Rieslings with which you're familiar.

MEDITERRANEAN

Chapel Hill–Durham

MEDITERRANEAN DELI $
410 W. Franklin St., Chapel Hill
(919) 967-2666

If you can't find something to eat at Mediterranean Deli, you must not be hungry. The fresh-baked pita, made on-site from local, organic, kosher flour forms the basis for all the familiar Middle Eastern sandwich combinations and lots of surprises. Falafel eggplant pita and chicken shawarma are always winners. Those looking to fill their bellies should try the fatayers, boat-shaped breads filled with fresh feta and mozzarella and a variety of other fillings including ground sirloin, lamb, and spinach. The deli is on Franklin Street, with big picture windows, if you're lucky enough to score a table. It's a busy lunch spot, but take-out is always an option.

Raleigh-Cary

NEOMONDE $
3817 Beryl Rd., Raleigh
(919) 828-1628

10235 Chapel Hill Rd., Morrisville
(919) 466-8100
www.neomonde.com

The Lebanese Saleh brothers have been baking bread and pita since they came to Raleigh in the 1970s. Their bread is found in restaurants throughout the Triangle, including their two locations of Neomonde, where they use it to make Mediterranean sandwiches topped with local tomatoes. Neomonde's staples, especially the hummus, are delicious, and their inventive specialty pies, made with their pita dough, contain a variety of scrumptious fillings including spinach, cheese, and tomato-and-olive. The Morrisville location is a popular RTP lunch spot while the Beryl Road spot, near the J.C. Raulston Arboretum, serves N.C. State and environs.

SITTI $$$
137 S. Wilmington St., Raleigh
(919) 239-4070
www.sitti-raleigh.com

The name means "grandmother" in Lebanese, and the restaurant goes beyond the usual Mediterranean deli setting to create an atmosphere of urbane hominess. A beautiful, long wooden table is the centerpiece of the renovated furniture store on a busy downtown corner. Sitti is a joint effort of the Saleh brothers, who run Neomonde, and Greg Hatem, a Raleigh developer and restaurateur who is also of Lebanese descent. The food is outstanding and includes traditional recipes not usually on the menu of more casual Mediterranean eateries. Try the okra stew with lamb and tomatoes served over Sitti rice, which includes vermicelli and is topped with almonds, or the kibbi nayyeh, Lebanese steak tartar with cracked wheat and spices. For dessert, don't miss the rice pudding, made with orange blossom water and sprinkled with pistachios and cinnamon.

Carolina Style

When the man making your hot dog or hamburger asks if you want it "all the way," what he means is Carolina style, which is topped with mustard, slaw, onions, and beef chili. Visitors unaccustomed to this standard are often surprised—or even delighted—to learn that, in North Carolina, topping meat with even more meat is the expected custom. You can add ketchup to the Carolina style burger if you like, but most people find it is overkill. If the burger or hot dog is made properly, a mélange of onion-spiked slaw, chili, and mustard will ooze out onto the plate or wax paper wrapper from which you're eating, giving you something to sop up with your fries or chips.

HAMBURGERS

Chapel Hill–Durham

ONLYBURGER $$
www.durhamcatering.com/onlyburger

Unless you luck out and the OnlyBurger truck happens to be parked at your street party or festival, you have to do a little homework to find one of the best burgers in the Triangle. OnlyBurger's restaurant-on-wheels changes its Durham location daily. But lots of fans follow them on Twitter and Facebook, keeping their big, fresh, juicy burgers on their lunchtime radar. Toppings include lettuce, onion, tomato, pickles, ketchup, and mustard, and if you ask, mayo. Cheese and bacon are extra. Specials can include burgers topped with fried green tomatoes and an egg. Fries or chips are the only sides. OnlyBurger also cooks up a pretty good veggie burger.

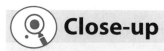

Close-up

Hot Dogs, Their Way

For years, competitive eaters have been one-upping each other, one hot dog at a time, at the oldest wiener house in Raleigh, **The Roast Grill**. A recent record of 24 wieners downed in one hour is considered unbreakable by anyone other than a professional gorger or a full-grown Yeti. Before the 24-dog mark was set, Adam Richman of the Travel Channel's *Man vs. Food* held the title for a while after putting away 17 hot dogs in one sitting during a taping of the show. The dogs come slathered in chili, stuffed between buns, and after a dozen, they go down the gullet like baseballs through a garden hose. Competitors have been known to stagger outside onto the sidewalk, gasping for fresh air and clutching their guts. Only the determined, and the gastrointestinally gifted, can compete.

Of course, The Roast Grill caters to diners who order hot dogs in single digits as well, just as long as the order is for hot dogs. That's all they sell. Toppings are limited to chili, mustard, slaw, and chopped onions. Ask for ketchup, relish, kraut or—gasp—mayonnaise, and you'll get scowls at best, a boot out the door at worst.

This shrine to hot wieners has shoveled them into downtown Raleigh customers since 1940. It's tucked back off the main streets in a single room a little larger than a walk-in closet, and to step inside is to bathe yourself in the odor of roasting meat. Traditions are held stubbornly. The Roast Grill takes no credit cards, serves no French fries or chips, and won't even brew a cup of coffee. The frankfurter is king, and Cokes come by the bottle. The Roast Grill is at 7 South West St. in downtown Raleigh, (919) 832-8292.

WIMPY'S $
617 Hicks St., Durham
(919) 286-4380

Wimpy's grinds the beef for its burgers fresh every morning and makes chili from scratch. That's helped make this take-out place near Duke's East Campus a Durham landmark for more than 20 years. The classic Carolina Burger—with chili, slaw, onions, and mustard—should be enough to satisfy most appetites. Those seeking a gullet challenge can order the Garbage Burger, a double cheeseburger topped with bacon, lettuce, tomato, pickles, onion, mayo, mustard, ketchup, chili, and coleslaw. If that's lunch, plan on a small dinner.

Raleigh-Cary

THE BERKELEY CAFE $
217 W. Martin St., Raleigh
(919) 821-0777
www.berkeleycafe.net

It's a narrow little dive sandwiched between downtown and the warehouse district where the service is prompt and friendly and the burgers are divine. The Berkeley's burgers come in 14 variations, from the Luau Lisa, with grilled pineapple and honey mustard, to the Del Mar, with guacamole and provolone. It's the kind of place where you can sit and eat your burger and keep to yourself or chat casually with the cooks and waiters behind the counter.

CHAR-GRILL $
618 Hillsborough St., Raleigh
(919) 821-7636

3211 Edwards Mill Rd., Raleigh
(919) 781-2945

4621 Atlantic Ave., Raleigh
(919) 954-9556

9601 Strickland Rd., Raleigh
(919) 845-8994

1125 W. N.C. 54, Durham
(919) 489-6900

3635 SouthW. Cary Parkway, Cary
(919) 461-7112
www.chargrillusa.com

This Raleigh institution marks half a century of burger slinging in 2010. Not much has changed about the place since the original Char-Grill opened on Hillsborough Street. Eager diners fill out their order forms and slide them under the glass to the cooks, who grill up sizzling burgers, fries, and chicken sandwiches. Hungry diners wait anxiously for their names to be called, then spread the grub out on a picnic table overlooking the traffic or eat behind the wheel. Burgers are fresh and juicy, and toppings are plentiful. Savvy burger lovers know to call ahead and cut down on wait times.

SNOOPY'S $

1931 Wake Forest Rd., Raleigh
(919) 833-0992

600 Hillsborough St., Raleigh
(919) 839-2176

3600 Hillsborough St., Raleigh
(919) 755-9022

2431 Spring Forest Rd. Unit 161, Raleigh
(919) 876-3775

Snoopy's has a big hot dog on its sign, the mark of its beloved footlongs, but its burgers rank among the best in Raleigh, too. It's walk-up, take-out stores are beloved for zippy service and the late hours they keep, which means you'll find a crowd lingering in a Snoopy's parking lot, waiting for burgers or wolfing them down, almost any time of day. Snoopy's has daily specials, including 99-cent hot dogs on Tuesdays. The original store on Wake Forest Road has been a landmark since 1978.

INDIAN

Chapel Hill–Durham

SITAR INDIA PALACE $$
3630 Durham-Chapel Hill Blvd., Durham
(919) 490-1326
www.sitarindiapalace.net
Sitar offers lunch buffets every day and dinner buffets on Friday and Saturday nights. Saturday nights also feature sitar and tabla music. Among

the favorites at Sitar are the naan stuffed with homemade cheese, the vegetable vindaloo, and the tender fish tikka. The large dining room features a brilliantly colored mural, and the bar area is cozy.

Raleigh-Cary

ROYAL INDIA $$$
3901 Capital Blvd. Suite 103, Raleigh
(919) 981-0849
www.royalindianc.com
You'd never guess how pretty the dining room of this restaurant is judging from the outside. Hand-carved wooden screens, vintage black-and-white portraits of Indian royalty, and illuminated mango-colored ceilings give an exotic air to Royal India. The food is some of the most popular in the city, with butter chicken and chicken tikka masala consistent favorites. The lunch buffet is popular, as are the specialty meals including the vegetarian platter and the sizzling grill, which features lamb and chicken kebabs and tandoori shrimp.

SAFFRON $$$$
4121 Davis Dr., McCrimmon Corners,
Morrisville
(919) 469-5774
www.saffronnc.com
This is a special-occasion spot that distinguishes itself from the many Indian restaurants in the Triangle with a modern, understated décor that still recalls the far-away origins of its cuisine. Carved wooden details, an onyx bar, red-and-gold tapestries, and soft lights make this a great place for a romantic night out. The service and presentation are as well-executed as the cuisine. Familiar favorites like vegetable samosa and tandoori chicken share space on the menu with grilled salmon and smoked lobster.

TOWER $$
144 Morrisville Square Way, Morrisville
(919) 465-2326
www.towernc.com
Vegetarians, your wishes come true at Tower. The chefs take incredible care in preparing vegetarian-

only dishes in the traditions of South India. Try the Medhu Vidai, a fried lentil doughnut with sambar and coconut chutney, to start. Move on to Gobi Manchurian with Rice, which is marinated and deep-fried cauliflower tossed in soy and spicy chili sauce, or the curries of eggplant or okra. The decor is nothing spectacular. What keeps the crowds returning is the excellent food.

ITALIAN

Chapel Hill–Durham

PANCIUTO $$$
110 S. Churton St., Hillsborough
(919) 732-6261
www.panciuto.com
Panciuto prepares Italian specialties with a Southern accent, using local and sustainably grown meat and produce. Touches like a smear of hot pepper jelly added to bruschetta topped with a duck egg and warm Carolina Moon cheese remind diners that they're in the South. The menu changes weekly and remains small so that the chef can attend to each dish carefully. The chef sources his ingredients from a cadre of 26 local farmers and cheese makers. The all-Italian wine list is sourced from small family vineyards. In Hillsborough's downtown historic district, the elegantly comfortable setting is welcoming and the service is spot-on, prompt without being fawning.

PIAZZA ITALIA $$$
905 W. Main St., Suite 18A
Brightleaf Square, Durham
(919) 956-7360
www.piazzaitalia.us
Piazza Italia's beautifully restored warehouse home, all warm wood and exposed brick, sets a lovely, rustic tone for meals that feature freshly made pasta and gelato. In Brightleaf Square, the restaurant is set up to recall an Italian village, with a fountain in the middle. Ravioli, stuffed with either ricotta and spinach or beef, pork, and veal, are always delicious. The kitchen also turns out good fish and shellfish dishes, including a filet

of sole Milanese. You can buy fresh pasta and other ingredients to take home from the market section.

POP'S $$$
605 W. Main St., Durham
(919) 956-7677
www.pops-durham.com
The wood-fired pizzas at Pop's are so good, it's a wonder they serve anything else. In fact, once you have the pie with house-made meatballs, broccoli rabe, Parmesan, and roasted garlic, you might not ever order anything else. But you should, because it would be a crime to miss Pop's Big Bowl of Mussels in their glorious white wine broth spiked with garlic, chile, and roasted tomato. Pop's uses local and seasonal ingredients to great effect, and changes its lasagna and soup selections daily. The interior is cozy-cool with old wood floors, exposed brick walls, and soft lights.

Raleigh-Cary

BELLA MONICA $$$
3121-103 Edwards Mill Rd., Raleigh
Olde Raleigh Village Shopping Center
(919) 881-9778
www.bellamonica.com
A menu of traditional Italian favorites made with care keeps the crowds coming to Bella Monica in North Raleigh. It's a family friendly spot, and has a large menu of gluten-free options that includes pasta dishes and flatbreads that give allergy sufferers interesting alternatives to pizza. The shopping center space is bright and cheery with yellow walls and purple accents. Bella Monica is also known for its line of frozen gluten-free flatbreads.

POSTA TUSCAN GRILLE $$$–$$$$
500 Fayetteville St., Marriott City Center,
Raleigh
(919) 227-3370
www.postatuscangrille.com
Posta Tuscan Grill, on the ground floor of Raleigh's downtown Marriott, underscores the hotel's air of

sophistication. Brothers from Tuscany run the restaurant, and the kitchen delivers cuisine authentic to their Italian home. Appetizers include impossibly thin beef carpaccio on arugula and insalata caprese made with imported buffalo mozzarella. Pasta dishes shine in their simplicity, boasting top-quality ingredients and proving careful preparation. The wood-fired pizzas come with mozzarella and tomato or prosciutto, no Americanized topping combinations. The wine list is vast with choices from Italy and the American west coast, and includes a selection of reserve wines by the glass. Set inside a large, airy space with dark wood floors, tall windows, and warm terra cotta walls, Posta is a little oasis of the Italian countryside in the middle of downtown Raleigh.

JAPANESE AND SUSHI

Chapel Hill–Durham

AKASHI $$$
2223 N.C. 54, Suite R
Durham, (919) 572-9444
www.akashisushi54.com
Half-price sushi that is always fresh, with service that is as impeccable as the fish, make Akashi a favorite for the RTP lunch crowd as well as nighttime diners seeking a deal. Favorites include the tuna jaw appetizer, the Romeo roll, and the Carolina roll. Ordering off the sushi menu is a good bet, too. Try the spinach-tofu soup and just about anything from the teppanyaki menu. The setting isn't posh, but the food is reliable and creative.

Raleigh-Cary

CAROLINA SUSHI AND ROLL $$$
6008 Falls of Neuse Rd., N. Ridge Shopping Center, Raleigh
(919) 981-5835
www.carolinasushi.com.whsites.net
On the end of a busy shopping center on a busy road in North Raleigh, Carolina Sushi has a strong following among neighbors who love its fresh sushi, flavorful noodle dishes, and excellent tempura. The prices are reasonable and the service

is prompt. The green walls and paper Japanese shades give the strip mall space a relaxing air. On the long hall that leads to the bathroom, a wall of graffiti written by frequent customers and first-timers attests to the loyalty Carolina Sushi inspires.

MURA $$$$
4121 Main St., N. Hills Shopping Center, Raleigh
(919) 781-7887
www.muranorthhills.com
Mura is the place to go for spectacular sushi and Kobe beef in a sleek, modern setting. The menu is extensive and well-executed with everything from seaweed salad to Kobe filets to yokisoba noodles to lobster salad sushi rolls. Lunch entrees can cost about half what dinner does, which makes a midday meal a great time to sample this high-end eatery.

MEXICAN

Chapel Hill–Durham

DOS PERROS $$$
200 N. Mangum St., Durham
(919) 956-2750
www.dosperrosrestaurant.com
The newest addition to the Triangle's collection of dressed-up Mexican restaurants, Dos Perros is sleek, comfortable, and delicious. The atmosphere is California contemporary, with mango-colored walls and spare adornment. The food, from Chef Charlie Deal, whose other restaurant is Chapel Hill's Jujube, is traditional Mexican with some American influences, but certainly not Tex-Mex. Mole poblano, sweet potato soup, and the chile rellenos all exceed expectations. Creative margaritas like the mango-cayenne are an unusual treat. Dos Perros is in downtown Durham within walking distance of the Durham Performing Arts Center, which makes it a good pre-show dining option. Just remember to give yourself plenty of time since it's not an in-and-out Mexican joint.

Raleigh-Cary

DOS TAQUITOS CENTRO $$$
106 S. Wilmington St., Raleigh
(919) 835-3593
www.dostaquitoscentro.com
This popular downtown eatery offers beautiful Mexican food, including mole and empanadas as well as some surprising fusion dishes like mussels steamed with Mexican chorizo, served in a white wine broth with bolillo toasts for sopping. The menu is a creative journey through Mexico, and the interior is a colorful cacophony of folk art. Wash it all down with an agua fresca or a cilantro-spiked margarita.

JIBARRA $$$
327 W. Davie St., Suite 102, Raleigh
(919) 755-0556
www.jibarra.net
One look at the appetizer menu—a selection of ceviches, pork confit carnitas, and a shredded duck tossed salad—lets you know you're in for a meal that is anything but simple Mexican. Just wait until you try the salmon poblana, grilled fish over a creamy roasted poblano chile sauce with potatoes, corn, zucchini, and tomatoes. The dishes are complex and executed beautifully. The setting, in a renovated rail depot building in the warehouse district, is urban chic with sheer curtains and a backlit bar. Make sure to have a margarita. The latest seasonal fruit concoction and the pear-cilantro are always delicious.

NEW SOUTH

Chapel Hill–Durham

CROOK'S CORNER $$$
610 W. Franklin St., Chapel Hill
(919) 929-7643
www.crookscorner.com
Bill Smith continues the traditions of this legendary restaurant, where Bill Neal presented ground-breaking dishes like shrimp and grits in the 1980s and made a new name for Southern cooking. It's a small space that used to be a fish market, then a barbecue joint, and now sports a cheery atmosphere with chrome details, local art inside, and its trademark pig statue flying high above the roof. The menu changes with the seasons to reflect the local harvest. Come in the fall to get grilled short loin steak and persimmon pudding or, if you're lucky, show up in the summer when honeysuckle sorbet is on the menu. After you've had the legendary shrimp and grits for brunch, go back and try the Eggs New Bern and see what a difference a biscuit makes to a Benedict. The outdoor patio, shrouded in bamboo and decorated with folk artist Clyde Jones's wooden critters, is a lovely place for a warm evening's dinner.

ELAINE'S ON FRANKLIN $$$–$$$$
454 W. Franklin St., Chapel Hill
(919) 960-2770
www.elainesonfranklin.com
Elaine's is a white tablecloth dining experience with a casual, comfortable vibe. The cuisine is imaginatively designed by Chef Brett Jennings, a Virginia native who melds his earliest food loves with his experience cooking throughout the world and the South. The menu changes daily and includes locally sourced produce and meats. North Carolina seafood gets wonderful treatment in the jumbo lump blue crab salad served on a crispy cumin popadum, and the North Carolina pan-seared flounder pairs wonderfully with a mélange of Maine lobster, potatoes, leeks, spinach, and chanterelles. The chef's specials are always surprising and delicious. The restaurant is intimate and cozy, and the service is attentive without being overbearing.

THE FEARRINGTON HOUSE RESTAURANT $$$$
2000 Fearrington Village Center, Pittsboro
(919) 542-2121
www.fearrington.com/house/restaurant.asp
Set in a restored farmhouse, surrounded by the immaculate and beautiful grounds of Fearrington Village, dinner at Fearrington House is a special occasion, whether or not it's your birthday. Lush linens, European antiques, and glowing wall sconces set the mood in each of the small dining areas. The menu changes frequently, and the

chef incorporates local produce, meat, and game. Traditional dishes like beef tenderloin come with smoked wild mushroom ragout and foie gras, atop a decidedly Southern mix of spaghetti squash, turnips, and sweet potatoes. Seared North Carolina mountain trout gets dressed up with herb gnocchi and a bed of leeks and butternut squash. The presentation and service are flawless, and the wine list is wide ranging. It often includes a few choices from North Carolina's growing wine region, one of the few in the area that does.

MAGNOLIA GRILL $$$$
1002 Ninth St., Durham
(919) 286-3609
www.magnoliagrill.net
A darling of the national food press, Magnolia Grill earns its stripes with consistently excellent New South cooking that turns traditional ingredients into dreamy works of culinary art. Start with the twice-baked grits soufflé covered in exotic mushroom ragout and shaved confit foie gras and you'll begin to understand why grits are sometimes more than just grits. Owner-chefs Ben and Karen Barker follow the seasons with their daily changing menu and incorporate local produce, meat, and seafood. Set in a converted grocery store, Magnolia Grill's façade belies its charming interior of warm wood floors, white tablecloths, and walls bedecked with modern art.

WATTS GROCERY $$$
1116 Broad St., Durham
(919) 237-3611
www.wattsgrocery.com
Chef Amy Tornquist turned the grocery store where she used to buy candy as a kid into a unique incarnation of Southern comfort cuisine. The menu has a lot of local offerings, including smoked pork and fish made nearby at Zuke's, house-made terrines with artichoke pickles, and pasta dishes spiked with local goat cheese. North Carolina seafood turns up as cornmeal-crusted fried oysters, catfish almandine, and shrimp and crab étouffée. The setting is casual and modern, with a wall of banquette seating, dark wood

tables, and a long bar illuminated by cylindrical lights. It's a comfortable place to experience updated Southern dishes prepared with great attention to detail.

Raleigh-Cary

18 SEABOARD $$$
18 Seaboard Ave., Seaboard Station, Raleigh
(919) 861-4318
www.18seaboard.com
Chef Jason Smith's resume includes an interesting range of experience, from cooking in New York's Union Square Cafe and Gramercy Tavern to working as a chef on an Antarctic research station. His roots are planted firmly in his native North Carolina, though, and at 18 Seaboard he shines his culinary light on Southern food. Presentations are often simple, letting the beauty of the ingredients, many of which are sourced locally, speak for themselves. The fried green tomatoes appetizer, dressed with corn relish tartar sauce and aged balsamic, is addicting, and any of the seafood or meats cooked over the hardwood fire grill and accompanied by one of six house-made sauces makes a memorable meal. The setting is modern with clean lines and spare decor, and a rooftop patio offers lovely views of the downtown Raleigh skyline. The wines are well-chosen and the cocktail list is inventive. It's the sort of place where a wide variety of appetites can find comfort and satisfaction.

HERON'S $$$$
100 Woodland Pond, Cary
(919) 447-4000
www.heronsrestaurant.com
Set inside the Triangle's grandest hotel, Heron's is informed by the same philosophy that guides the Umstead Hotel and Spa—high-quality luxury in a setting that is uniquely North Carolinian. The beautiful sleek lines of the hotel's stone exterior continue through the lobby and into the dining room at Heron's. Low lights create alcoves of privacy and call attention to the elegant pottery pieces by North Carolina artists. The chef uses

locally grown produce and meats as well as herbs from the restaurant's on-site garden. Dishes like pan-roasted monk fish with white corn polenta in brown butter illustrate the chef's commitment to detail and precise execution. The service is attentive, with teams of waiters meeting every need promptly. Wine recommendations are perfect, and desserts like lime-scented pound cake with chilled white port muskmelon soup are one-of-a-kind. Heron's serves dinner, brunch, and lunch.

PIZZA

Chapel Hill–Durham

MELLOW MUSHROOM   **$$**
410 Blackwell St., Durham
American Tobacco Historic District
(919) 680-8500

601 W. Peace St., Raleigh
(919) 832-3499

2125 S. Main St., Wake Forest
(919) 556-8884

This Atlanta-based chain has three popular outposts in the Triangle that serve up good pizza and beer selections in fun, laid-back atmospheres. The crusts are hand-tossed and the toppings are fresh and inventive. The salad selection is respectable and the ingredients are fresh. Vegetarians can take heart in the tempeh subs on the menu. Psychedelic decor, including the signature mushrooms, convey a hippie-inspired playfulness. The patio at the Raleigh location, at the corner of Peace and Glenwood, is packed anytime the sun shines and the mercury ekes above 55 degrees.

PEPPER'S   **$$**
127 E. Franklin St., Chapel Hill
(919) 967-7766
www.myspace.com/pepperspizza666
A longtime Franklin Street institution, Pepper's boasts wonderful pies on house-made crusts delivered by colorful characters in a uniquely Chapel Hill environment. White pizza, pesto-based pies, and creatively named combinations like the all-veggie Euell Gibbons and the Regular

Guy—mushrooms, onions, bell peppers, pepperoni, fresh Italian sausage, fresh ground chuck, and diced ham—are always delicious. Strombolis, calzones, gazpacho, and salads are great, too. A word of caution: Your server might be dressed eccentrically. It's all part of the college-town vibe.

Raleigh-Cary

CAPITAL CREATIONS   **$$**
1842 Wake Forest Rd., Raleigh
(919) 836-8000

3055 Medlin Dr., Raleigh
(919) 782-7080
A take-out or delivery only pizzeria, Capital Creations delights in concocting pizzas that make you say, "Hmmm?"; one taste and a "yum" quickly

follows. Try the muffaletta, a white pizza crust topped with chopped black and green olives and carrots, garlic, herbs and olive oil, provolone cheese, salami, Canadian bacon, red onions, and banana peppers. Or the Arizona Chicken, a cornmeal crust slathered in a sour cream–picante sauce topped with Pepper Jack cheese, grilled chicken, corn, white onions, and green peppers. If you fall outside their delivery area, their locations are convenient to much of Raleigh, whether you're inside the Beltline or out.

LILLY'S $$
1813 Glenwood Ave., Raleigh
(919) 833-0226
www.lillyspizza.com
A Five Points landmark with a funky and bohemian atmosphere, Lilly's features thick or thin crusts made with organic whole wheat flour, organic toppings, and interesting combinations such as the Corporate Greed, which involves homemade Alfredo sauce, cremini mushrooms, mozzarella, artichoke hearts, and grilled chicken. Lilly's also serves gluten-free pies, calzones, Stromboli, and pasta dishes. Local artwork hangs on the wall, and there's a small patio where you can watch the traffic on Glenwood.

MOONLIGHT $$
615 W. Morgan St., Raleigh
(919) 755-9133
www.moonlightpizza.com
A few blocks from the south end of Glenwood Avenue, Moonlight is a neighborhood joint that serves some of the best pizza in Raleigh. The interior is cozy-cool, with wooden booths, walls hung with local art, and a small bar that draws an eclectic group. The small patio is lovely in warmer months, hung with Christmas lights and shaded by large umbrellas. Once you've had their Four Seasons pie—essentially four pizzas in one that includes shrimp, black olives, and sundried tomatoes—it's hard to resist getting it over and over. But there are plenty of other tempting selections on the menu.

SEAFOOD

Chapel Hill–Durham

FISHMONGER'S $$–$$$
806 W. Main St., Durham
(919) 682-0128
A downtown institution for more than 25 years, Fishmonger's feels like a beachside oyster bar, only the plate glass windows open onto the traffic near Brightleaf Square instead of the sand. Wide wooden booths have a weathered feel, and the staff is laid back. Fishmonger's Friday oysters special ($7 for a dozen between 2 and 6 p.m.), makes it a popular early-weekend start. Fried, steamed, and broiled seafood of many varieties populates the menu. If you feel like a messy, delicious feast, order the Frogmore Stew, a South Carolina low country tradition. It's a mess of shrimp, sausage, corn, and potatoes cooked in Old Bay and beer that you eat with your hands.

Raleigh-Cary

BUKU $$
110 E. Davie St., Raleigh
(919) 834-6963
www.bukuraleigh.com
Set in one of Raleigh's most beautiful dining rooms, buku offers a realm of flavors inspired by the street foods of the world. Indian curry hot pot, Moroccan lamb meat balls, Columbian arepas, Chinese pork buns, and grilled octopus are among the standouts on a can't-miss litany of small plates. Formerly the nationally renowned Fins, buku retains the shimmering wall of water that separates the bar from the dining area. Overhead, long tube-shaped, paper-shaded lanterns combine with hundreds of pinpoint lights to illuminate the soft gold walls and create an atmosphere of intimacy and serenity. Chef William D'Auvray's deft touch with the global menu of tapas-like treats extends to the sashimi selection and full-size entrees as well. Entertainment underscores the global theme. On a given night the bar could be thumping to the sounds of a DJ or moving to the music of an African drum group. If you don't feel like stepping inside, grab a bite from buku's cart on the sidewalk for a true street food experience.

42ND STREET OYSTER BAR $$$
508 W. Jones St., Raleigh
(919) 831-2811
www.42ndstoysterbar.com

The spot at the corner of Jones and West streets, a few blocks from downtown's state office district and one block off Glenwood South, has been serving oysters and beer since Prohibition ended. At that time it was a grocery store whose nickname recalled a memorable New York trip some of its regulars took. In the 1950s, it became a restaurant, keeping the name. Once owned in part by longtime N.C. Secretary of State Thad Eure, 42nd Street is a popular legislative watering hole and meeting place. A large mural depicts North Carolina politicos who frequented the place. The menu includes a vast variety of seafood, broiled, fried, or sautéed, and several cuts of steak served with sides of traditional Southern vegetables such as black-eyed peas, collard greens, and the restaurant's famous cheese-baked potato.

MICHAEL DEAN'S SEAFOOD GRILL $$$
6004 Falls of Neuse Rd., Raleigh
(919) 790-9992
www.michaeldeans.com

In the parking lot of a North Raleigh shopping center, Michael Dean's is a lively spot for well-made seafood dishes with a popular after-work bar inside. The fish is fresh, and the menu offers a variety of presentations including traditional favorites like Seafood Newburg and more modern options like fish tacos and shrimp pizza with pesto cream sauce and fontina cheese. Meat eaters will find a number of entrée and appetizer selections as well. The wine list is fairly wide-ranging with plenty of by-the-glass choices.

STEAKHOUSES

Chapel Hill–Durham

BIN 54 $$$$
1201-M Raleigh Rd., Chapel Hill
(919) 969-1155
www.bin54restaurant.com

If you're looking for the best steak money can buy in the Triangle, Bin 54 is your ticket. The cuts are top-quality and carnivores have plenty of choices, from the dry-aged Kansas City strip to the roasted Kurobuta pork loin to the wood-grilled duck breast. Choose from a dozen sauces and as many side dishes. The setting is sleek and clubby with golden wood floors, leather banquettes, white tablecloths, and exposed brick. As the name implies, the wine is a main attraction, so be prepared to spend a little time finding the right wine to accompany your meal. The cellar contains more than 1,400 bottles in 300 varietals.

Raleigh-Cary

ANGUS BARN $$$$
9401 Glenwood Ave., Raleigh
(919) 781-2444
www.angusbarn.com

The Angus Barn is the Triangle's original special-occasion restaurant, having hosted countless anniversary, birthday, and graduation celebrations since 1960. It's a rambling 550-seat place that houses a country store, a 30,000-bottle wine cellar, and the Wild Turkey Lounge along with the many dining rooms. Every meal starts with the Barn's cheese spread on crackers and ends with a free apple from one of the barrels near the door, the Barn's answer to after-dinner mints. Chef Walter Royal, an *Iron Chef* winner, delivers the goods when it comes to well-prepared corn-fed Midwestern beef entrees, but he also offers interesting choices such as ostrich satay. Once located in the middle of nowhere between Raleigh and Durham on U.S. 70, the Angus Barn is now convenient to RDU and RTP. The clubby Wild Turkey Lounge, adorned with dark leather chairs, more than 600 Wild Turkey decanters, and a glass case containing one of the largest collections of single-action colt revolvers on the East Coast, is a popular after-hours gathering spot for park workers.

NIGHTLIFE

You can't say the Triangle is hopping every night of the week, but between the college bars on Franklin Street in Chapel Hill and Ninth Street in Durham and the Glenwood South district in Raleigh, the nightlife scene offers something to explore Thursday through Sunday to be sure. Options range from a few swanky dance clubs with dress codes to laid-back neighborhood bars to old-school dives that revel in their grittiness. In addition to the downtown nightlife, Raleigh's suburban areas have watering holes where apartment dwellers mingle with moms and dads out for a night without the kids.

The Triangle also boasts a handful of great music venues where a couple hundred fans can get together and see the latest buzz band on its way up or their old club-scene favorites. Salsa, swing, and ballroom dancers have a scene, too, one that frequently takes over the Durham Armory.

North Carolina's liquor laws can take some getting used to. It was one of the last states in the union to repeal Prohibition, and the Byzantine set of rules that remains in place can confound newcomers. An establishment that sells alcohol and makes less than 40 percent of its money from food sales is required to operate as a private club. This means you may be asked to join or find a member to sign you in at the door. Usually this amounts to a charge of about $5, and filling out a form. This rule isn't followed religiously though, so you never know when the bouncer will skip this step and let you in with just a check of your ID to make sure you're legal. The drinking age is 21.

Alcohol sales are approved by municipal governments, and some pockets of North Carolina remain dry, but none of these remain in the Triangle. Beer, wine, and liquor are available throughout the area. Some places may be licensed to sell only beer and wine, though.

Another quirk is that no alcohol can be served or sold before noon on Sunday, meaning the state is effectively dry on this day of the week from the time the bars close at 2 a.m. until lunchtime. Keep this in mind when you're headed for Sunday brunch. Mimosas and bloody Marys are off-limits until 12 o'clock.

As of January 2010, smoking became forbidden in North Carolina bars and restaurants, a thought that until a few years ago was considered impossible in a state where tobacco had long dominated the economy and where farmers still grow more tobacco than in any state in the country. Cigar bars and private clubs are exempted from the rule.

In North Carolina, the law considers you impaired if your blood alcohol level is higher than 0.08 percent, so call a cab or designate a driver if you plan to have more than a drink or two.

BARS, PUBS, AND LOUNGES

Chapel Hill and Carrboro

HELL
157 E. Rosemary St., Chapel Hill
(919) 932-4997

Anyone looking for an alternative to the argyle-and-loafers vibe that prevails at so many Chapel Hill bars can find an underground haven in Hell. Dingy and graffiti-covered, Hell takes great pride in its grittiness. The crowd is diverse, but a fondness for pitchers of beer served in dark places seems to be the common denominator. The beer selection is better than you might expect, going beyond the domestic staples. Thursday trivia night is a popular event, as is the twice-monthly dance party, which attracts straight and LGBT dancers in even numbers. A lifetime membership is $5.

MILLTOWN
907 E. Main St., Carrboro
(919) 968-2460

The pairing of beer and meat are the specialties at Milltown, with the emphasis on the beer. Their selection is designed to impress beer geeks, and it does, with a number of Belgians on tap and a rotating menu of great choices from North Carolina as well. Burgers, fish tacos, and curry fries are among the favored choices for soaking up the suds. The atmosphere is laid back and no one cares if you wind up spilling a little beer on the floor. It's just on the Chapel Hill side of Carrboro and close to the Cat's Cradle, which makes it a good pre- or post-show nosh.

ROBERTS AT THE FRANKLIN
311 W. Franklin St., Chapel Hill
(919) 442-9000
www.franklinhotelnc.com

In the lobby of the posh Franklin Hotel, the Roberts is upscale-comfy chic. Deep sofas and pillowback chairs beckon you to sink in while you listen to someone tickle the ivories of the baby grand or soak in the warmth of the gas logs. It's a bit like being in a friend's well-appointed living room, if your friend also offered a well-chosen wine list and a menu of specialty cocktails. French doors open onto a sidewalk patio illuminated by gas lights. It's busy at cocktail hour and on weekend nights when diners meet for pre-dinner drinks or after-dinner nightcaps and dessert.

Durham

DAIN'S PLACE
754 Ninth St., Durham
(919) 416-8800
www.dainsplace.net

A laid-back pub where you can get together with pals to watch the game and drink beer or take

the family for a burger-intensive dinner, Dain's Place accommodates many needs. The beer list is extensive and the menu of cheese fries, steak sandwiches, burgers, and veggie burgers is consistently well-executed. On the college kids' favorite, Ninth Street, it can get packed late nights.

THE GREEN ROOM
1108 Broad St., Durham
(919) 286-2359
www.myspace.com/greenroomdurham

The original incarnation of this longtime Bull City barroom served as the setting for the climactic scene in *Bull Durham*, where Tim Robbins' Nuke tells Kevin Costner's Crash that he's "going to the show." Nuke might have thought the place was a dump, but it's a Durham institution that's been pulling locals in for decades. A diverse crowd, from construction workers to Duke scientists, comes in to hone pool skills or just bend the bartender's ear and throw back a few cold ones. If you don't like pool, you can play shuffleboard, darts, or foosball. Dogs are welcome. It's close to Durham's East Campus.

THE PINHOOK
117 W. Main St., Durham
(919) 667-1100
www.thepinhook.com

The Pinhook takes its name from a rough 19th-century Durham neighborhood where debauchery ruled. Opened in 2009, it embraces a basement-chic aesthetic, with exposed duct work, second-hand couches, and painted block walls hung with rotating displays of local artists' work. Local bands and DJs provide the music by which hip kids play pool or retro arcades games like Galaga. Once a month, the chef cooks up a vegan Sunday brunch.

WHISKEY
347 W. Main St., Durham
(919) 682-6191
www.whiskeydurham.com

Dark wood paneling, tufted leather couches, softly glowing copper lamps, and Sinatra coming through the speakers make you feel like ordering a proper cocktail. The bartenders happily oblige with a list of classics and special creations made with top shelf liquor. Whiskey also offers a range of North Carolina beers on tap. It's a comfortable place to have a well-made drink, especially if you go early in the evening. Late nights can get packed, so be prepared to elbow your way through the crowd.

Raleigh—Downtown/ Warehouse District/Glenwood South

THE BOROUGH
317 W. Morgan St., Raleigh
(919) 832-8433
www.theburoughraleigh.com
On the ground floor of a new downtown high rise, the Borough is a sleek but comfortable watering hole that attracts an eclectic mix of patrons. Drinks like the Short Little Span of Attention, a combination of amaretto and pomegranate, and the Schmitty's Schnapps reflect the owners' quirky sensibilities. The food menu includes matzo ball soup, carne asada quesadillas, and homemade "What's In a Name" chips and salsa. Smartly arranged seating areas and a street-front patio give everyone plenty of room to spread out. It's gay friendly, a place where drag queens feel comfy letting their hair down.

FOUNDATION
213 Fayetteville St., Raleigh
(919) 896-6016
www.foundationnc.com
A small, underground space, Foundation takes mixology to a higher level with its dedication to fresh ingredients, rare liquors, and innovative drink recipes. Inspired by the locavore movement, Foundation dedicates most of its taps and space on its wine shelf to beer and wine from North Carolina. Drinks include the Queen Anne's Revenge, a blend of spiced rum, egg whites, and cinnamon named for the ship that belonged to the pirate Blackbeard, which was sunk along the North Carolina coast. The decor is renovation-minimalist with exposed masonry and ceiling beams dominating

the dark cozy space. The sidewalk patio upstairs is great for people-watching while you sip.

HAVANA DELUXE
437 Glenwood Ave., Raleigh
(919) 831-0991
Half a block off the sidewalk along Glenwood, you might miss Havana Deluxe if you didn't know it was there. It's a scotch-and-cigars lounge where you can settle into a leather chair and have a waitress refresh your drinks all night. Several televisions turned to sports often dominate crowd attentions, but the vibe is also conducive to board games and chatting.

HIBERNIAN
311 Glenwood Ave., Raleigh
(919) 833-2258

1144 Kildaire Farm Rd., Cary
(919) 467-9000
www.hibernianpub.com
Of Raleigh's Irish pubs, this one feels the most authentic, with its dark wood interior, close spaces, and fans watching soccer matches on TV. It's in the heart of Glenwood South, which means it can get packed on weekend nights. But in the evenings, it's a cool place to sit and have a pint or a cider and a bit of conversation, as the music isn't too loud. The menu features Irish staples such as bangers and mash or fish and chips. The black and blue salad, with blackened steak and bleu cheese, is a popular favorite. The pub also has a Cary location.

HUMBLE PIE
317 S. Harrington St., Raleigh
(919) 829-9222
www.humblepierestaurant.com
A longtime staple in Raleigh's flourishing warehouse district, Humble Pie makes great use of its interior spare, wide-open space and its outdoor patio area. The tiki bar, which features parachute-cloth sails and strings of globe lights, fills up regardless of the time of year. Popular items on its small-plates menu include tuna tartar tostados—a blend of barely seared tuna, wasabi, and torti-

llas—and tempura asparagus. The atmosphere is relaxed, and it's a great place to grab a nosh or have a drink after a barbecue dinner at The Pit, around the corner.

LYNNWOOD GRILL
4800 Grove Barton Rd., Raleigh
(919) 785-0043
www.lynnwoodgrill.com
Neighbors become regulars of this North Raleigh bar thanks to the great pizza with imaginative toppings like shrimp and potatoes, cheap wing specials, good beer selection, and welcoming atmosphere. It's a good place to grab a bite before heading to a movie at the multiplex next door, to watch a Canes game, or to show up in costume on Halloween night. The crowd is friendly and the service is reliable.

PLAYER'S RETREAT
105 Oberlin Rd., Raleigh
(919) 755-9589
www.playersretreat.net
A few steps from the corner of Hillsborough and Oberlin, the PR, as old timers call it, is an old-school N.C. State fan hangout and Raleigh's oldest bar. Basketball memorabilia recalls Coach Everette Case's 1950s era as well as Jim Valvano and the 1982 NCAA championship team. Decor includes fish tanks, a vast collection of obscure beer cans, and wooden tables carved with patrons' initials. These days the PR is a gathering spot for hockey fans who can watch the Carolina Hurricanes action on flat-screen TVs on the sidewalk patio.

THE RALEIGH TIMES BAR
14 E. Hargett St., Raleigh
(919) 833-0999
www.raleightimesbar.com
On the wall by the door, a floor-to-ceiling, vintage photographic mural of early-1900s newsboys, some of them barefoot, pays homage to the days when the narrow space was home to the ink-stained journalists of a now-defunct city paper. Today it's one of downtown's busiest bars, drawing the crowds with a well-chosen selection of beer, wine, and cocktails and a bar menu of deli-

cious standards like pulled pork nachos, chicken-fried pickles, and fried green beans. Decorative touches like glowing drop lights combine with the restored pressed tin ceiling and exposed masonry for a chic but relaxed atmosphere. Among the photos above the bar tables is a shot of Barack Obama, taken when he stopped in for a Pabst Blue Ribbon and a chat during the 2008 campaign.

SADLACKS
2116 Hillsborough St., Raleigh
(919) 828-9190
www.sadlacks.blogspot.com
Before its recent renovation, Sadlacks was best-known for its grit, which fans adored. In fact, some Sadlacks fans worried the makeover would ruin the place, a Raleigh institution for more than 30 years. But their concerns were unfounded. Refreshed with new paint and a larger kitchen, it still draws a loyal mix of bikers, N.C. State students, blue collar workers, and Carolina Rollergirls and their fans. The most popular pastime is sitting at the picnic tables on the deck, drinking Pabst Blue Ribbon and listening to great local music. The sandwiches are fresh and delicious, too.

BLUES CLUBS

BLUE BAYOU CLUB
106 S. Churton St., Hillsborough
(919) 732-2555
www.bluebayouclub.com
On the main street in Hillsborough, the Blue Bayou is a small, laid-back place that hosts jazz and blues acts. National names like Tab Benoit, the Asylum Street Spankers, and the Reverend Billy C. Wirtz have played Blue Bayou. They serve hot dogs and Zapp's chips, and plenty of beer. Covers vary depending on the act and can be as much as $25 or as little as $6.

PAPA MOJO'S ROADHOUSE
5410-Y N.C. 55, Greenwood
Commons Shopping Center
Durham
(919) 361-2222
www.papamojosroadhouse.com

Papa Mojo's re-creates a little bit of Chef Mel Melton's beloved Louisiana Cajun country. The chef takes the stage to rock the crowd with his harmonica-infused zydeco band, but also makes room for local and national acts to crank out party music like R&B and Big Easy–tinged blues. It's the best place in the Triangle to eat étouffée, sip a hurricane, close your eyes, and imagine you're in the Big Easy.

BREWERIES AND BREW PUBS

Chapel Hill

CAROLINA BREWERY
460 W. Franklin St., Chapel Hill
(919) 942-1800

120 Lowes Dr., Suite 100, Pittsboro
(919) 545-2330
www.carolinabrewery.com
Both locations of this brewery offer great, fresh beer and a menu of better-than-average staples to accompany them. Try the award-winning Copperline Amber Ale with a homemade pizza and finish it off with the stout ice cream float. Ales are brewed seasonally, so you'll be able to try new flavors throughout the year. The downtown Chapel Hill location is in the heart of busy West Franklin Street. The Pittsboro brewery is near the intersection of U.S. 15-501 and U.S. 64, about 2 miles from downtown.

TOP OF THE HILL
100 E. Franklin St., Chapel Hill
(919) 929-8676
www.topofthehillrestaurant.com
A popular spot for college kids and alumni returning for football games or homecomings, Top of the Hill has a great third-floor patio with awesome views of downtown Chapel Hill. The beer brewed on site regularly brings home awards, and when it's time to tap the kegs on a new season's batch, lines have been known to form outside the door. The menu includes salads and belly-filling entrees like king crab mac' and cheese and buttermilk fried chicken.

Durham

FULLSTEAM BREWERY
726 Rigsbee Ave., Durham
(620) HOG-WASH
http://fullsteam.ag
Fullsteam Brewery is the newest addition to the Triangle beer scene and aims to be its most inventive. The brewery features locally grown ingredients in its beers—sweet potato, scuppernong, Carolina grits, rhubarb, even kudzu—and brews a smoky beer called Hogwash specifically to go with North Carolina pulled-pork barbecue. Fullsteam also offers more common brews like India pale ale, stout, and the flagship Carolina Common. The on-site tavern, Fullsteam R&D, serves test batches and one-time-only incarnations along with the regular brews and bullies, which are small savory pies made with seasonal ingredients. The gathering space also features local music, really bad movies, and other community events. The brewery is in downtown Durham near Central Park.

Raleigh

BOYLAN BRIDGE BREW PUB
201 S. Boylan Ave., Raleigh
(919) 803-8927
www.boylanbridge.com
Opened in 2009, this popular spot fits right into the old neighborhood, just a mile from downtown. Groups love to gather around the wide deck's many picnic tables where they can soak in the views of downtown, and the railroad tracks that pass under the Boylan Bridge. The interior is bright and airy with lots of windows and warm wood. The beer is brewed on site, and includes seasonal specials. Fare like fish and chips, spaghetti and meatballs, burgers, and an excellent veggie burger fills out the menu. The atmosphere is comfortable and convivial.

HORNIBLOW'S TAVERN
1249-A Wicker Dr., Raleigh
(919) 834-0045
www.horniblowstavern.com
In an industrial area just north of downtown off Atlantic Avenue, you have to go looking for

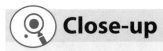

Close-up

Brewing Companies

The growth of craft-brewed beers has turned many a casual beer quaffer into a brewing enthusiast. The Triangle has a handful of breweries that sell and distribute artisanal beverages where beer lovers can get an up-close look at the process. While these tours are usually in the afternoon, they could serve as a precursor to a lively night of fun. **Carolina Brewing Company** has built a wide and loyal following for its craft-brewed ales in the decade and a half it has been around. Shoppers can find CBC Pale Ale, IPA, and Nut Brown Ale year-round in Triangle area stores and on tap at local restaurants. Seasonal brews, available only at the brewery, include a summer wheat, a spring bock, a fall lager, and a special holiday beverage that varies from year to year. Fans can take a free tour and sample the products Saturday at 1 p.m. at 140 Thomas Mill Rd., Holly Springs, (919) 557-BEER, www.carolinabrew.com. **Triangle Brewing Company** specializes in Belgian and American style ales, and also offers a number of seasonal specialties, including a white ale, a stout, and an abbey ale. Kegs are available at the brewery. The brewers host a tour most Saturdays and occasionally put on larger events like multiple-brewery tastings, at 918 Pearl Street, Durham, (919) 683-BEER, www.trianglebrewery .com. **LoneRider Brewing Company**, which opened in 2009, makes a small assortment of beers including Shotgun Betty, a Hefeweizen, and DeadEye Jack, a porter. Kegs and growlers are available at their brewery. Tours are offered on alternating Friday evenings and Saturday afternoons. Check the Web site or call for hours. It's located at 8816 Gulf Court, Suite 100, Raleigh, (919) 442-8004, www.loneriderbeer.com.

Horniblow's to find it. It's the tasting room for Big Boss Brewery, and the bar sits inside the metal warehouse above the brewing tanks. The interior is divided into three rooms. One has a typical bar, one is a game room with worn-out couches, and a third has a Ping Pong table, a pool table, and a couple of video games. All the games are free, and once you see the condition of the equipment, you'll know why. It's like hanging out in a buddy's basement, if your buddy happened to brew some of the best beer made in North Carolina.

NATTY GREENE'S PUB & BREWING CO.
505 W. Jones St., Raleigh
(919) 232-2477
A block off Glenwood South, Natty Greene's is a newcomer to the downtown bar scene, having opened in March 2010. It is an outpost of the popular downtown Greensboro pub of the same name. The Raleigh bar brews its own beer on site, offering a combination of six standard beers and six rotating seasonal brews. Standouts

on the regular beer menu include the Southern Pale Ale and the Buckshot Amber, and be sure to taste the Freedom American Strong Pale Ale if its on tap. The menu offers solid renditions of bar-food staples like wings and fried calamari and sandwiches served with Natty Green's outstanding homemade potato salad. Pool tables, dart boards and table-top shuffle board add to the house-party atmosphere.

COMEDY AND IMPROV CLUBS

Chapel Hill and Carrboro

DSI COMEDY THEATER
200 N. Greensboro St.
Carr Mill Mall, Carrboro
www.dsicomedytheater.com
Improv players present sketch and stand-up comedy and team events at DSI—Dirty South Improv—Comedy Theater. DSI hosts festivals, presents family friendly shows, invites audience participation with true-story night, and offers improv instruction to actors, business people, and teachers.

Raleigh

COMEDY WORX
431 W. Peace St., Raleigh
(919) 829-0822
www.comedyworx.com

On the edge of the Glenwood South district, Comedy Worx aims to entertain a wide range of audiences. Prime time shows pit two teams of improv players against one another, while late-night involves players riffing off audience suggestions long form. The prime time shows are family friendly while the 10:30 p.m. shows are for mature audiences only. Comedy Worx also has a traveling improv team that is available for private parties as well as an annual talent show series. The club is open Friday and Saturday only.

GOODNIGHT'S COMEDY CLUB
861 W. Morgan St., Raleigh
(919) 828-5233
www.goodnightscomedy.com

A staple of the national touring comedian club scene, Goodnight's stage has hosted Jerry Seinfeld, Chris Rock, Ray Romano, and a host of other greats on their way to comedic glory. In the basement, Old Bar serves up the legendary fajitas and margaritas Wednesday special and $30 Thursday deals, which include dinner for two and the comedy show.

DANCE CLUBS

Durham

THE SIRENS LOUNGE
1803 W. Markham Ave., Durham
416-6684
www.sirenslounge.com

Restored tin ceilings, an oak bar, a fireplace, and a centerpiece aquarium offer a swanky vibe to this hotspot on Ninth Street near Duke's East campus. DJs spinning tunes on Friday and Saturday nights pack the kids onto the dance floor. Sip a martini made with seasonal fresh fruit infusions while relaxing on a plush couch between spins on the dance floor.

i Swing dancing survives in the Triangle with the constant help and support of the Triangle Swing Dance Society. The group maintains a list of swing dance teachers and hosts regular dances that feature local and regional bands. The venue changes from week to week, with dances scheduled at the Durham Armory one week and at the Triangle Dance Studio the next. Entry is usually about $10. Find swing events at www.triangleswingdance.org.

SOLAS
419 Glenwood Ave., Raleigh
(919) 755-0755
www.solasraleigh.com

Solas is where all the dressed-up kids go on Glenwood South to shake a tail feather. It's sleek, with deep red banquets and long sheer curtains bathed in neon light. There are three floors for dining, lounging, and taking in the rooftop air. The see-through dance floor on the second story is a big draw, as is the menu of haute cuisine appetizers. Solas is one of the few clubs on Glenwood South that has a dress code, with no T-shirts, boots, or baseball caps allowed. The $10 cover also sets it apart.

GAY AND LESBIAN CLUBS

Durham

CLUB STEEL BLUE
1426 S. Miami Blvd., Suite A, Durham
(919) 596-5876
www.clubsteelblue.com

Club Steel Blue is one of the Triangle's most popular gay and lesbian bars and also has some of the best DJs in the area. Set in an industrial area in southeast Durham, it is a big barn of a place with an expansive dance floor. Sleek touches like drop lights over the bar help lend a modern-loft feel. Events like women's-only speed dating, *American Idol*–style drag singing contests, dancing, and an annual Toys for Tots fundraiser make it a popular LGBT meeting spot.

The White Rabbit Books & Things

The White Rabbit Books & Things is a hub of LGBT activity and information in downtown Raleigh's warehouse district. The store relocated in 2010 to the ground floor of the new Hue apartments building at 300West Hargett St. White Rabbit sells CDs, books, magazines, gay pride-wear, and T-shirts, and has one of the best selections of funny greeting cards anywhere, regardless of the recipient's sexual orientation. The store prints free postcard maps of the warehouse district with points of interest in the "Gayborhood." Reach the store at (919) 856-1429 or online at www.whiterabbitbooks.com.

Raleigh

FLEX
2 S. W. St., Raleigh
(919) 832-8855
www.flex-club.com
Flex is primarily a men's bar, with different nights drawing different age crowds. Music alternates between hip-hop, country, and karaoke, depending on the night of the week. Thursday is Trailer Park Prize Night, with drag queens competing for the title. The first Saturday of the month is the Carolina Bear Lodge dinner. It's a dark, low-ceilinged building in Raleigh's warehouse district, and the music reverberates off the walls when it's cranked up. The bar stocks an extensive menu of beers including lagers from Laos and microbrews by Raleigh's Big Boss Brewery.

LEGENDS
330 W. Hargett St., Raleigh
(919) 831-8888
www.legends-club.com

The most established LGBT bar in the downtown Raleigh's warehouse district, Legends is a collection of dance floors and bars where you can let your hair down, or put it up. The warrenlike complex includes a large dance floor, a video bar, a gaming room and theater for cabaret performances. Featured entertainment changes nightly to include drag reviews, goth night, video game night, and industrial night. A housecast of favorite drag performers takes to the stage on a rotating basis. The patio offers a respite for dancers who want to relax between songs.

MUSIC VENUES

Chapel Hill

CAT'S CRADLE
300 E. Main St., Carrboro
(919) 967-9053
www.catscradle.com
The Triangle's best-known club music venue, the Cradle is a staple on the national club circuit. Indie bands, hip-hop acts, and punk rockers—bands on their way up and established genre veterans—make the Cradle part of any tour. Nirvana played there in the early 1990s, a time when Chapel Hill's music scene was prompting industry watchers to label it "the next Seattle." Acts like Ben Folds Five and Archers of Loaf built momentum with their early Cradle shows. Chapel Hill didn't wind up being the new center of the music universe, but the Cradle remains a star. Inside, it's dark and loud and grungy. Seats are scarce, but nobody goes to the Cradle to sit down anyway. The beer selection is pretty good.

THE CAVE
452 W. Franklin St., Chapel Hill
(919) 968-9308
www.caverntavern.com
A beloved basement dive on Franklin Street's west end, The Cave has been serving beer and giving local musicians a stage for more than 40 years. Musical acts range from pop to rock to country to funk. They serve beer, and that's all. Dogs are welcome. Cover charge is usually

between $3 and $5. Memberships are $5. It's open every day of the year, and if you get lucky you might find a potluck on Christmas.

Raleigh

THE BREWERY
3009 Hillsborough St., Raleigh
(919) 838-6788
www.brewerync.com

The Brewery is an intimate little box of a club near N.C. State's campus on Hillsborough Street where you can see local bands and some national acts gaining buzz. The acoustics are good and the club often packs the bills so you get to see a lot of music for a little money. There is, in fact, no brewery on site, but they sell beer and liquor.

LINCOLN THEATRE
126 E. Cabarrus St., Raleigh
(919) 821-4111
www.lincolntheatre.com

In a quiet corner of downtown Raleigh, the Lincoln Theater is a great place to get up close to your favorite bands. The graduated flooring offers terrific views on many levels, and in the pit, you can get close enough to look into the singers' eyes. The place holds about 500, and there's never a wait for a beer even when it's packed. You'll never pay more than $25 for a show, and usually you'll pay much less. Indie bands popular with college-age kids, and club-scene staples like Robert Earl Keene and the Reverend Horton Heat, fill the bills.

THE POUR HOUSE
224 S. Blount St., Raleigh
(919) 821-1120
www.the-pour-house.com

An eclectic mix of mostly local acts dominates the stage at this small, dark club, where bluegrass on Wednesday might give way to funk and hip-hop on Thursday. The beer selection is above average and comes in cups the size of 7-Eleven Big Gulps. In downtown Raleigh on the edge of Moore Square, Pour House is a good place to catch a show without dropping a load of cash.

Basketball Keeps Bouncing

The great thing about living in the Triangle is that the game is always on. Say, for example, that a good friend has inexplicably scheduled her wedding to take place during the Atlantic Coast Conference tournament, which means you'll be clinking champagne glasses and eating wedding cake while your team is on the court. No worries. There's a bar somewhere at the reception site where a tender is keeping tabs on the game. If you find the sports bars crowded when you show up for tip-off, you might find even better viewing options at a restaurant with a couple of TVs, where you won't have to fight the crowds and can actually hear the announcers. It's rare to walk into a bar or restaurant in the Triangle and not be able to get an instant report on the score.

SPORTS BARS

Chapel Hill

FOUR CORNERS
175 E. Franklin St., Chapel Hill
(919) 968-3809

The tiered seating levels help give Four Corners an airy feel, which is rare among sports bars. The many televisions allow game viewing from any seat in the house, and the menu delivers all the fried food you expect, along with some better-than-average nachos. The name pays homage to the defense strategy former UNC basketball coach Dean Smith invented, the one that gave rise to the shot clock. And yes, it's crowded on game days.

HAM'S
310 W. Franklin St., Chapel Hill
(919) 933-3767
www.hamsrestaurants.com
Part of a Greensboro-based chain, the Chapel Hill outpost of Ham's has anchored the West Franklin Street bar scene for decades. The televisions are myriad, the fried food is served crispy-greasy just as it should be, and the beer specials are cheap. No one leaves without ordering a basket of homemade potato chips, served with a side of ranch dressing. Daytime specials often include free meals for the kids, while nighttime is dedicated to discounted Irish car bombs and Coors Light bottles. Ham's is a raucous place to watch the game, or all the games at once.

Durham

DEVINE'S RESTAURANT & SPORTS
904 W. Main St., Durham
(919) 682-0228
A few blocks from Duke's East Campus, Devine's is a comfy old watering hole with 19 televisions that gets loud and rowdy on game days. It draws a loyal crowd especially on Duke basketball game days and after Bull Durham baseball wins. In the summer, the patio is a popular place for a pub fare and cold brews. Great onion wings, burgers, and a juicy chicken Parmesan sandwich are menu stand-outs. Beer specials include deals on Miller Light tall boys as well as discounts on the microbrews and specialty beers on tap.

Raleigh

HI5
510 Glenwood Ave., Raleigh
(919) 834-4335
www.hi5raleigh.com
A large underground space on Glenwood South, Hi5 has small TVs at just about every table in addition to the large flat-screens. Their menu includes burgers and an array of chicken wing flavors, and they offer $5 food specials every day. It's one of the most popular places in Raleigh to watch whatever game you need to see.

TOBACCO ROAD SPORTS CAFE
222 Glenwood Ave., Raleigh
(919) 832-3688
www.tobaccoroadsportscafe.com
Tobacco Road's centerpiece is a sunken row of easy chairs set about 5 feet from a wall of televisions. The sensory-overload-meets-comfort scenario is worth showing up early to grab one of these primo seats. The menu includes some unexpected surprises like carne asada taquitos, and the nachos are delicious. There's a small patio if you prefer people-watching to sports.

WINE BARS

Chapel Hill and Carrboro

GLASSHALFULL
106 S. Greensboro St., Carrboro
(919) 967-9784
www.glasshalfullcarrboro.com
A great selection of 25 wines by the glass and small plates of seasonal, Mediterranean-inspired dishes to nibble alongside make Glasshalfull popular with grown-ups looking to have a lively conversation over delicious food and drink. The bright, airy dining room is a great place to mix and match wine and food pairings or simply to nibble on olives and grilled artichokes while sipping something simple at the marble bar. Glasshalfull is also a wine shop, so if you find something you like while you're there, you can take home a bottle.

Durham

SIX PLATES
2812 Erwin Rd., Suite 104, Durham
(919) 321-0203
www.sixplates.com
Six Plates offers a daily menu of six half-size entrees, each paired with wine. The food is seasonally fresh, and the menu changes frequently, so that one day's matching of North Carolina shrimp a la diabla with a Portuguese terras do sado is even more tempting since it won't likely be there on your next visit. It's a warm and cozy

atmosphere, with comfy chairs arranged in conversation areas around tables, where entrée sharing inevitably takes place. Six Plates also has 150 wines by the bottle and 30 beers by the bottle.

Raleigh

MOSAIC
517 W. Jones St., Raleigh
(919) 829-5886
www.mosaicwinelounge.com
Candlelight and silk curtains set an exotic mood in this wine lover's haven half a block off Glenwood Avenue. The low-slung couches are deep and supple, and the vibe is Casablanca-meets-urban-chic with the glow from lacy metal lanterns bouncing off exposed brick walls. Dance nights get the floor moving with Moroccan-inspired electronica, but the music doesn't take over the whole club. The wine selection is extensive, and the bar also serves beer and martinis. An outdoor patio buzzes in warm months.

MOVIES

The Triangle has a host of modern multiple-screen cineplexes equipped with surround sound and stadium seating where you can see the latest releases. Here is a list of smaller independent theaters where you can see smaller films and classic cinema.

Cary

GALAXY CINEMA
770 Cary Towne Blvd., Cary
(919) 463-9989
www.mygalaxycinema.com
The Galaxy specializes in showing independent, foreign, and small films, with a special emphasis on Bollywood cinema. There's always at least one title in Hindi with English subtitles. The concessions are inventive and include Indian samosas and kurkure snacks.

Chapel Hill

CHELSEA THEATER
1129 Weaver Dairy Rd.
Timberlyne Shopping Center, Chapel Hill
(919) 968-3005
www.thechelseatheater.com
The Chelsea has three small screens that feature art-house movies and independent films. There's no stadium seating or surround sound, but the Chelsea has movies no one else in town is showing. The concession stand sells beer and wine and European chocolate. The theater accepts cash only.

LUMINA THEATER
700 Market St., Chapel Hill
(919) 960-5765
www.thelumina.com
A five-screen theater in Southern Village, Lumina shows first-run movies in an intimate setting that provides an alternative to the multiplexes. The theaters have stadium seating and digital surround sound. Family-oriented programming includes morning shows for kids when school is out and baby-friendly shows on Monday nights. In the summer, you can watch movies on the lawn and bring your own picnic.

THE VARSITY
123 E. Franklin St., Chapel Hill
(919) 967-8665
www.varsityonfranklin.com
A longtime Franklin Street staple, The Varsity was shuttered for a while in 2009 before reopening late in the year as a $3-all-shows theater. New owners renovated the 1927-era space, where they screen classic films and new releases. The theater also serves as a meeting place for corporate functions and private events.

Durham

THE CAROLINA THEATRE
309 W. Morgan St., Durham
(919) 560-3030
www.carolinatheatre.org

A performance venue as well as a movie theater, the Carolina was built in 1926, making it the Triangle's most historic setting for cinema. In downtown Durham, the theater screens art house fare and independent films and is a central venue for the annual Full Frame Film Festival.

Raleigh

THE COLONY
5438 Six Forks Rd., Raleigh
(919) 847-5677
www.therialto.com
The Colony features mostly independent and foreign films on its two screens in North Raleigh. The theater also features special series of modern classics including *Pee Wee's Big Adventure* and *Fargo*. Concessions include beer and wine.

RALEIGHWOOD CINEMA GRILL
6609 Falls of Neuse Rd., Raleigh
(919) 847-0326
www.raleighwoodmovies.com
Raleighwood features a good mix of children's and adult movies in a movie-pub setting that allows patrons to eat dinner and drink a beer in front of the screen. Menu includes nachos and other pub grub staples. The theater also screens Monday Night Football.

RIALTO THEATER
1620 Glenwood Ave., Raleigh
(919) 856-8683
www.therialto.com
In the heart of Raleigh's tony Five Points neighborhood, about a mile from downtown, the Rialto's single screen shows independent films. The recently renovated 1942 theater retains an historic charm. Bar concessions include microbrews and wine. *The Rocky Horror Picture Show* screens on Friday nights.

WACHOVIA IMAX THEATER AT MARBLES KID MUSEUM
201 E. Hargett St., Raleigh
(919) 882-4629
www.imaxraleigh.org
The Triangle's only IMAX theater shows historical and documentary shows as well as blockbusters in the IMAX format. The 50-foot screen is 3-D capable, and the theater's sound system includes 44 speakers. At press time, tickets were $8.95 for documentaries, $11.95 for features for adults; $6.50 and $9.50 for children under 12.

PERFORMING ARTS

The intellectual life that thrives at the universities in Raleigh, Durham, and Chapel Hill has for decades fueled a corresponding cultural vitality. Though scientific research, entrepreneurship, and college basketball grab the larger headlines, the theater, ballet, and music scenes gain much from the progressive people who call the Triangle home.

Artists at the area's universities have a long history of using their work as catalyst for social change. Among these notables was Pulitzer Prize–winning playwright Paul Green, whose name graces the premiere theater on the UNC campus. In the 1920s, Green was one of the first Southerners to examine issues of race and the legacy of slavery in his work. Today in the Triangle, artists of all stripes find outlets for the kind of politically and socially engaging work that Green pioneered. Triangle audiences also make room on the community's stage for classics, comedies, and experiments of many sorts.

Music soars here, from banjos ringing through open-air amphitheaters to perfected chorales reaching for Duke Chapel's Gothic rises. Its thriving music scene has made the Triangle an inviting home for a number of internationally known musicians, including saxophonist Branford Marsalis, jazz singer Nnenna Freelon, hip-hop producer Ninth Wonder, and rapper Christopher Martin, aka Play of Kid-n-Play. The many venues for orchestral and choral music provide opportunities for professionals and keen amateurs to continue nurturing their talents throughout their lives while aficionados of the region's musical heritage work to keep the legacies of Piedmont Blues and banjo-fueled bluegrass alive.

But it's not just the local talents that shape the arts in the Triangle. With its reputation for engaged, well-educated audiences, the area has the cultural cachet to draw big acts and an eclectic mix of smaller, cutting-edge artists. Every spring, the Full Frame Documentary Film Festival draws master filmmakers, promising ingénues, and Hollywood stars to Durham. Likewise every summer, the American Dance Festival brings the most innovative virtuosos of the form to teach and perform at Duke University and in venues throughout Durham.

Perhaps the most inspiring aspect of the Triangle's art scene is its grassroots responsiveness. Once a small group of motivated theater fans or opera or ballet lovers gets it into their collective heads that the scene is void of the art form they crave, stand back and watch the fundraising begin. Upstart cultural groups find themselves marking a quarter of a century before they know it.

A WORD ABOUT THIS CHAPTER

In general, the venues and organizations featured in this chapter have established themselves as dependable providers of professional-grade entertainment. There simply wasn't room to list the plethora of smaller community groups and cultural centers that contribute to the Triangle's vibrant and evolving arts scene.

Phone numbers provided are for the box office. Many of the larger venues, including the RBC Center and the outdoor amphitheaters, sell tickets via Ticketmaster and other ticket services. Where no number is listed, the venue's tickets are available through a third party service only. Most venues and presenting organizations offer discounts for seniors, student, and groups. Call or consult the Web site to find out.

VENUES

THE ARTSCENTER OF CARRBORO
300-G E. Main St., Carrboro
(919) 929-2787
www.artscenterlive.org

The ArtsCenter serves amateurs and professionals with a slate of classes in various media as well as a concert schedule that brings popular professionals to the center's two theaters. Past seasons have included national favorites like Ricki Lee Jones, along with local talent-on-the-rise like the Avett Brothers. The performance space is intimate and nonsmoking, which contributes to the civilized feel of the shows. It's a step above the night-club scene. Theater from local and national groups plays at the ArtsCenter, and the group organizes several series just for children. The ArtsCenter is also home to the Center Gallery and East End Gallery for visual art.

CARTER-FINLEY STADIUM
4600 Trinity Rd., Raleigh
www.gopack.com

The home of the N.C. State University's Wolfpack football team, Carter-Finley is a giant bowl that holds more than 55,000 spectators. It is located on the school's West Campus, adjacent to the RBC Center, between Hillsborough Street and Wade Avenue. Built in 1966, the stadium was updated with a press tower and skyboxes in the early 2000s. As the largest venue in the Triangle, Carter-Finley plays host only to the biggest name entertainers that draw outsize crowds. When U2 played there in 2009, ticket sales totaled more than 55,000, and getting all those cars into the parking fields proved challenging. The best solution is to carpool, leave early, and look for routes that avoid exits off I-40/Wade Avenue.

THE CLAYTON CENTER
111 E. Second St., Clayton
(919) 553-1737
www.theclaytoncenter.com

A 600-seat theater is the standout feature of the Clayton Center, a pair of 1920s school buildings restored in 2002 to serve as the growing town's

cultural apex. The venue hosts theater, magicians, comedians, and musicians ranging from blues to bluegrass. Seasons average about eight shows and recent lineups have included Ricky Skaggs and international "pop opera" group Destino.

DURHAM PERFORMING ARTS CENTER
123 Vivian St., Durham
(919) 688-3722
www.dpacnc.com

One of the pillars of downtown Durham's ongoing renaissance, the DPAC opened in 2008. It's a gleaming, glass-and-steel structure that seats 2,700, with no seat more than 135 feet from the stage. The DPAC has hosted big-name comics Robin Williams and Kathy Griffin and musicians including Leonard Cohen and Vince Gill, and is home to the SunTrust Broadway Series, which features touring productions of current Broadway hits. Among the shows to play the DPAC in its first seasons have been *Wicked*, *Hairspray*, and *Mamma Mia!*

J.S. DORTON ARENA
1025 Blue Ridge Rd., Raleigh
www.ncstatefair.org/dorton.htm
(919) 821-7400

The Triangle's most provocatively designed entertainment venue is J.S. Dorton Arena, on the N.C. State Fairgrounds. Built in 1952, the 7,600-seat arena is a lasting tribute to the influence of mid-century modernist design in Raleigh. Architect Matthew Nowicki of the N.C. State Department of Architecture gave the building an elliptical shape that brings to mind a concrete and glass butterfly. During the State Fair, Dorton hosts a concert series of mostly country and Christian rock acts. It is also home to the Carolina Rollergirls Flat Track Roller Derby team.

KOKA BOOTH AMPHITHEATRE, CARY
8003 Regency Parkway, Cary
(919) 462-2052
www.boothamphitheatre.com

A 7,000-foot amphitheater built in 2001, Koka Booth's design makes beautiful use of its forested, lakeside setting. Guests can bring chairs and blankets to spread out on the sloped lawn or choose seats in the upper deck. The amphitheater is home to the N.C. Symphony's Summerfest series and several other annual events, including Cary's Diwali festival in the fall and the Great Grapes Wine Art & Food Festival in the spring. Recent touring acts have included Bonnie Raitt and John Legend. The amphitheater hosts an outdoor movie series and creates an outdoor skating rink for the holidays.

MEMORIAL HALL
200 W. Cameron Ave., UNC–Chapel Hill
(919) 843-3333
www.carolinaperformingarts.org
Built in 1931, Memorial Hall is a proscenium-arch, 1,400-seat theater that has long served as the UNC campus's main stage. A three-year renovation was completed in 2005. Left untouched were the marble slabs commemorating university benefactors who helped pay for construction of the original Memorial Hall in 1885. Those still grace the lobby. Memorial Hall hosts the Carolina Performing Arts series as well as performances and productions of student groups.

NC MUSEUM OF ART'S JOSEPH M. BRYAN THEATRE
2110 Blue Ridge Rd., Raleigh
(919) 715-5923
www.ncartmuseum.org
Between reserved seating and the lawn, the museum's amphitheater can accommodate as many as 2,400. It is situated between the new museum building, completed in 2010, and the museum's outdoor sculpture park, which features 150-foot arches, a towering whirligig, and other outsized works of art. The venue is family friendly with space for children to explore, including a giant map of the state decorated with plaques commemorating historic events, and giant three-dimensional letters that spell out the words "Picture This" when viewed from the air. Touring musicians in recent seasons have included alterna-pop stars They Might Be Giants! and bluegrass legend Doc Watson. The museum hosts an outdoor movie series in the summer, with a mix of adult and kid-friendly fare.

PROGRESS ENERGY CENTER
2 E. S. St., Raleigh
(919) 831-6060
www.progressenergycenter.com
The Progress Energy Center is home to four distinct venues: Memorial Auditorium, with 2,277 seats; Meymandi Concert Hall, with 1,700 seats; Fletcher Opera Theatre, with 600 seats; and Kennedy Theatre, with 170 seats. Memorial Hall is home to Carolina Ballet, the big musical productions of North Carolina Theatre, and the touring shows of Broadway Series South. Meymandi Concert Hall was specifically designed to showcase the North Carolina Symphony. Fletcher Opera Theater hosts touring and local opera productions. Kennedy Theatre is a black-box space that is home to the Hot Summer Nights theater series. The original Greek Revival building, Memorial Auditorium, dates to 1932, but renovations in 1990 brought the facilities up to date.

RBC CENTER
1400 Edwards Mill Rd., Raleigh
(919) 861-2323
www.rbccenter.com
The indoor arena was built in 1999 as a home for the N.C. State men's basketball team and the recently acquired National Hockey League's Carolina Hurricanes, formerly the Hartford Whalers. The arena is just off I-440 west of downtown. The RBC in the name stands for Royal Bank of Canada, which has its U.S. headquarters in Raleigh. The arena holds 18,000 for hockey, more than 19,000 for basketball, and between 18,000 and 19,500 for concerts. The venue has hosted big-name entertainment, from Disney on Ice shows to comedian Dane Cook to Christian rockers Casting Crowns.

ST. JOSEPH'S HISTORIC FOUNDATION
Hayti Heritage Center
804 Olde Fayetteville St., Durham
(919) 683-1709 ext. 3
www.hayti.org
The foundation takes its name from the former church where it is housed. Built in 1891, the Victorian masterpiece was a crowning achievement of the prosperous, turn-of-the-20th-century African-

American business community in Durham. The restored St. Joseph's AME Church is now the home for the Hayti Heritage Center, which is named after the surrounding African-American community. The foundation sponsors several annual events aimed at preserving and furthering the area's African-American cultural heritage. Among them are the Bull Durham Blues Festival, the Jambalaya Soul Slam poetry competition, and the Juneteenth Celebration and Unity March. Throughout the year, the foundation hosts plays, concerts, art exhibits, lectures, and educational and artistic programs for youth.

TIME WARNER CABLE MUSIC PAVILION AT WALNUT CREEK
3801 Rock Quarry Rd., Raleigh
(919) 831-6400 ext. 1
www.livenation.com
Between the 6,800 seats and the space on the lawn, Walnut Creek can hold about 20,000 people. Built in 1991, the amphitheater is south of downtown Raleigh just off I-40. The summer concert series features a range of acts from Kenny Chesney to New Edition to Dave Matthews Band. Expect to see the Allman Brothers Band on the lineup every year. The blues rockers have played the venue every summer since it opened.

THEATER

BURNING COAL THEATRE
3056 Barrow Dr., Raleigh
(919) 834-4001
www.burningcoal.org
Each season, Burning Coal takes on a half-dozen meaty plays with social relevance, from *Waiting for Godot* to *The Love Song of J. Robert Oppenheimer*, with casts of Equity and professional actors. As part of its emphasis on community involvement, the company commissions playwrights on staff to pen works specific to Raleigh. The most recent was *1960*, a historical drama examining the desegregation of Raleigh's school system. The Burning Coal Lab program gives new playwrights and directors the chance to have their works staged and reviewed. The company

conducts several arts education programs in conjunction with local schools. Burning Coal's home venue is the Meymandi Theatre in the restored 1913 Murphey School at 224 Polk St. in downtown Raleigh. The reconstructed auditorium, which seats between 140 and 175, can be configured in the round or as a thrust stage and offers an intimate and architecturally engaging setting for the company's equally engaging work.

Burning Coal Theatre's Oakwood Plays

Setting a play in a cemetery might seem macabre, but it works to great effect with Burning Coal Theatre's cycle of Oakwood Plays. Playwright Ian Finley takes his inspiration for characters in these original works from the people who are buried in Oakwood Cemetery. The historic graveyard is the second-oldest in the city. Set on a hillside, its rolling paths, centuries-old hardwoods, and graying monuments offer a beautiful backdrop for the *Spoon River*-like productions. Among the many colorful characters buried in Oakwood are Rachel Bauer, the Cherokee wife of a 19th-century architect who died of a broken heart after being shunned by Raleigh society; Berrien Kinnard Upshaw, the first husband of author Margaret Mitchell, who served as inspiration for *Gone With the Wind*'s Rhett Butler; and national-championship-winning basketball coach and TV personality Jim Valvano. The plays are an enchanting mix of historical tour and ghost story. In a similar vein are the original plays based on Raleigh history that Burning Coal stages occasionally on the sidewalk in downtown. The Oakwood Plays are staged in May.

COMMON GROUND THEATRE
4815B Hillsborough Rd., Durham
(919) 698-3870
www.cgtheatre.com

Common Ground is not a company but a venue where some of the Triangle's smaller, edgier theater companies stage their works. Among the groups that make use of Common Ground are Both Hands Theatre Company, a pair of female playwrights that create original works often involving community-generated content; Ghost & Spice, which focuses on modern classics from playwrights like David Mamet and Edward Albee; and New Traditions Theater, a mostly African-American ensemble of young actors and playwrights that focuses on consciousness-raising works. Common Ground is a spare black-box that seats about 50. The theater also sponsors workshops and hosts performances of improv and music.

i Like many Durham destinations, Common Ground is hard to find. The address is Hillsborough Road, but the entrance is actually on the adjacent Brenrose Circle. Parking is available on the theater's lot, accessible from Brenrose Circle and in the CWJ Heating and Cooling lot.

DEEP DISH THEATER
University Mall
201 S. Estes Dr., Chapel Hill
(919) 968-1515
www.deepdishtheater.org

The fact that Deep Dish stages its four-play seasons in a shopping mall tells you that the company's goal is to put theater where the masses can get at it. Ibsen and Brecht, Wendy Wasserstein and David Mamet have all been produced in the store space wedged between a hobby shop and a frame store in University Mall. Deep Dish pairs its productions with a suggested book for community reading and hosts discussions groups of the book and play during the run. Post-performance discussions also follow some of the productions.

LITTLE GREEN PIG THEATRICAL CONCERN
646 Lawndale Ave., Durham
(919) 286-0456
www.littlegreenpig.com

Each season Little Green Pig stages four or five plays inspired by the culture of a different country. Some of the titles and playwrights may sound familiar, but the company sets them on their ear. That might mean an all-African-American cast for *The Cherry Orchard* during the Russia season or a staging of *A Streetcar Named Desire* set in a macabre fun house environment as part of the German season, for reasons untold. Puppets or nudity could be part of the show, and it's seldom what you expect. Original works and premieres get attention as well as classics. Little Green Pig selects stages to suit its needs, whether that means the loft performance space of Golden Belt, a restored textiles warehouse in downtown Durham, or the stage of another company's theater.

MANBITES DOG THEATER
703 Foster St., Durham
(919) 682-3343
www.manbitesdogtheater.org

Manbites Dog's mission is to provide an outlet for new works and fresh presentations of established plays. Founded more than 20 years ago, the company presents regional and state premieres and the occasional world debut and new plays created in-house. Topics of social and political relevance find a home here, and past memorable productions have included Edward Albee's *The Goat or Who Is Silvia?* and Linda Griffith's *Age of Arousal*. With its Other Voices series, Manbites co-hosts productions by other companies. Manbites' venue is a 1920s-era printing factory in downtown Durham that the company bought and restored in the late 1990s. The theater seats between 80 and 120, and the configuration changes with each production.

NORTH CAROLINA THEATRE
1 E. S. St., Raleigh
(919) 831-6941
www.nctheatre.com

North Carolina Theatre puts on big Broadway musicals with casts of Equity actors and Broadway veterans—sometimes marquee names—as well as local non-Equity talent. Fare includes family favorites such as *Annie* and *High School Musical*, classics like *West Side Story* and *The Sound of Music*, and more current productions like *Bat Boy* and *The Full Monty*. Recent stars have included Lou Diamond Phillips as the King in *The King and I* and Sheena Easton as the Narrator in *Joseph and the Amazing Technicolor Dreamcoat*.

The not-for-profit company is an anchor tenant in Memorial Auditorium, one of three venues in downtown Raleigh's Progress Energy Center, owned by the city. North Carolina Theatre tied its fortunes to the revitalization of downtown more than 25 years ago and aims to please the crowds by crafting seasons that include something for everyone.

PAPERHAND PUPPET INTERVENTION
306 Saxapahaw Church Rd., Saxapahaw
(919) 923-1857
www.paperhand.org
Using giant puppets, shadow play, masked actors, dancers on stilts, music, and a variety of other media, Paperhand tells stories and fables that express the company's dedication to progressive social and political ideals. Performances might involve a 15-foot Buddha puppet, a troupe of jugglers on stilts, or marionettes in the form of crows. Enormous Paperhand Puppets lead the People's Procession, a parade open to spectators, during Raleigh's First Night New Year's Eve celebration, and they frequently appear at outdoor festivals. Paperhand stages performances outdoors as well, mainly at the Forest Theater on the UNC–Chapel Hill campus and the N.C. Museum of Art's Joseph Bryan amphitheater in Raleigh.

Paperhand's creations inspire the imagination, but their plays are not always appropriate for children. Many have adult themes that leave younger audiences struggling to keep up. Make sure the performance is geared toward children before you go.

PLAYMAKERS REPERTORY COMPANY
150 Country Club Rd., Chapel Hill
(919) 962-7529
www.playmakersrep.org
Playmakers Repertory Company is the professional theater company associated with the University of North Carolina at Chapel Hill's Department of Dramatic Art. The company, which is more than 90 years old, has won national recognition for being a top-notch regional theater with lavish productions of classics and modern works. Shakespeare, Oscar Wilde, Arthur Miller, and Susan Lori-Parks have all been produced in the Mainstage series in recent seasons. With its PRC2 series, the company offers more cutting-edge fare in a more relaxed setting that encourages post-show discussions.

Mainstage shows take place in the 500-seat, thrust-stage Paul Green Theater, which manages to feel more intimate than its size should allow. PRC2 presentations take place in the smaller Kenan Theater, which seats 265. Both are housed in the Center for Dramatic Art, alongside rehearsal space and classrooms. As with anything on the UNC campus, give yourself plenty of time to find parking. The Cobb Parking Deck behind the Center for Dramatic Art, the visitors lot on N.C. 54, and the School of Government parking deck are nearby options.

RALEIGH ENSEMBLE PLAYERS
213 Fayetteville St., Suite 202, Raleigh
(919) 832-9607
www.realtheatre.org
The founders of Raleigh Ensemble Players got together almost three decades ago to offer the theater that went beyond the existing scene's mostly family-friendly fare. The company stages three or four plays per season featuring Equity and non-Equity actors. Recent years have included productions of *Hedwig and the Angry Inch* and *The Best Little Whorehouse in Texas* as well as more serious offerings such as Caryl Churchill's *The Skryker*. Company players also stage the popular REP Sings/REP Rocks cabaret series. For years, Raleigh Ensemble Players staged perfor-

mances at Artspace, a downtown Raleigh center for visual artists, or in the auditoriums of private highs schools. In 2009, the company moved to 213 Fayetteville St., a historic building in the heart of downtown Raleigh, which is being renovated to become its permanent venue.

RALEIGH LITTLE THEATRE
301 Pogue St., Raleigh
(919) 821-3111
www.raleighlittletheatre.org
Raleigh Little Theatre has been staging community theater in Raleigh for more than 70 years. The company puts on 11 shows per season and runs theater education programs for adults and children. Lineups include a wide variety, from musicals such as *Altar Boyz* and *Pump Boys and Dinettes* to tragedies like *Wit* and *'night Mother*. Productions are staged in one of the company's three venues—two indoor theaters and one outdoor amphitheatre, beautifully situated beside the city's rose garden. The company's annual holiday performance of *Cinderella*, which it stages at the 600-seat Fletcher Theater in the Progress Energy Center, has been running for more than 20 years.

THEATRE IN THE PARK
107 Pullen Rd., Raleigh
(919) 831-6058
www.theatreinthepark.com
Don't let the name confuse you: all of the action takes place indoors. The building is located in Pullen Park, just by N.C. State University's main campus. Theatre in the Park began more than 60 years ago as a children's theater but has since grown to present a variety of works including musicals (*Master Class*), drama (*Angels in America*, *Who's Afraid of Virginia Woolf?*), and Shakespeare. Theatre in the Park presents original works and regional premieres as well. The company is best known for its presentation of artistic director Ira David Wood III's *A Christmas Carol*, a musical comedy adaptation of the Charles Dickens work. The annual production runs for weeks at Memorial Auditorium in downtown Raleigh's Progress Energy Center.

TRANSACTORS IMPROV COMPANY
P.O. Box 2295, Chapel Hill, 27515
(919) 824-0937
www.transactors.org
Transactors, a group of professional actors and playwrights, has been around for more than 25 years. The troupe began as a children's theater, but morphed into an improv group long ago. Transactors appears regularly at its home venue, the ArtsCenter in Carrboro, where it stages intimate evenings of one- and two-act long-form improvisation theater pieces and musicals. The group also presents a monthly serial medical show, called *City of Medicine*, at Common Ground Theatre in Durham. Transactors conducts workshops for performers and for educational and professional development groups. The actors are quick on their feet and funny, and their performances can make for an evening of surprising entertainment.

CLASSICAL AND TRADITIONAL MUSIC

CHAMBER ORCHESTRA OF THE TRIANGLE
1213 E. Franklin St., Chapel Hill
(919) 360-3382
www.chamberorchestraofthetriangle.org
The Chamber Orchestra of the Triangle's 30-plus musicians, granted admission by audition, perform five concerts a year in the Carolina Theatre's Fletcher Hall in Durham. Performances often focus on rarely heard pieces of music and may feature visiting guest musicians. The orchestra's conductor, Lorenzo Muti, is a native of Spoleto, Italy, and has led orchestras throughout Europe. The group also sponsors a competition for young string soloists.

CIOMPI QUARTET
Duke University Department of Music
Box 90665, Durham 27708
www.ciompi.org
Italian violinist Giorgio Ciompi founded the quartet that bears his name at Duke University more than 40 years ago. The group draws its members from the Duke University faculty and is renowned

in classical music circles. The quartet performs masterpieces as well as works by modern composers in venues in major cities around the world. Its schedule includes frequent performances at Duke, Duke Gardens, and UNC–Chapel Hill as well as other spots around the state.

DUKE CHAPEL CHOIR
1 Chapel Dr.
Box 90974, Durham 27708
(919) 684-3898
www.chapel.duke.edu

The choir leads the hymns during Sunday worship services at Duke Chapel, the Gothic centerpiece of Duke's campus, every Sunday of the academic year. But the 150-member group is best known for its Christmastime presentation of Handel's *Messiah* in the chapel. The well-rehearsed and inspiring voices combine with the dramatic architecture of the chapel to create a holiday tradition that has packed the church every year since 1932. In addition to *Messiah*, the choir takes on other challenging sacred music such as Bach's *St. Matthew Passion* and Mozart's *Requiem*. It also stages a spring performance. Membership is open to Duke students and faculty and members of the community by audition.

DURHAM SYMPHONY ORCHESTRA
P.O. Box 1993, Durham 27702
(919) 560-2736
www.durhamsymphony.org

The Durham Symphony Orchestra's paid and volunteer musicians perform 10 concerts per year in and around Durham. The repertoire is classical and pops and features an annual holiday performance and an annual outdoor concert. William Henry Curry is the conductor and artistic director. Curry is also a resident conductor for the North Carolina Symphony and artistic director of the N.C. Symphony's Summerfest program.

MALLARMÉ CHAMBER PLAYERS
120 Morris St., Durham
(919) 560-2788
www.mallarmemusic.org

The Mallarmé Chamber Players focus on seldom-performed works of traditional chamber music with an eye toward highlighting the compositions of African-American, Asian, Latino, Indian, Middle Eastern, and female artists. The group presents works of the masters and celebrates new music as well. It has commissioned more than 25 pieces from American composers. Grammy-nominated jazz singer Nnenna Freelon is among the 30 or so professional musicians who perform in the group. Mallarmé presents about half a dozen concerts in the Triangle each year and some in other parts of the state. The group also works with local schools and community groups on music education programs.

NORTH CAROLINA SYMPHONY
4350 Lassiter at N. Hills Ave., Suite 250, Raleigh
(919) 733-2750
www.ncsymphony.org

The North Carolina Symphony performs 175 concerts every year across the state, but the Triangle benefits from the group's home base being Meymandi Concert Hall in downtown Raleigh's Progress Energy Center. Between Meymandi and Koka Booth Amphitheatre in Cary, where the symphony performs its Summerfest series, Triangle residents don't have to go far to see the best symphonic music in the state. Grant Llewellyn leads the group of 65 full-time musicians with inspired programs. Recent seasons have included the examination of cultural connections between Europe and America through the compositions of leading modern composers and the premieres of original works by North Carolina composers.

The symphony frequently collaborates with other cultural organizations to program music that complements current projects, such as the recent "El Greco to Velazquez" exhibit at the Nasher Museum of Art at Duke University. Yo-Yo Ma, André Watts, and Lynn Harrell are among the many notable artists who have performed with the North Carolina Symphony. During the Summerfest series, guest performers may range from the Preservation Hall Jazz Band to flying aerialists.

NORTH CAROLINA MASTER CHORALE
P.O. Box 562, Raleigh 27602
(919) 856-9700
www.ncmasterchorale.org
The 170 singers in the North Carolina Master Chorale perform choral masterpieces with orchestral accompaniment. Many of the singers in the volunteer group are professional musicians or music teachers. Admission is by audition. In recent seasons, the chorale has performed works by Prokofiev and William Walton with the North Carolina Symphony, and has provided accompaniment for the Carolina Ballet. The chorale performs six concerts per season in Raleigh and some in other parts of the state. The most popular is the *Joy of the Season* concert of holiday corals in Meymandi Concert Hall. The smaller, more elite 22-member North Carolina Chamber Choir, a subgroup of the chorale, performs works from the Renaissance to modern day and presents programs on music history in the public schools.

PINECONE PIEDMONT COUNCIL OF TRADITIONAL MUSIC
P.O. Box 28534, Raleigh 27611
(919) 664-8333
www.pinecone.org
PineCone supports traditional music in genres including blue grass, Irish, swing, folk, and blues. The non-profit group organizes concerts, sponsors sessions for musicians, hosts the weekly PineCone Bluegrass Show on WQDR-FM, and generally supports efforts to keep older forms of music alive. The group puts on 150 events each year, some of which are free. Recent seasons have included a two-day festival featuring Kris Kristofferson, Tift Merritt, and Ricky Skaggs at Meymandi Concert Hall, as well as a series of free Americana concerts at the N.C. Museum of History.

RALEIGH CHAMBER MUSIC GUILD
P.O. Box 2059, Raleigh 27602
(919) 821-2030
http://rcmg.org
The Raleigh Chamber Music Guild presents concerts, commissions new work, and promotes music education in the community. The group

presents a dozen concerts per year, in two series. In recent years, the guild has brought Eroica Trio and the Harlem String Quartet to the Fletcher Theater of the Progress Energy Center and sponsored local groups at the North Carolina Museum of Art. The touring groups often lead master classes for local musicians.

OPERA

CAPITAL OPERA RALEIGH
P. O. Box 1206, Raleigh 27602
(919) 760-8237
Capital Opera presents two works per year in the Jones Auditorium of Meredith College in Raleigh. Begun in 2003, the company focuses on traditional masterworks of the genre. The company also performs in the Wake County public schools, where it presents its most popular work, an Engelbert Humperdinck–scored version of *Hansel and Gretel.*

DURHAM SAVOYARDS
108 Barenwood Circle, Durham
www.durhamsavoyards.org
For more than 45 years, this theater troupe has presented the works of Gilbert & Sullivan. With one or two productions per year, the group has staged every Gilbert & Sullivan operetta at least once. Charmed by the writing and composing duo's wit and music, the Savoyards respect many traditions to honor Gilbert & Sullivan, including singing "God Save the Queen" at the start of each performance and "Hail Poetry" at the end of each. The operettas are staged in the Carolina Theatre in downtown Durham. The Savoyards' enthusiasm for the work is infectious and the performances are consistently fun, as are the community sing-a-longs.

LONG LEAF OPERA
P.O. Box 2683, Chapel Hill 27515
(919) 240-8782
www.longleafopera.org
Long Leaf Opera is dedicated to presenting and promoting operas written in English by American composers. At its annual festival, staged in N.C.

State's Stewart Theatre, the company presents vocal recitals, opera premieres, works in progress, and a national vocal competition.

THE OPERA COMPANY OF NORTH CAROLINA
414 Fayetteville St., Suite 100, Raleigh
(919) 792-3850
www.operanc.com

Founded in 1996, the Opera Company of North Carolina is the most established presenter of the art form in the Triangle. The company offers three or four operas per season, with classic works like *La Boheme, Carmen*, and *Rigoletto* dominating the schedule. Seasons often include an outdoor concert guided by less formal structure presented at the N.C. Museum of Art's Joseph Bryan amphitheater in Raleigh. Guest singers have included Luciano Pavarotti and Victoria Livengood, among others, and the opera has joined forces with the North Carolina Symphony and the North Carolina Master Chorale in previous seasons. The group's About Town singing group performs at community events. Operas are staged in Memorial Auditorium or in Fletcher Opera Theater in the Progress Energy Center.

DANCE

CAROLINA BALLET
3401-131 Atlantic Ave., Raleigh
(919) 719-0800
www.carolinaballet.com

Artistic director Robert Weiss infuses the Carolina Ballet with energy through his assertive programming choices as well as his inspired choreography. The ballet has presented more than 45 premieres since its inception in 1997, many of them created by Weiss himself. Weiss often takes inspiration from cultural currents in the community, as with his recent creation of a piece titled *Picasso*, which coincided with the exhibition "Picasso and the Allure of Language" at the Nasher Museum of Art at Duke University. Story ballets receive plenty of attention from the ballet as well, and the annual performance

of *Nutcracker* is a traditional favorite. The ballet performs most often in either the Fletcher Opera Theater or Memorial Auditorium, both at the Progress Energy Center in downtown Raleigh, with some stagings of *Nutcracker* at UNC–Chapel Hill's Memorial Hall, and limited touring. Carolina Ballet has earned accolades from critics in the local, national, and European press for it ambitious agenda and talented dancers.

CHOREO COLLECTIVE
P.O. Box 52264, Durham 27717
(919) 259-4686
http://choreo.devel.rainsdance.org

A coalition of modern dancers and choreographers based in the Triangle, Choreo Collective presents an annual concert of members' new works or works-in-progress and several other performances annually. The group also hosts workshops and works with other arts organizations in collaborations that may involve dance, theater, or visual arts. Choreo Collective sponsors a weekly laboratory for dancers and choreographers that focuses on modern dance technique.

CHUCK DAVIS AFRICAN AMERICAN DANCE ENSEMBLE
120 Morris St., Durham
(919) 560-2729
www.africanamericandanceensemble.org

The troupe of five dancers and five musicians performs modern dance and music informed by traditional African rhythms, traditions, and history. Internationally acclaimed choreographer Chuck Davis founded the group in 1984 after moving his Chuck Davis Dance Company from New York City to Durham at the behest of the American Dance Festival. Davis creates and tours original pieces throughout the world. His company is a perennial presence at community events, including Durham's Fourth of July Festival for the Eno, Raleigh's First Night New Year's celebration, and KwanzaaFest, which the African American Dance Ensemble presents in Durham. The performances are arousing, colorful affairs and audience members often dance in the aisles.

EVEN EXCHANGE
114 St Mary's St., Raleigh
(919) 828-2377
www.evenexchange.com
Even Exchange is a Raleigh-based modern dance company that presents original works several times per year. One of the group's missions is to collaborate with non-dancers in creating and presenting dance, and their partners in these endeavors have included senior citizens and pre-schoolers. The group presents community workshops and forums and rehearses at ArtsTogether school in downtown Raleigh.

ARTS ON CAMPUS

ARTS NC STATE
Campus Box 7306, Raleigh 27695
(919) 513-1820
www.ncsu.edu/arts
Arts NC State presents performances and exhibits to enhance North Carolina State University's visual and performance art programs. The group schedules two or three series of performing arts events per year, one of which is designed for children. Recent seasons have included genre-bending violinist Daniel Bernard Roumain and Mermaid Theatre of Nova Scotia's performance of *The Very Hungry Caterpillar & Other Eric Carle Favourites*. Arts NC State also coordinates events associated with exhibits at the school's Crafts Center, its Gregg Museum of Art & Design, and productions of the music and theater departments. Most events are open to the public.

CAROLINA PERFORMING ARTS
University of N. Carolina at Chapel Hill
Third Floor Carr Building, CB# 3233,
Chapel Hill
(919) 843-7776
Carolina Performing Arts schedules performers to appear in the University of North Carolina at Chapel Hill's main performance venue, Memorial Hall. Seasons average about 30 shows during the academic year. The emphasis is on cutting-edge performance art with a good mix of international stars. Recent seasons have included avant-garde

musicians Bang on a Can All-Stars, the Maly Drama Theatre of St. Petersburg's presentation of *Uncle Vanya*, and Senegalese pop star Baaba Maal. Performances are open to the public.

DUKE PERFORMANCES
Smith Warehouse, Bay 8, Suite 227, Durham
(919) 660-3356
http://dukeperformances.duke.edu/
The main performing arts organization at Duke, Duke Performances brings nationally and internationally acclaimed musicians and dancers to the campus. The seasons average about 50 shows during the academic year, and recent seasons have included artists as diverse as a capella group Sweet Honey in the Rock, guitarist Alejandro Escovedo, the Saint Lawrence String Quartet, and the dance troupe Urban Bush Women. Events are held in various venues on campus and are open to the public.

MEREDITH COLLEGE MUSIC DEPARTMENT
3800 Hillsborough St., Raleigh
(919) 760-8600
www.meredith.edu/music/events.htm
A private college for women, Meredith has a well-respected music program and offers many opportunities for involvement to the community. Among these are performances on campus, many of which are free and open to the public. Meredith hosts performances of Capital Opera and the Raleigh Symphony Orchestra, presents faculty and student performances, and schedules guest musicians from the Triangle and other parts of the state.

i If you're headed to a cultural event at one of the Triangle's larger universities, give yourself plenty of time to find parking. Space for cars is particularly scarce at Duke, UNC, and N.C. State, where the cities have grown up around the campuses. Parking is seldom close to the venue. For larger events, such as arena concerts, you may want to scout out remote parking possibilities and take a shuttle to the venue.

NORTH CAROLINA CENTRAL UNIVERSITY
1801 Fayetteville St., Durham
(919) 530-6100
http://webevent.nccu.edu

A historically black state university, N.C. Central offers performances, lectures, and forums that are frequently open to the public, mainly through its departments of theater and music. The school's jazz ensembles and jazz vocal ensembles are nationally respected and frequently appear on campus and at international and national festivals.

PEACE COLLEGE
15 E. Peace St., Raleigh
(800) 732-2347
www.peace.edu

Peace College, a private school for women, presents student and alumni performances of dance, music, and theater and hosts performances of professional musicians and actors on campus. Many events are open to the public, including the Manning Chamber Music Series and presentations of the school's drama and dance department and photography exhibitions.

SHAW UNIVERSITY
118 E. S. St., Raleigh
(919) 546-8200
www.shawuniversity.edu

Shaw is a private, historically black university in downtown Raleigh. Its drama and music departments present events on campus and at nearby venues including the Progress Energy Center and downtown churches that are often open to the public. . Performing groups include the University Choir, Shaw University Band, Platinum Sound Marching Band, Jazz Ensembles I and II and the Shaw Players. Recent theater performances by the Shaw Players, a troupe of students and professors, have included "Livin' Fat," a slice-of-life comedy set in the 1970s.

ARTS SUPPORT ORGANIZATIONS

CHATHAMARTS
P.O. Box 418, Pittsboro 27312
(919) 542-0394
http://chathamarts.org

CHATHAMARTS GALLERY
115 Hillsboro St., Pittsboro
(919) 542-4144

ChathamArts supports the work of artists in Chatham County by staging community events and festivals, providing a directory for artists, working with the area schools on arts education programs, and offering art and craft classes. The organization operates a gallery in downtown Pittsboro's historic district that features the work of more than 90 Chatham County community artists and writers. An opening reception on the first Sunday of each month introduces a new art exhibition.

DURHAM ARTS COUNCIL
120 Morris St., Durham
(919) 560-2787
www.durhamarts.org

The Durham Arts Council maintains the Arts Council Building in downtown Durham, a renovated 1906 space that today holds three galleries, two theaters, rehearsal spaces, and studios. The council also operates the Clay Studio at 546 Foster St. in downtown, where some of its many classes are held. In addition to the networking and informational services it offers artists and art lovers, the Arts Council stages CenterFest, the city's annual fall arts festival, and the Edible Arts Festival of Food and Art held in June.

HILLSBOROUGH ARTS COUNCIL
102 W. King St., Hillsborough
(919) 643-2500
www.hillsboroughartscouncil.org

The organization sponsors Hillsborough's Last Friday events on the final Friday evening of each month. Last Friday consists of concerts on the old courthouse lawn in warm weather and indoor concerts or movies in cooler weather, sidewalk exhibitions of arts and crafts, a pie contest, gallery receptions, poetry readings, and similar artistic displays. Also an Arts Council project is Handmade Parade, an annual autumn march through town that features costumes, masks, and giant puppets created by local artists and parade marchers. The Arts Council promotes exhibits at local galleries, offers classes in various media, sponsors musical performances, and is actively pursuing the creation of a cultural center to serve Hillsborough and northern Orange County.

JOHNSTON COUNTY ARTS COUNCIL
231 E. Second St., Clayton
(919) 553-1930
www.johnstoncountyarts.org
The Johnston County Arts Council administers grants, promotes the work of artists, and sponsors arts education in the schools. It also hosts Music for the Lunch Bunch, a summertime concert series at various venues downtown that showcases local musicians with an emphasis on classical music.

ORANGE COUNTY ARTS COMMISSION
110 E. King St., Hillsborough
(919) 245-2335
http://artsorange.org/index.html
The Orange County Arts Commission awards grants to fund projects proposed by artists, art organizations, and schools in the county twice a year. The commission is a co-sponsor, along with other area arts councils, of the Piedmont Laureate program, which names a laureate annually. The commission has a special focus on emerging artists, high school artists, and funding works of public art.

UNITED ARTS COUNCIL OF RALEIGH & WAKE COUNTY
110 S. Blount St., Raleigh
(919) 839-1498
www.unitedarts.org

The council distributes thousands of dollars in grants to organizations and individual artists in Wake County every year. The council also works with the Wake County Schools and with parks and recreation departments across the county to promote arts education through grants and programs. It promotes collaboration between artists and seeks display placement for artwork in public buildings.

LITERARY EVENTS

MCINTYRE'S FINE BOOKS
2000 Fearrington Village Center, Pittsboro
(919) 542-3030
www.fearrington.com

QUAIL RIDGE BOOKS AND MUSIC
3522 Wade Ave., Raleigh
(919) 828-1588
www.quailridgebooks.com

THE REGULATOR BOOKSHOP
720 Ninth St., Durham,
(919) 286-2700
www.regulatorbookshop.com
Between the universities and a trio of well-run independent bookstores, the Triangle draws a large and diverse slate of authors on a regular basis. The Regulator Bookshop in Durham, McIntyre's Fine Books in Fearrington Village, and Quail Ridge Books in Raleigh consistently bring authors in for readings and discussions. It's not unusual to pop into one of these stores and find a small group in rapt attention to a bestselling writer or a crowd overflowing into the aisles. Visitors have included Pulitzer Prize winner Michael Chabon, international culinary star Patricia Wells, UNC men's basketball coach Roy Williams, Duke men's basketball coach Mike Krzyzewski, and bestselling authors Sue Monk Kidd and Sarah Vowell. Local bestsellers, historians, scholars, and musicians also appear frequently.

MUSEUMS

Museums and galleries help drive the social and cultural calendar in the Triangle, from the annual kid-centered BugFest extravaganza put on by the North Carolina Museum of Natural Sciences, to the monthly schedules of gallery crawls that bring art lovers out in force. Each of the largest towns boasts a major state-funded science museum—the Museum of Natural Sciences in Raleigh, the North Carolina Museum of Life and Science in Durham, and the Morehead Planetarium and Science Center at UNC–Chapel Hill. Likewise, each has a noteworthy art museum—the North Carolina Museum of Art in Raleigh, the Nasher Museum of Art at Duke University, and the Ackland Museum of Art at UNC.

Beyond these giants, smaller art galleries thrive, shaped by many influences, from North Carolina's strong pottery craft tradition to N.C. State's innovative and highly regarded School of Design. Art lovers of all sorts can satisfy their appetites at scores of venues that offer everything from traditional Southern landscapes to provocative installation pieces. Between the permanent collections and the touring shows, a visitor to one of the Triangle's museums could expect to see ancient Egyptian artifacts, works by European master Raphael, paintings by Picasso, and sculpture by Henry Moore. Science museum programs offer opportunities for lifelong learning and engagement with the natural world.

Strong arts support organizations provide educational and enrichment opportunities, which helps sustain a community appetite for the visual arts. Monthly open-house gallery crawls in Raleigh, Cary, Durham, Chapel Hill, and Hillsborough inspire fresh presentations and repeat visits. As the Triangle has grown, its visual arts scene has kept pace, moving beyond the traditional to embrace the cutting-edge. Galleries like the internationally known Lump help bring outside, avant-garde talent to the area while organizations like Designbox support local artists who embrace a similar edgy aesthetic.

As Durham's downtown renaissance rolls on, the community is working to define itself as the arts hub of the Triangle. French artist Georges Rousee's 2006 trompe-l'oeil installation project in four about-to-be-renovated downtown warehouses certainly bolstered those ambitions and invigorated the arts community. Artists continue to find affordable studio and exhibition space in downtown, and Durham's semi-annual Art Walk, held in April and November, draws thousands. The opening of the Nasher Museum in 2005 also enhanced Durham's arts status. In 2010, Raleigh got a similar boost from the opening of the new North Carolina Museum of Art. And at N.C. State's School of Design, plans simmer for a contemporary art museum to anchor the blooming arts scene in Raleigh's warehouse district.

A NOTE ABOUT THIS CHAPTER

This chapter attempts to offer a solid overview of the museums, galleries, and centers that inform the Triangle's arts and culture scene. Not every gallery could be included due to space constraints. The area's eight universities and colleges provide a number of smaller, on-campus exhibition in addition to the listing here. A number of galleries that focus more on crafts than arts can be found in the Shopping chapter, while more information on the larger science museums is found in the Attractions chapter.

VISUAL ART MUSEUMS

ACKLAND ART MUSEUM
101 S. Columbia St., University of N. Carolina, Chapel Hill
(919) 966-5736
www.ackland.org
The Ackland Art Museum, the University of North Carolina at Chapel Hill's premier art space, sits on the edge of campus on Columbia Street. Completed in 1958, the museum's Georgian design echoes the lines of the university's oldest buildings. As per his wishes, the body of the museum's namesake benefactor is interred within.

Renovations completed in 2007 have brought the galleries up to 21st-century speed. The Ackland is home to 15,000 works of art, of which 10,000 are works on paper. Works from the paper collection rotate through the "Upstairs at the Ackland" space and include rare prints, photographs, and Chinese calligraphy, among others. Other key elements of the Ackland's permanent collection include European masterworks, Asian art, and African art, which also rotate on gallery exhibits. In addition to the permanent collection, the Ackland schedules several exhibitions of traveling exhibits annually. Those may include anything from Early Modern portraits to photography to European paintings to video installations.

With its renovation in 2007, the Ackland renewed its efforts to embrace the community and today places priority on innovative programs to lure visitors. Admission is free and participation in the programs is usually $5 or less. Among them are lunchtime lectures, music and dance performances, and yoga classes amid the artwork. The frequency with which the museum's works and the traveling art move through the galleries means that there is usually something new to see.

GREGG MUSEUM OF ART & DESIGN AT N.C. STATE UNIVERSITY
Talley Student Center, N.C. State University, Raleigh
(919) 515-3503
www.ncsu.edu/gregg

As a land-grant university, N.C. State defines part of its mission as the promotion of the creation of objects that are both useful and attractive. The Gregg Museum helps fulfill this mission with its collections of textiles, ceramics, architectural drawings, photography, modern furniture, and outsider art. The museum was born of a need to support State's renowned School of Design, but its scope has grown in the past four decades to include the works of other university departments as well. Emphasis is on North Carolina artists and craftsmen and N.C. State alumni and faculty.

The museum stages between six and eight exhibits annually in the Talley Student Center and in various venues around campus. Admission is free. Recent shows have examined contemporary fiber art, the history of building in North Carolina, the works of individual potters and metalsmiths, and the war photography of an N.C. State alum. Museum-curated examinations of such topics as quilts, Japanese woodblocks, and appliqués have traveled to other museums.

NASHER MUSEUM OF ART $
2001 Campus Dr., Duke University, Durham
(919) 684-5135
www.nasher.duke.edu
The Nasher, which opened in 2005, is a spectacular setting for some of the most innovative exhibitions that appear in the Triangle. From the outside, the Rafael Viñoly–designed museum appears as a series of white concrete boxes set among the hardwoods. Inside, its glass-roofed, soaring great hall sets the stage for the cutting-edge art the museum presents in the surrounding galleries. Recent seasons have seen a giant, four-screen video installation by internationally known artist Christian Marclay, a retrospective of photographs from Duke University's Special Collections Library, and an examination of how Picasso's art was informed by the artist's relationship with language. Programming includes lectures and discussions that complement current exhibitions as well as frequent children's programs and occasional free admission.

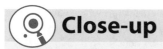 **Close-up**

The Plensa Kerfuffle

While Raleigh's city leaders are progressive thinkers on many issues, their tentative approach to public art recently cost the city what could have been a nationally renowned attraction.

In 2006, as the city was nearing completion of its renovation of downtown's Fayetteville Street, local media mogul Jim Goodmon, owner of Capitol Broadcasting, offered to put up $2.5 million for a piece of public art. The proposed project was to be a massive sculpture installation by internationally renowned Spanish artist Jaume Plensa, best known in the United States for Chicago's Crown Fountain. That Plensa work, in Chicago's Millennium Park, is a mesmerizing piece that features 50-foot video projections of Chicago residents' faces spouting water.

But when the artist's proposal was unveiled, the project derailed. It was a high-concept piece that would have involved a display of flashing lights and misting water above the new City Plaza. Questions about maintenance—who would be responsible for changing the light bulbs, for instance—arose. Critics complained that you would no longer be able to see from Memorial Auditorium, at Fayetteville Street's east end, to the State Capitol, at its west end. Eventually city leaders' demands for alterations to the artists' vision prompted both artist and benefactor to withdraw.

Today, the view from Memorial Hall to the Capitol remains unobstructed. City Plaza is home to four 55-foot, color-changing light towers decorated with stainless steel oak leaves and a rotating display of outdoor sculptures. If you want to see a Plensa sculpture, you can go to Duke University. The artist's "Tattoo," a 9-foot sculpture of a glowing, kneeling figure, adorns the school's West Campus Plaza. The Crown family of Chicago announced its loan of the sculpture to the school shortly after the Plensa debacle in Raleigh. But Plensa does have a presence in Raleigh. In 2009, Goodmon gave the North Carolina Museum of Art three of the sculptor's glowing works, "The Doors of Jerusalem I," "II," and "III." They greet visitors entering the lobby of the new North Carolina Museum of Art.

The museum enjoys frequent loans of masterwork sculpture from the other museum that shares its benefactor's name, the Nasher Sculpture Center in Dallas. Recent loans have included works of Henry Moore, Marino Marini, and Mimmo Paladino, which grace the great hall. In the Nasher's permanent collection are more than 13,000 works of art, with concentrations in contemporary art as well as the medieval and renaissance period, African art, Greek and Roman antiquities, and ancient American art.

The Nasher Museum Cafe, which does not require admission to the museum, offers an elegant, internationally inspired menu of salads and sandwiches that uses seasonal ingredients. Wine and North Carolina beer are available. Most entrees cost less than $10.

NORTH CAROLINA CENTRAL UNIVERSITY ART MUSEUM
Lawson St. between the Fine Arts and Music buildings
N. Carolina Central University, Durham
(919) 530-6211
www.nccu.edu
The permanent collection of the N.C. Central University Art Museum is devoted to the works of African-American artists and others who focus on the African-American experience. This includes artists from the late 19th and early 20th centuries, such as Romare Bearden and Jacob Lawrence, as well as contemporary artists including Barkley Hendricks, Geoffrey Holder, and North Carolina native Minnie Evans. Curators create exhibitions to make use of the permanent collection and host occasional touring works. Recent exhibits have included a

retrospective of the works of 19th-century still life painter Charles Ethan Porter, an examination of African-American modernism through the work of William H. Johnson, and a look at the career of Gordon Park. Admission to the museum is free, with the exception of occasional special programs.

NORTH CAROLINA MUSEUM OF ART
2110 Blue Ridge Rd., Raleigh
(919) 839-6262
www.ncartmuseum.org

The North Carolina Museum of Art's new gallery space is a wondrous blend of thoughtful design and ambitious vision. From its anodized aluminum exterior to its glass walls and innovative use of muted sunlight, the 127,000-square-foot building seamlessly melds a grassy, wooded setting and a luminous interior. The stands of birch and magnolia, shimmer pools, and lily pond outside are visible through the glass walls, creating a natural backdrop for the museum's varied permanent collection. The open floor plan allows visitors to get a sense of the breadth of the collection from many vantage points, as its bright modern murals, European paintings, African textiles, and Egyptian artifacts can be glimpsed together.

The new museum building complements the existing, adjacent 164-acre sculpture park. Crisscrossed by several trails, the sculpture park is part open meadow, part woods. Among the highlights are a series of 150-foot arches, a giant whirligig, a cloud chamber, and a pedestrian bridge that spans I-440 at the park's perimeter.

When it began the museum in 1947 with $1 million, North Carolina became the first state in the country to use public money to fund an art collection. Since then, the North Carolina Museum of Art's permanent collection has grown to span 5,000 years and include 30 Rodin sculptures—the largest collection in the Southeast—one of the few galleries in the country dedicated to Judaica, and pieces from a range of renowned artists—Georgia O'Keeffe, Frank Stella, Jacob Lawrence, Thomas Hart Benton, Henry Moore, and Bill Viola among them.

Admission to the museum is free, but tickets are required for the frequent touring exhibitions.

It's advisable to get tickets early, as crowds come from a radius of hundreds of miles. Popular exhibitions of previous seasons have included a retrospective of Monet in Normandy, an exploration of ancient Egyptian artifacts, and a collection of impressionist-era landscapes.

The museum's Blue Ridge Cafe serves fancy sandwiches and salads. As part of its mission as the state's foremost purveyor of art, the museum offers regular programs for children and adults.

ART GALLERIES AND STUDIOS

ADAM CAVE FINE ART
15½ E. Hargett St., Suite 240, Raleigh
(919) 838-6692
www.adamcavefineart.com

Adam Cave Fine Art represents a diverse slate of between 15 and 20 artists working in mediums including photography, painting, sculpture, glassmaking, and printmaking. Most live in the Southeast but their art focuses on a range of subjects that surpasses regionalism, with the streets of New York, abstract animal portraits, and impressionist portraits of Midwestern landscapes among them. The gallery is on the second floor of a restored turn-of-the-century office building downtown, between Fayetteville Street and Moore Square. Owners Adam Cave and Cynthia Cave are trained artists with many years of experience working with artists and galleries. The gallery features exhibits that change monthly.

ANIMATION AND FINE ART GALLERY
201 S. Estes Dr., University Mall, Chapel Hill
(919) 968-8008
www.animationandfineart.com

A trio of young art collectors runs this hip gallery, which specializes in high-quality prints of 20th-century masterworks and original cels and drawings of animation from studios including Warner Bros. and Disney. It's also a good place to check for autographed memorabilia. Their inventory has included pieces signed by such varied celebrities as Jim Cary, Tiger Woods, and Menachem Begin. Near A Southern Season gourmet food store, the gallery is a study in bold colors and bright presentation. If you're worried about spending too much, relax. The gallery has a 10-month, no-interest layaway payment plan.

ARTSOURCE FINE ART GALLERY AND FRAMING
509 W. Whitaker Mill Rd., Suite 105, Raleigh
(919) 833-0013

4351 The Circle at N. Hills, Suite 101
(919) 787-9533

ArtSource Fine Art Gallery sells the work of almost 100 artists—painters, glassworkers, sculptors, potters, photographers, and jewelers—most of whom live and work in the Southeast. The gallery's inventory numbers 3,000 pieces. One of the gallery's most popular genres is landscape portraits of North Carolina landmarks, beaches, and street scenes.

ARTSPACE
201 E. Davie St., Raleigh
(919) 821-2787
www.artspacenc.org

Artspace is a collection of open artists' studios, exhibition areas, and a gift shop housed in a 30,000-square-foot downtown building that was once a Ford dealership. A hub of arts activity in Raleigh, Artspace is home to 35 working artists, all of whom are juried members of the Artspace Artist Association. Mediums include clay, digital media, fiber art, jewelry, mixed media, painting, photography, printmaking, and sculpture. Artspace offers lessons and marketing support services for artists, entertainment, and a range of outreach workshops and projects for adults and children.

Exhibitions of members' work and shows of traveling work rotate through the galleries. The space is especially vibrant during Raleigh's First Friday gallery art walk, when new exhibitions most often open. During a stroll through the studios, you can see traditional portraiture, marble sculpture, and animation-inspired painting while downstairs in the galleries a show of nationally renowned lowbrow painters might be unveiled. Artspace also sponsors performances of spoken

word and poetry, music, and film, and the occasional high school party. Admission to exhibits is free with donations suggested. Most programs charge a fee.

BEV'S FINE ART
7400 Six Forks Rd., Peachtree Market, Raleigh
(919) 870-5342
www.bevsfineart.com

Bev's Fine Art has 2,000 works by more than 60 artists on hand, ranging from landscape oils to contemporary wood sculpture. The gallery also deals in lithographs and engravings of antique British paintings and antique French furniture. The gallery hosts events for art lovers, including local art history lectures on site. First Friday art crawlers can see exhibits of the gallery's artist at the Fayetteville Street offices of Remax Realty.

CARY GALLERY OF ARTISTS
200 S. Academy St., Ashworth Village, Cary
(919) 462-2035

The Cary Gallery of Artists features more than 25 local artists whose media include pottery, digital photography and art, handcrafted books, stained glass, clay sculpture and pastel, watercolor, acrylic, and oil painting. The gallery also offers lessons in painting, pottery, drawing, and how to use artistic techniques and approaches as tools for living. In 2009, the gallery staged its first juried art show, with plans for more in the future.

CENTER FOR DOCUMENTARY STUDIES AT DUKE UNIVERSITY
Lyndhurst House, 1317 W. Pettigrew St., Durham
(919) 660-3663
http://cds.aas.duke.edu/

The Center for Documentary Studies offers courses to students and post-grads in video, photography, and audio documentary practices. Its galleries showcase the work of students, instructors, and professional documentarians on a rotating basis. The center, housed in a renovated turn-of-the-century home, contains four galleries. Work might include modern photographs of immigrants presented with their handwritten biographies, historical photographs of farm and factory life, and art installations created by young people in Durham. The exhibitions change regularly, and the center presents a crowded calendar of lectures, workshops, and screenings. Admission to most events is free.

CHATHAMARTS GALLERY
115 Hillsboro St., Pittsboro
(919) 542-4144
www.chathamarts.org
Scores of artist and crafts makers who work in studios scattered about the wooded countryside of Chatham County show their works at ChathamArts Gallery in historic downtown Pittsboro. The Chatham County Art Council operates the gallery and exhibiting artists must live or work in the county. Art includes painting, photography, glassworks, textile art, metal work, stained glass, and more. The gallery exhibits new works monthly, and holds an opening reception on the first Sunday of each month from noon to 5 p.m.

CHURTON STREET GALLERY
100 S. Churton St., Hillsborough
(919) 732-2685
A 2009 addition to the downtown Hillsborough arts scene, the gallery focuses on art and crafts in North Carolina, including painting, pottery, and jewelry. Fans of North Carolina landscape painting can find some of the most popular artists in the genre, including Bob Rankin, Melissa Miller, Jennifer Miller, and Shannon Bueker.

CRAVEN ALLEN GALLERY
1106½ Broad St., Durham
(919) 286-4837
Craven Allen features the work of about 30 nationally recognized artists, most of whom defy easy categorization. Photography includes stunning black-and-white seascapes of beaches from around the world, photograms of organic materials enlarged to abstraction, and the work of artistic duo Nanny Studios, which includes wry tableaus of Barbie dolls and sock monkeys. Paintings include abstract landscapes in soothing palates, collages of nudes, and watercolors that feature oversized disembodied limbs or headless beachcombers. The selection and exhibits are always provocative at Craven Allen, which makes it a must-stop on Durham's monthly gallery crawl.

DESIGNBOX
323 W. Martin St., Raleigh
(919) 834-3552
www.designbox.us
Designbox isn't just a gallery, but a communal workspace for creative professionals that hosts exhibits of art and design during the First Friday Art Walk. Works on view might include animated short films, a comparative study of commissioned versus non-commissioned design work, or paintings of sparse urban landscapes. The space is in the transforming warehouse district and it's a good place to find the work of local artists and designers. If you stop in for the opening receptions you can also sneak a peek at what the graphic designers, architects, and other design-types are up to.

DURHAM ARTS COUNCIL
120 Morris St., Durham
(919) 560-2787
www.durhamarts.org
The Durham Arts Council works with the Durham Arts Guild to schedule exhibits in the three galleries in the council's historic building. The organizations issue a call for artists annually and judge works submitted, which are usually two-dimensional or small three-dimensional pieces. Artists need not be from North Carolina, but most are.

FISH MARKET
133 Fayetteville St., Raleigh
www.ncsu.edu/www/ncsu/design/sod5/
fishmarket
The Fish Market is the N.C. State University's College of Design Student Gallery. Open for Raleigh's First Friday gallery walks and on the Saturday and Sunday afterward. A below-ground gallery, it is one of the more raucous stops on the First Friday circuit as DJs frequently provide the music, which serves as more than background. Shows feature a

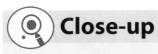 **Close-up**

Gallery Crawls

Cities in the Triangle have adopted the popular custom of art walks, coordinated evenings of exhibit openings and receptions to drive traffic to galleries, businesses that set aside exhibition space, and museums. Musical performances, film screenings, and restaurant specials are often scheduled to coincide. Raleigh kicks off the schedule with First Friday, which includes galleries from downtown to the warehouse district to Glenwood South. Chapel Hill and Carrboro follow with Second Friday events from the galleries of University Mall to Pilates studios in Carrboro. Durham holds its walk on Third Friday in and around downtown. And Hillsborough and Cary each host a walk on the Last Friday of the month.

Gallery crawls are a great way to take in a lot of art and get a feel for many different venues. Many curators and programmers seek to schedule show openings to coincide with the crawls. It's a free cultural experience you don't have to plan for. All you have to do is remember which city's walk is when.

variety of media, including photography, textiles and landscape plans. A recent community installation project invited students to bring found objects to be hung from the studio ceiling.

FLANDERS ART GALLERY
302 S. W. St., Raleigh
(919) 834-5044
www.flandersartgallery.com

FLANDERS 311
311 W. Martin St., Raleigh
(919) 821-2262
Flanders represents more than 40 contemporary artists, from the Triangle and across the country. Mediums include installation art, painting, drawing, photography, and sculpture, and works may include abstract landscapes, an oil-on-linen still life of a cluttered kitchen counter, and bleak digital photographs of farm animals lit like stage actors. The gallery's main space has recently relocated to the warehouse district. Flanders occupies a second gallery in front of studio and print space at 311 West Martin St. Exhibits rotate frequently at both spaces.

GALLERY C
3532 Wade Ave., Raleigh
(919) 828-3165
www.galleryc.net

Gallery C represents more than 30 artists of national and international reputation. Among the gallery's specialties are traditional and abstract Southern landscapes, original production animation art, folk art, Haitian art, Asian art, North Carolina artists, and antique prints and art. The gallery hosts eight exhibitions annually, including a showcase of significant 19th- and 20th-century North Carolina artwork every March. Gallery C is in Ridgewood Shopping Center, just inside the Beltline. The brightly colored sculpture installed near the exterior sign makes it easy to pick out of the strip mall lineup.

GOLDEN BELT
807 E. Main St., Durham
(919) 967-7700
www.goldenbeltarts.com
One of a spate of former warehouse renovations in downtown Durham, Golden Belt is a former textile mill turned into a multiuse complex. Along with loft apartments, and retail space are 35 artists' studios, a store featuring contemporary arts and crafts, and exhibition and event spaces that host art and performance events. It's a popular stop on Durham art walks. Exhibitions have included a student-and-mentor photography show of portraits of adults with mental illness, a mixed-media examination of the effect President Obama's election has had on perceptions of race,

and sketches from a professor's recent trip to Papua New Guinea. Golden Belt works with arts organizations in the community on an artist-in-residence program and show schedules.

HILLSBOROUGH GALLERY OF ART
121 N. Churton St., Suite 1D, Hillsborough
(919) 732-5001
www.hillsboroughgallery.com
A co-operative of 15 local artists and crafts makers runs the Hillsborough Gallery of Art. Membership is by jury. Members work in a variety of media, including paint, ceramics, photography, textiles, glass, metal, and wood, and the gallery hosts monthly shows featuring member works. The gallery's storefront location in historic downtown makes it a high-traffic stop during the town's monthly art walk.

HORACE WILLIAMS HOUSE
610 E. Rosemary St., Chapel Hill
(919) 942-7818
www.chapelhillpreservation.com
The Horace Williams House stages monthly exhibits of local artists' work in its striking Octagon Room gallery. Owned and operated by the Preservation Society of Chapel Hill, the house was built in 1850 in the Colonial Revival style. In the antebellum period, it was the home of Benjamin Hedrick, a professor fired from the university for his strident support of abolition. It was last home to philosophy professor Horace Williams. The society presents lectures, musical performances, and author readings at the house as well. Admission to the house and art exhibits is free.

LEE HANSLEY GALLERY
225 Glenwood Ave., Raleigh
(919) 828-7557
www.leehansleygallery.com
Lee Hansley's experience as a former curator at the Southeastern Center for Contemporary Art in Winston-Salem has informed his gallery's artistic sensibilities since its creation in 1993. It is housed in a restored bungalow on Glenwood South, a revitalized section of the city a few blocks from downtown. The gallery represents 35 artists, with a concentration on contemporary regional and North Carolina artists, living and historical. Mediums include painting, sculpture, mixed-media, ceramics, works on paper, and photography. Frequent exhibitions feature the work of gallery artists as well as others by invitation. Hansley recently opened a second gallery space nearby at 126 Glenwood Ave.

LITTLE ART GALLERY
432 Daniels St., Cameron Village, Raleigh
(919) 890-4111
www.littleartgalleryandcraft.com
One of Raleigh's oldest galleries, the Little Art Gallery opened in 1968 and is in Cameron Village, the city's oldest shopping center. Today it carries the works of more than 100 artists, mostly from the Southeast. The gallery also carries sculpture and crafts, including Brian Andreas's Story People.

LOCAL COLOR GALLERY
22 S. Glenwood, Raleigh
(919) 754-3887
www.localcoloraleigh.com
A co-operative of women artists created Local Color in the early 2000s as a place to show their art. Today, the co-op includes 14 members who operate store-front gallery space in the Glenwood South arts and entertainment district. In addition to monthly exhibitions of work by members and others, Local Color sponsors an annual event called Plein Air Paint Out in April. On one day, entrants paint a designated section of the city, then submit the paintings to a jury for judging.

LUMP
505 S. Blount St., Raleigh
(919) 889-2927
www.teamlump.org
Lump is the Triangle's most provocative artist collective and the best known in national and international contemporary art circles. Housed in a small former garage a few blocks from Shaw University in downtown Raleigh, the gallery presents mostly installation works. Lump features artists from around the country and world. The

emphasis is on emerging artists and those who fly beneath the radar. Members of Team Lump, the collective, exhibit nationally and internationally. Members work in a range of mixed media, addressing a range of political and social themes. This is no place to look for your grandmother's Christmas present.

THE MAHLER
228 Fayetteville St., Raleigh
(919) 896-7503
www.themahlerfineart.com
One of the newer additions to Raleigh's arts scene, the Mahler opened in 2009 in a sleekly renovated Fayetteville Street storefront that once housed a silversmith shop. Golden wood floors and natural light give the long, narrow space a warm glow and exposed plaster recalls its history. The Mahler specializes in modern art, in genres including abstract, architectural, figurative, landscape, and still life painting as well as glassworks, photography, and sculpture. Artists are regional and national, emerging and established.

MISSY MCLAMB GALLERY
403 W. Camden, Fearrington Village,
Pittsboro
(919) 755-1117
www.missymclamb.com/exhibitions
The de facto official wedding photographer for Fearrington Village, Missy McLamb features her work and the work of other photographers in her gallery in the village. McLamb, whose clients have included Stephen King and former U.S. Senator John Edwards, employs a documentary approach in her wedding photography. Past exhibits have included a retrospective of 10 years' worth of wedding cake photos and candid portraits of children.

NICOLE'S STUDIO AND ART GALLERY
715 N. Person St., Raleigh
(919) 838-8580
www.nicolestudio.com
Nicole Kennedy features her paintings and the work of about 35 other artists in her gallery, in a shopping center a block from Peace College.

Pastoral North Carolina and European landscape paintings dominate, but the gallery also deals in glass art, jewelry, and ceramics. Nicole's Studio stages monthly exhibits of artists' works in the studio and on occasion in the Capital Bank Plaza Lobby on Fayetteville Street. The studio offers workshops in painting and drawing.

POINTS OF VIEW PHOTOGRAPHY GALLERY
20 Glenwood Ave., Raleigh
(919) 819-1000
www.povphoto.tripod.com
Points of View is home to more than 20 photographers who concentrate on fine art and documentary photography using a variety of processes and approaches. Most are regional artists who have achieved national distinction. Images on display could range from abstract studies of light and line to historical black-and-white street scenes.

REBUS WORKS
301-2 Kinsey St., Raleigh
(919) 754-8452
www.rebusworks.us
Rebus Works' gallery sits at the Boylan Heights end of the Boylan Street Bridge, overlooking downtown Raleigh in what used to be the neighborhood's family-owned grocery store. The gallery represents more than 35 artists and crafters from the Southeast and beyond. Among them are local surrealist painters, digital portraitists, visionary and folk artists, mixed-media sculptors, ceramicists, and glass blowers. Rebus Works presents frequent exhibits and an annual show called "Via Penland" of works inspired by their creators' relationships with the renowned Penland School of Crafts near Asheville. Rebus Works also hosts Rebus Fest, an annual arts fair in the studio parking lot, on the same May weekend as Artsplosure downtown, and other community art events during the year.

ROSENZWEIG GALLERY
Judea Reform Congregation
1933 W. Cornwallis Rd., Durham
(919) 668-5839
www.jhfnc.org/rosenzweig-gallery

The Jewish Heritage Foundation of North Carolina operates the Rosenzweig Gallery, an exhibition space for Jewish art and artifacts inside Judea Reform Congregation. The gallery collects and exhibits Jewish artifacts from across the state. History exhibitions examine the ebb and flow of Jewish communities in towns throughout North Carolina. The gallery presents the art of Jewish artists in exhibits that change every month or two.

SOMERHILL GALLERY
303 S. Roxboro St., Durham
(919) 688-8868
www.somerhill.com

After 36 years in Chapel Hill, Somerhill Gallery moved to a dazzling new 9,600-square-foot space in the Venable Center, one of downtown Durham's renovated tobacco warehouse projects. The gallery is lit by more than 40 skylights and provides a sleek setting for the paintings, sculptures, mixed-media, photography, glass, ceramics, and jewelry on display. Somerhill represents more than 275 artists, regional and national, whose styles range from representative to abstract.

311 WEST MARTIN STREET GALLERIES AND STUDIOS
311 W. Martin St., Raleigh
(919) 821 2262
www.311galleriesandstudios.org

A slate of half a dozen rotating artists specializing in mainly printmaking, photography, and painting occupies this space in the warehouse district. The 311 West gallery has evolved from owner Judy Jones's original The Print Studio into a multi-genre arts center that stages collaborative efforts with painters from within and without. Abstract expressionist paintings and photos, mezzotints, intaglio, and lithography prints are among the offerings. Classes are offered through The Print Studio.

TYNDALL GALLERIES CHAPEL HILL
University Mall, 201 S. Estes Dr., Chapel Hill
(919) 942-2290
www.tyndallgalleries.com

Tyndall Gallery represents contemporary painters, sculptors, ceramicists, and textile artists whose work has achieved national acclaim. Most live and work in the Southeast. Works range from bas relief wooden sculptures of regional flora to Rothko-inspired watercolors. Exhibitions of gallery artists' work change every month to two months. In University Mall, the gallery is a white-walled, wooden-floor respite from its surroundings.

VISUAL ART EXCHANGE
325 Blake St., Raleigh
(919) 828-7834
www.visualartexchange.org

VAE is a private non-profit whose mission is to provide opportunities for emerging artists to exhibit their work and hone their skills. Membership in the exchange is not juried, but exhibits at VAE's gallery space are. In addition to regular exhibitions of member and non-member work, the gallery offers lessons in technique and networking opportunities for artists and art supporters, holds an annual exhibition of student art, and presents the annual Raleigh Street Painting Festival in September in conjunction with the Sparkcon festival. The gallery is a longtime resident of City Market, a renovated historic commercial district in the heart of downtown.

WOOTINI
Carr Mill Mall
200 N. Greensboro St., Carrboro
(919) 933-6061
www.wootini.com

If you appreciate the sensibilities of Tim Burton, you'll find much to like at Wootini, an art gallery focusing on Pop Pluralism art and designer toys. Burton is one of the scores of artists Wootini carries, but you'll also find anime-inspired designs, Hello Kitty–like posters, robot paintings on wood, and much more. The gallery's show openings can be lively affairs, with musicians wearing devil masks inspired by the art, for instance, or robots dancing across the hardwood. It's a fun place to explore on any day.

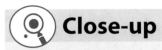

Close-up

Scrap Exchange

Take a quick look inside the Scrap Exchange and you may wonder if you've misread the listing. Art gallery isn't the first thing that comes to mind. It's a cluttered warehouse filled with wires, nails, broken picture frames, bits of tile, machine parts, rolls of fabric—the list seems endless. The Scrap Exchange is where old things come to find new life. More than a recycling center in the traditional sense, it serves as a supply center for artists and craft workers clever enough to turn trash into treasures. In addition to supplies, the Scrap Exchange sells the wares of local artists who use reclaimed materials—jewelry, handbags, sculpture, and the like. Scrap Exchange workers also promote the creation of "scrap art" at festivals and children's events. They bring the scraps and sticky stuff and spur kids on to action.

Although it seems impossible, the Scrap Exchange does refuse some things. Clothes, bedding, appliances, food containers, toxic substances, and a few other things are no go's. Exchange workers collect from businesses within 250 miles of Durham.

The Scrap Exchange is at 548 Foster St. in Durham; (919) 688-6960; www.scrapexchange.org.

HISTORY MUSEUMS

CHAPEL HILL MUSEUM
523 E. Franklin St., Chapel Hill
(919) 967-1400
www.chapelhillmuseum.org

Housed in a stone-walled 1968 structure that previously served as the town's library, the Chapel Hill Museum tells the story of the university town through a dozen exhibits, some changing, some permanent. Exhibits are dedicated to early 20th-century playwright Paul Green, who attended and taught at UNC; singer James Taylor, who grew up in town; and clothing designer Alexander Julian, a native son. Other exhibits examine the history of Chapel Hill, including the town's civil rights struggle in the 1950s and '60s and the changing face of Franklin Street, the main street that abuts campus.

Curators create programs for different children's age groups, with varying themes: Puppets sing about fire safety and show off a 1914 fire truck for younger children, while fourth-graders can perform a short version of playwright Paul Green's *The Lost Colony*. The museum also sponsors a series of adult-oriented fundraising events with historical and cultural enrichment themes, including walking tours led by costumed guides, progressive dinners, and cabaret performances of songs of earlier eras. Admission to the museum and programs are free.

JOEL LANE HOUSE MUSEUM
728 W. Hargett St., Raleigh
(919) 833-3431
www.joellane.org

Joel Lane was an influential Revolutionary-era plantation owner and lawmaker who helped Raleigh secure its unlikely bid to become the state's capital. In 1770, Lane petitioned the Colonial government to create Wake County, and in 1792 sold the state 1,000 acres that would become Raleigh. Legend holds that a drink called cherry bounce helped sway lawmakers in their real estate dealings, but this is not a part of the official historical record. The 1770s-era Joel Lane House stands at the edge of what is now Raleigh's warehouse district. It has been restored and furnished to reflect the period.

March through mid-December, costumed interpreters lead tours, starting at the visitors' center at 160 South St. Tours begin hourly from 10 a.m. to 1 p.m. Wednesday through Friday and from 1 to 3 p.m. Saturday. Group tours are available on Sunday by appointment. The museum has a gift shop and also sponsors special events and lectures that focus on Colonial life.

JOHNSTON COUNTY HERITAGE CENTER
241 E. Market St., Smithfield
(919) 934-2836
www.co.johnston.nc.us

A renovated bank in downtown Smithfield serves as the home for the Johnston County Heritage Center. The center is home to the county's collection of local history artifacts and genealogical records. Exhibits chronicle life in the county, including the role gristmills played in social and commercial development and the history of First Citizens Bank, which donated its former home to the museum. Admission is free.

NORTH CAROLINA COLLECTION GALLERY
Louis Round Wilson Library, University of
N. Carolina–Chapel Hill.
(919) 962-1172
www.lib.unc.edu/ncc/gallery.html

On the second floor of the serene and stately Wilson Library, the gallery rotates displays of its 22,000-piece collection. The gallery focuses on the history of the university, the political history of North Carolina, natural history, and numismatics, but has also accumulated a number of striking odds and ends through its two centuries. Among them are a plaster death mask of Napoleon Bonaparte and items owned by Eng and Chang Bunker, the conjoined twins who toured with circuses and retired to rural North Carolina in the 19th century. Among the permanent exhibits is a chronicle of the settlement of Roanoke Island and its native people and a display on the life of novelist Thomas Wolfe, a university alum. The gallery is open 9 a.m. to 5 p.m. Monday through Friday, 9 a.m. to 1 p.m. Saturday, and 1 to 5 p.m. Sunday. Admission is free.

NORTH CAROLINA MUSEUM OF HISTORY
5 E. Edenton St., Raleigh
(919) 807-7900
www.ncmuseumofhistory.org

Any child who attended elementary school in North Carolina no doubt spent a field-trip day at the North Carolina Museum of History. The three-story museum occupies a city block between the State Capitol and the Legislative Building and shares a plaza with the North Carolina Museum of Natural Sciences. See the Attractions chapter for more on the museum.

ORANGE COUNTY HISTORICAL MUSEUM
201 N. Churton St., Hillsborough
(919) 732-2201
www.orangenchistory.org

The museum tells the story of Orange County and Hillsborough, its county seat, one of the oldest English settlements in North Carolina. While the traditional narratives of the Revolutionary War and Civil War eras are represented, the museum also does a good job of bringing attention to the roles of women and slaves in eras when they are often overlooked. Temporary exhibits have looked at the life of jazz legend Billy Strayhorn, whose grandparents lived in Hillsborough, and the desegregation of Orange County's public schools. The museum is open 11 a.m. to 4 p.m Tuesday through Saturday and 1 p.m. to 4 p.m. Sunday. Admission is free.

RALEIGH CITY MUSEUM
220 Fayetteville St., Raleigh
(919) 832-3775
www.raleighcitymuseum.org

The redbrick, white-trimmed Briggs Hardware Building that houses the Raleigh City Museum was considered a skyscraper—the tallest in eastern North Carolina—when it was built in 1874. It is the only 19th-century commercial building in the city to escape significant changes, as most were altered or razed in the 20th century. The city museum collects artifacts of Raleigh's history and organizes exhibits and programs that illuminate Raleigh's past and define its present. Recent exhibits have included submitted photographs of the city by amateurs and professionals, and a look at the role the media has played in Raleigh's development. The museum leads a historical walking tour of Fayetteville Street and the surrounding area every Thursday morning at 10. An annual theatrical production produced with Burning Coal Theatre Company presents a mobile historical play on Fayetteville Street. Admission and tours are free.

PARKS

For much of their histories, the urban centers that dot the Triangle were small towns separated by vast tracts of rural land dedicated to farms and woods. It has only been in recent decades that Raleigh, Durham, and Chapel Hill have accrued population numbers that put them on the national map. As this growth occurred, forward thinking planners and ecologically minded residents set aside pockets of wilderness, protecting them from development. Urban growth has marched right up to the gates of Umstead State Park and Durham's West Point on the Eno city park, but within the park boundaries, nature flourishes and remnants of the quieter life of centuries past remain to be discovered. Having such oases in the middle of metropolitan life lends a gentleness to its pace.

Not every park space is dedicated to contemplative moments, of course. City and county governments continue to create and maintain scores of parks that cater to the changing needs of their residents. The past five years have seen the opening of several new dog parks around the Triangle, spurred on by pet owners' urgings. Both Durham and Raleigh have created public skate parks in recent years, providing havens for boarders weary of being chased out of parking lots and shopping centers.

Educational and recreational programming is strong at the parks in the Triangle, so it's worth exploring what the nearest recreation center or park has on tap. This list aims to cover the breadth of the parks scene in the Triangle. Space limitations make it impossible to list every park, as neighborhoods throughout the Triangle enjoy playgrounds and ball fields that suit community needs. Hours of operation and fees are always subject to change, so it's a good idea to call or check the Web site before heading out on your day trip. Most parks have water sources, but carrying extra H_2O is also wise.

STATE PARKS

ENO RIVER STATE PARK
6101 Cole Mill Rd., Durham
(919) 383-1686
www.ncparks.gov
As the name implies, the shallow waterway that winds through this park is its defining feature. Canoeing and tubing are popular ways to see the beauty of the river and its surrounding steep banks and woodlands. Within the 3,900-acre park are five access points to the water: Cabe Lands, Cole Mill, Few's Ford, Pleasant Green, and Pump Station. The Eno is a tricky river to gauge. If you put a canoe in when the water is too low, expect to get caught on the rocks. If you put in after heavy rains, prepare for swift currents that

move you rapidly through its many twists and turns. Rapids are usually short, but it's easy to be surprised by them. The park's Web site offers a "Current Conditions" tab to help canoeists and kayakers determine if water levels are appropriate for their skill levels. Park rangers are always happy to advise by phone.

For those who want to remain on dry land, the Eno River State Park has more than 24 miles of trails that range in difficulty from the easy 1-mile Fanny's Ford trail along the river in the Few's Ford area to the strenuous, 4-mile Cox Mountain Trail. The Few's Ford and Cole Mill areas have backcountry camping sites for individuals and families. No drinking water is available at the sites.

Settlements on the Eno date back to long before European exploration when American

Indians lived and traveled along its banks. During Colonial and post-Revolutionary times, the river powered a series of mills and fostered logging operations that gave rise to small communities. Evidence still stands at a few of those settlements. The area became a state park in 1972.

Admission to the park is free. Reservations are required for group camping areas and strongly advised for individual areas. Permits, which cost $12 per day, must be obtained either online or at the park office. The office is open weekdays 8 a.m. to 4:30 p.m. November through February. Friday hours are extended until 8 p.m. March through October. Saturday hours are 9 a.m. to 6 p.m. and Sunday hours are noon to 5 p.m. March through October. Saturday and Sunday hours are noon to 4 p.m. November through February.

FALLS LAKE STATE RECREATION AREA
13304 Creedmoor Rd., Wake Forest
(919) 676-1027
www.ncparks.gov

North of Raleigh, where the counties of Granville, Wake, and Durham meet, 12,000 acres of water and 26,000 acres of woodlands comprise Falls Lake Recreation Area. Beginning in 1978, the U.S. Army Corps of Engineers dammed the Neuse River to create Falls Lake and control flooding in the area. Boating and fishing are popular pastimes. For more details on those, see the Recreation chapter of this book.

The area surrounding the lake offers opportunities for hikers, mountain bikers, and campers as well. RV and tent campers can drive to more than 300 campsites, while backpackers can hike to 47 sites and two group areas. Hikers can follow the southern shore of the lake for more than 20 miles on the Falls Lake Trail, which is part of the statewide Mountains-to-Sea Trail. Parts of the trail traverse game lands, so take precautions during hunting season. Shorter walks into the woods or along the lake start at the Rolling View, Sandling Beach, Beaverdam, and Holly Point recreation areas. Swimmers can jump into the lake from sandy areas at Sandling Beach, Rolling View, and Beaverdam. Falls Lake's woodlands include 13 trails for single-track mountain biking. Half are designated as easy to intermediate, and half are advanced. The trailheads are at the Beaverdam area.

The recreation area charges a $5 per car fee for day use of the park between Memorial Day and Labor Day and on weekends and holidays in April, May, and September. Camping fees range from $18 to $23 per day. The area is open 8 a.m. to 6 p.m. November through February; 8 a.m. to 8 p.m. March, April, September, and October; and 8 a.m. to 9 p.m. May through August. The park is closed on Christmas Day.

JORDAN LAKE STATE RECREATION AREA
280 State Park Rd., Apex
(919) 362-0586
www.ncparks.gov

Jordan Lake, in eastern Chatham County, is a 14,000-acre, man-made lake that serves as a water source, wildlife habitat, and recreational area. The most popular activities are boating and fishing. For details on these, see the Recreation chapter of this book. The surrounding 33,000 acres of wooded lakeshore also draws campers, hikers, and bird watchers as Jordan Lake is home to the largest concentration of bald eagles on the East Coast.

The recreation area has 1,000 family campsites, including hundreds of sites for RVs, spread among the Crosswinds, Parker's Creek, and Poplar Point campgrounds. The New Hope Overlook has 24 hike-in primitive campsites all within half a mile of the parking lot. The park also has 11 group tent camps and a group RV camp with 50 sites. Reservations are encouraged for all campsites. Beaches at the Ebenezer Church, Seaforth, Parker's Creek, and White Oak Recreation areas are open to day visitors for swimming, while beaches near the campgrounds are reserved for campers.

Rangers offer bird watching programs regularly, for those wanting to get a look at the bald eagles and other wildlife. The best time to spot the birds is early in the morning or late in the afternoon. The eagles migrate north during spring and early summer, which is a good time to see them on the move. Vista Point, Ebenezer, and Seaforth recreation area offer good views for bird watching.

The recreation area charges a $5 per car fee for day use of the park between Memorial Day and Labor Day and on weekends and holidays in April, May, and September. Camping fees range from $12 to $23 per day. The park is open 8 a.m. to 9 p.m. May through August; 8 a.m. to 8 p.m. September, October, March, and April; and 8 a.m. to 6 p.m. November, December, January, and February.

Parkgeek.com

A great way to stay abreast of scheduled activities at Triangle area parks is to subscribe to the parkgeek .com electronic newsletter. http:// Parkgeek.com covers several states' worth of parks, but it targets its newsletters to specific areas, so you'll get only information about events within an hour's drive. The newsletter goes out on Thursdays and outlines the weekend's events. At the Web site, you'll find reviews of hundreds of parks in the area, which help with planning for the trip. The subscription is free and most of the events, put on by public parks, are free as well.

OCCONEECHEE MOUNTAIN
STATE NATURAL AREA
6101 Cole Mill Rd., Durham
(919) 383-1686
www.ncparks.gov
At 867 feet above sea level, Occoneechee Mountain is the highest point in Orange County and serves as an anomalous example of mountain ecology in North Carolina's piedmont. The hike to the top is a workout but affords views of plants and animals usually found much farther west. Catawba rhododendron grows alongside a ravine whose slopes are covered in mountain laurel. Deer and wild turkey inhabit the area's three acres, which also provide a home for one of the few communities of brown elfin butterfly found outside of the mountains. The views along the river and from scenic bluffs are unequaled in the Triangle. Two ponds and the Eno River provide a place to fish, and picnickers are welcome. The natural area has no camping facilities, so it's a day-trip destination only.

Occoneechee is named for the American Indian tribe that settled near the mountain along the Eno River in the 17th century. The natural area is administered by the Eno River State Park. Admission is free.

UMSTEAD STATE PARK
8801 Glenwood Ave., Raleigh
(919) 571-4170
www.ncparks.gov
Crawling along I-40 in rush hour traffic between Durham and Raleigh, commuters can take comfort as they pass the signs for Umstead State Park. They may be stuck in traffic at the moment, but a wooded oasis is just a turn off the highway. Only the planes taking off at RDU shake the quiet in the deepest parts of Umstead's 5,579 acres, located in the midst of the Triangle between I-40 and U.S. 70. The park has two entrance points, the Reedy Creek entrance off I-40 and the Crabtree Creek entrance off U.S. 70.

Within the park, 20 miles of trails are dedicated to hiking, and 13 miles are reserved for mountain bikers and horseback riders. Boaters and anglers can rent canoes and rowboats for a float on Big Lake, in the northwest corner of the park, or picnic beside it. The park has 28 tent and trailer campsites, two primitive campsites for groups, and two group campsites with dining halls and bathhouses. Reservations are required for group sites.

One of the most popular walks in Umstead is the Company Mill Trail, a hilly 5.8-mile trail that takes hikers to the densest parts of the hardwood forest. It is popular with both hikers and runners. About a mile in, you can stop at the Company Mill site along Crabtree Creek. An old millstone recalls the park's earlier days, when European settlers had moved in to farm and log the land. By the early 20th century the soil was depleted and logging had taken a toll on the forests. In 1935, the federal and state governments bought the land that was to become the heart of the park and relocated its residents. Civil Conservation Corps and Works Progress Administration workers built the original park structures. At first, the land was divided into two parks, Reedy Creek for African Americans and Crabtree Recreational Area for whites. In the 1960s, the two parks were united under one name and equal access was granted to everyone.

Admission to the park is free. The park is open daily from 8 a.m to 6 p.m. November through February; 8 a.m. to 8 p.m. March, April, September, and October; and 8 a.m. to 9 p.m. May through August. The Crabtree Creek gate opens at 7 a.m. daily. Umstead is closed on Christmas Day. Boathouse hours are from 8:30 a.m. to 4:30 p.m. Boat rental is $5 for the first hour and $3 every hour after that.

COUNTY AND CITY PARKS

FRED G. BOND METRO PARK
801 High House Rd., Cary
(919) 469-4100
www.townofcary.org

The 310-acre Bond Park includes ball fields, the Sertoma Arts Center and amphitheater, a community center, the Cary Senior Center, and Bond Lake. More than 4 miles of trails crisscross the park, including one that circles the lake. It also includes the large Lazy Daze playground, a ropes course for adults, and a compost education center. Admission is free.

HARRIS LAKE
2112 County Park Dr., New Hill
(919) 387-4342
www.wakegov.com/parks

Harris Lake County Park sits on a peninsula of land jutting out into the cooling lake that serves the Shearon Harris Nuclear Power Plant in southwestern Wake County. Its 680 acres include two playgrounds, a primitive campground for supervised groups, a mountain bike trail, 5 miles of hiking trails, and an 18-hole disc golf course. Canoeing

and kayaking are allowed on the lake. The park has a handicapped-accessible fishing pier and a rod-loan program.

HEMLOCK BLUFFS NATURE PRESERVE
2616 Kildaire Farm Rd., Cary
(919) 387-5980
www.townofcary.org

Amid the busy throughways and subdivisions of south Cary, Hemlock Bluffs is a quiet space where birds and humans can take refuge. The park takes its name from a stand of rare Eastern Hemlock trees among the pines and hardwoods. It is home to about 3 miles of trails and elevated observation platforms that provide good vantage points for birders. Within the preserve is the Stevens Nature Center, which includes educational indoor exhibits and a wildflower garden. It is a good place to catch a glimpse of the brown-headed nuthatch and the red-headed woodpecker. Admission to the park is free. It is open daily 9 a.m. to sunset.

HISTORIC YATES MILL
4620 Lake Wheeler Rd., Raleigh
(919) 856-6675
www.wakegov.com/yatesmill

Anyone who drives around the Triangle will notice the number of streets named for the gristmills and sawmills that dotted the area long ago. Seventy of these mills once stood in the county. Yates Mill is the surviving artifact. Founded in 1750, the mill operated until the 1950s, then fell into disrepair. It was restored and reopened as the centerpiece of a county park in 2006. Visitors can tour the mill March through November. Demonstrations of the mill grinding corn into meal are held on the third weekend of those months. Yates Mill cornmeal is also available for sale online and at the park. Surrounding the mill are 174 acres of woodlands, including several trails of less than 1 mile each, and the mill pond, where fishing is allowed. The A.E. Finley educational center holds displays about the natural and political history of the site. The park is open 8 a.m. to sunset. The center closes at 5 p.m. Admission is free.

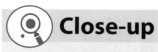 **Close-up**

Park Dreams Deferred

To the south of downtown Raleigh, opposite Western Boulevard from the historic Boylan Heights neighborhood, sits one of the most coveted plots of land in the Triangle. Set on a hill, it affords beautiful views of the city skyline. It's home to the state psychiatric hospital, known commonly around North Carolina as "Dix Hill." Mentally ill patients have found a haven on its wooded campus since the 1850s when activist Dorothea Dix traveled to North Carolina to lobby for better state-supported care for the insane. When state lawmakers made plans in the early 2000s to move the hospital to a new facility north of Durham, the lobbying by real estate developers and green space advocates began. Commercial developers would love to see housing and retail space on the plot. Park supporters want to see its 300-odd acres dedicated to green space. The lobbying is liable to continue for years, as the state has since postponed plans to close the hospital. Wrangling between the state and city governments is bound to continue after that. But yard signs throughout Raleigh boast park supporters' rallying cry of "Dix 306," a reference to the plot's acreage.

The campus is open to visitors who want to explore its open meadows and hills. Along with the hospital buildings are more than 100 other state offices, some related to mental health services, some not. It's a lovely place for a walk and it might make a nice park, someday.

LAKE CRABTREE
1400 Aviation Parkway, Morrisville
(919) 460-3390
www.wakegov.com/parks
The park's 215 wooded acres sit next to the 520-acre lake. In the park are paved and rugged trails, including a 6-mile loop of the lake and a mountain bike trail. The park is connected to Umstead State Park by Umstead's Lake Trail. The lake itself is open to electric motor boats. Boaters can rent sailboats, rowboats, pedal boats, canoes, and kayaks at the park during warmer months. Park hours are 8 a.m. to sunset. Admission is free.

LAKE JOHNSON
4601 Avent Ferry Rd., Raleigh
(919) 233-2121
www.raleighnc.gov
The 5½ miles of paved and natural paths that circle Lake Johnson are popular with runners who appreciate both the challenge of the lakeside hills and the shade of the woods. Boaters can rent Jon boats, pedal boats, canoes, kayaks, and small sailboats or bring their own non-motorized small crafts to the 150-acre lake. Anglers can fish for largemouth bass, shell cracker, crappie, bream, catfish, and carp. The lake sponsors a free

outdoor concert series during the summer. The park is open dawn to dusk, except on Monday October through March. Admission is free.

LAKE WHEELER
6404 Lake Wheeler Rd., Raleigh
(919) 662-5704
www.raleighnc.gov
South of downtown, and convenient to Cary and Raleigh, 650-acre Lake Wheeler is a water source for the city. Boaters can bring motorized or non-motorized craft to the lake or rent Jon boats, canoes, or pedal boats. Jet skis are not allowed. The 150 acres of park surrounding the lake offer a volleyball court and picnic areas, fishing access points, a conference center for rent, and a concession stand. The park is open daily from sunrise to sunset. Admission is free but fees are charged for boat launches, picnic shelter rentals, and the volleyball court.

LITTLE RIVER REGIONAL PARK
301 Little River Park Way, Guess Rd.,
Hillsborough
(919) 732-5505
www.enoriver.org

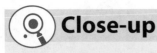

Close-up

Ghosts of Mordecais Past

The Mordecai family may have left behind more than just their ancestral home in Raleigh. Some believe a specter remains as well. Through the years, site staff members have claimed to see Mary Willis Mordecai Turk, appearing as a gray apparition and sometimes playing the piano downstairs in her family's home. The Sci-Fi channel's *Ghost Hunters* featured the Mordecai house, but found no evidence of the paranormal. But interest in the spirits is so great that the city of Raleigh must limit access by awarding contracts to paranormal investigators.

The contract allows one team of ghost busters per year overnight access to the historic site. They must report on their paranormal research at the annual Haunted Mordecai event in October. Other activities at the festival include music and games on the lawn, a late-night tour of the house, and late-night Historic Raleigh Trolley tours with an emphasis on all things spooky.

The 376 pristine acres of Little River Regional Park offer visitors a chance to see deer, turkey, beaver, bobcat, red-backed salamanders, and possibly black bear. Stands of hardwoods that have never been logged dot the steep slopes that rise from the Little River. Historic buildings, including an early 20th-century farmhouse, recall parts of the tract's history as a tobacco farm. The park has 7 miles of single-track mountain bike trails and 7 miles of hiking trails. It is located north of Hillsborough off Guess Road. Park hours are 7 a.m. to dusk, May through September, and 8 a.m. to dusk October through April. The park is closed Christmas Eve, Christmas Day, and New Year's Day. Admission is free.

MORDECAI PARK
1 Mimosa St., Raleigh
(919) 857-4364
www.raleighnc.gov
In centuries past, the Greek Revival Mordecai House was a farmhouse set on one of Wake County's largest plantations. Today it sits off busy, four-lane Wake Forest Road half a mile from the State Capitol. Moses Mordecai, for whom the house is named, married into the family of Raleigh founder Joel Lane. Through the generations, the 5,000 acres that made up the original farm were sold for development. Alongside the Mordecai House stand several historic buildings that have been moved to the site, including the small wood-plank house where Andrew Johnson, 17th president of the United States, was born. Admission to the grounds is free, but fees are charged for tours. Historic Raleigh Trolley Tours, which offer one-hour, narrated trips past downtown Raleigh's historic sites, leave from Mordecai House park Saturdays March through December. Call the site for information about tours and fees.

i In this case, the correct pronunciation of the name is MOR-duh-kee, according to both the 19th-century patriarch and the modern-day residents of the neighborhood that surrounds his historic home.

SOUTHERN COMMUNITY PARK
1300 U.S. 15-501 S. and 1000 Dogwood Acres
Dr., Chapel Hill
(919) 968-2784
www.townofchapelhill.org
The centerpiece of this 72-acre Chapel Hill Park, one of the newest in the city, is an inline skate hockey rink. Also on site are picnic shelters, a playground, basketball courts, a two-acre dog park, hiking and running trails, and an 18-hole disc golf course. More than half of the park's acres are dedicated to natural areas. Six art installations using elements like boulders and downed trees, which were saved during the construction of the park, will dot the area when they are complete.

WALNUT CREEK WETLAND CENTER AND PARK
950 Peterson St., Raleigh
(919) 831-1961
www.raleigh-nc.org
Walnut Creek Park offers a rare opportunity to experience a wetland ecosystem within an urban area. Its 59 acres are southeast of downtown Raleigh along a once-polluted stretch of Walnut Creek. Opened in 2009, the site is home to a $1.2 million environmental education center, greenway trails, and a deck overlooking the floodplain. Visitors can get a better understanding of the value of wetlands for water quality and wildlife preservation through exploration and programs offered by the park's naturalists.

WEST POINT ON THE ENO
5101 N. Roxboro Rd., Durham
(919) 471-1623
www.enoriver.org
Six miles north of downtown Durham, this 400-acre city park preserves the social history and natural heritage of the Eno River. A number of trails run parallel to the river and offer impressive views from the steep, wooded terrain that abuts it. The park takes its name from the community that grew up here with the first mill's establishment in the mid-1700s. A working reconstruction of the mill recalls the history. Before European settlers, the West Point area was home to the Shocco and Eno Indians, who found fertile hunting grounds near the river.

Also in the park are an environmental education center, a restored mid-19th-century farmhouse, and the Hugh Mangum Museum of Photography, housed in an old tobacco packhouse. Mangum's family lived at West Point, and he captured the early 20th-century development of the South on film. The museum houses a permanent collection of Mangum's photos and hosts changing shows of modern regional photographers. Historic buildings are open 1 to 5 p.m. Saturday and Sunday, mid-March through mid-December. Weekday tours can be arranged by calling the parks department.

The Eno River Association contributes to the survival of the park and furthers the protection of wild lands through its annual Festival for the Eno on July Fourth. (See the Annual Events chapter for more on the festival.) The park is open daily from 8 a.m. to sundown. Admission is free.

SKATE PARKS

CHAPEL HILL SKATE PARK
100 Northern Park Dr., Chapel Hill
(919) 932-7399
www.chapelhillskatepark.com
Vertical Urge, a longtime Triangle skateboard shop, has operated Chapel Hill's city-owned skate park since 2006. The 10,000-square-foot concrete park, inside Homestead Park, has wooden ramps and quarter-pipes and includes a concession stand and pro shop. Instructors offer lessons on site. Waivers signed by parents are required for those younger than 18. The park charges $7 per session for Orange County residents and $8 for non-residents. Annual memberships that bring down the cost of individual sessions are available.

DURHAM SKATE PARK
Durham Central Park
502 Foster St., Durham
(919) 560-4355
Durham's 10,000-square-foot concrete skate park opened downtown in late 2009. It includes three sets of seven-step stairs, launch boxes, a quarter pipe, a street clam, and an eight-inch trog bowl. Helmets, knee pads, and elbow pads are required, and no bicycles are allowed. The park is open dusk to dawn. Admission is free. No concession stand or pro-shop is associated with the park, but Ujamaa Boardhouse skate shop is nearby at 719 North Mangum Street.

MARSH CREEK SKATE PARK
3016 New Hope Rd., Raleigh
www.raleighnc.gov
A waterfall bowl, a half-pipe, a volcano, rails, and hubba ledges are among the features skateboarders can grind on at the outdoor concrete skate park the city of Raleigh opened in 2009.

Admission is free, but skaters must sign a waiver or, if they are 18 or younger, have their parents sign one. The park is unsupervised. Pads and helmets are required. No bicycles are allowed. Adjacent to the skate course is an inline hockey rink.

i Skaters who frequent the Marsh Creek site post photos and news items at its blog, http://marshcreek.blogspot.com.

SK8 CARY
2040 NorthW. Maynard Rd. in Godbold Park, Cary
(919) 380-297
www.townofcary.org

Bicyclists, skateboarders, and inline skaters are welcome at the town of Cary's 12,000-square-foot outdoor skate park. The course includes rails, banks, grind ledges, quarter-pipes, and half-pipes that range from 3 to 9 feet. The park also includes a pro shop and concession area. Young and novice skaters and bikers can take lessons from pros. The park hosts contests in the spring and fall.

Time at the park is divided into sessions for skateboarders and inline skaters and cyclists, so check the Web site or call the park. Helmets, pads, and signed waivers are required. The park charges $9 per session for skaters and $10 per session for bikers. Annual memberships and multi-session passes are available and bring down the per-session fee.

DOG PARKS

Cary

CARY DOG PARK
2050 NorthW. Maynard Rd.,
Godbold Park, Cary
(919) 469-4064, (919) 462-3970 (after 5 p.m.)
www.townofcary.org, www.carydogpark
club.org

The town of Cary operates the one-acre dog park and requires owners to register pets at one of the town's community centers before using the park. Entrance fees are $5 per day for Cary residents, $10 per day for non-residents. Annual passes for residents are $40 for one dog, $60 for multiple dogs; non-residents pay $80 for one dog and $120 for multiple dogs. Separate areas are provided for large and small dogs. The park is lighted and hours are 7 a.m. to 10 p.m. daily. No children younger than 12 are allowed in the dog park.

Chapel Hill

HOMESTEAD PARK
100 Northern Park Dr., Chapel Hill
www.chapelhilldogpark.com, www.townof
chapelhill.org

SOUTHERN COMMUNITY PARK
1000 Dogwood Acres, Chapel Hill
www.townofchapelhill.org

Separate areas are provided for large and small dogs. Parks are open dawn to dusk. No dogs younger than six months. No dog owners younger than 12 allowed without adult supervision. Pet owners must scoop poop. No digging. No dogs in heat. Admission is free.

Durham

NORTHGATE DOG PARK
300 W. Club Blvd., Northgate Park, Durham
(919) 560-4355
www.durhamnc.gov

PINEY WOOD PARK
400 E. Woodcroft Parkway, Piney Wood Park, Durham
(919) 560-4355 ext. 27220
www.durhamnc.gov

Durham operates two dog parks, and requires pet owners to obtain an admission tag for each dog from the city. Tags cost between $15 and $22 per dog, depending on whether the pet owner is a city resident. Pet owners can register by mail or in person at the Durham Parks and Recreation Department at 400 Cleveland St. Each dog park includes separate areas for large and small dogs. No dogs younger than three months old are allowed.

Raleigh

CAROLINA PINES
2305 Lake Wheeler Rd., Raleigh
(919) 872-4156
www.carolinapinesdogpark.com, www
.raleighnc.gov

MILLBROOK
1905 Spring Forest Rd., Raleigh
(919) 872-4156
www.millbrook-dog-park.com, www
.raleighnc.gov

OAKWOOD
910 Brookside Dr., Raleigh
(919) 872-4156
www.oakwooddogpark.com, www.raleighnc
.gov

The city operates three dog parks. Admission is free. Owners must scoop poop. No dogs in heat allowed. No dogs younger than four months old. No digging. No food or toys allowed inside the park. Each park includes a separate area for small dogs and large dogs. Hours are sunrise to sunset, except for Millbrook, which has lights and is open until 10 p.m. Each park is supported by a volunteer citizens' group that helps maintain the parks and provides an online forum for news and issues important to pet owners who frequent the parks. Some groups organize events at their parks as well.

WAKE FOREST
Flaherty Dog Park
1150 N. White St.
(919) 554-6180
www.wakeforestnc.gov

Opened in 2007, Wake Forest's dog park provides separate areas for large and small dogs. Dogs must be at least six months old and current on rabies shots. No dogs in heat. Owners must fill in any holes dug by dogs and scoop poop. No food or treats are allowed inside the park. The park is open from dawn to dusk.

RECREATION

About the only sports not available in the Triangle are those that require heavy snowfalls and constant below-freezing temperatures. So, don't look for cross-country skiing or ice fishing competitions, though indoor hockey is quite popular. Mild winter temperatures mean most pastimes can be pursued year-round, whether it's golf in December or canoeing in February. Sports leagues for adults and children thrive and communities work to ensure that facilities are attractive and well-maintained.

This chapter aims to provide a look at the range of recreational activities available in the Triangle and to offer starting points for exploring them. When possible, the emphasis is on public facilities. Some of these activities are free, but it's best to consult the phone number or Web site to determine if a fee is charged.

LAKES

All of the Triangle's recreational lakes are man-made, created in the past century in response to the area's ever-growing need for residential water. Their artificial creation has no bearing on their natural beauty, though, and many are havens to a range of wildlife. Whether you're looking to roar across the water on a jet-ski or glide into a quiet cove on a canoe, you can find it within reach. Most of the Triangle's lakes are open year-round. Exceptions are noted.

FALLS LAKE
Raleigh
(919) 676-1027
www.ncparks.gov
North of Raleigh, Falls Lake's 12,000 acres spread across the Durham, Wake, and Granville county lines. The state parks system manages the lake and its recreation areas. Most of the lake is dedicated to motor boats and jet-skis, which can launch from the Highway 40 or Rolling View boat ramps. Beaverdam recreation area is a haven for canoeists and kayakers since gasoline-powered boats are prohibited. Non-motorized boats can also launch from Sandling Beach. Anglers can find bass, bluegill, catfish, and crappie in Falls Lake.

HARRIS LAKE
2112 County Park Dr., New Hill
(919) 387-4342
www.wakegov.com/parks/harrislake
Harris Lake is a 4,000-acre cooling pool for Progress Energy's Shearon-Harris Nuclear Power Plant, 22 miles southwest of Raleigh on the Chatham-Wake county line. Wake County's Harris Lake Park permits launches of only non-motorized boats from its recreation center. The county leases 680 acres of the lake.

The North Carolina Wildlife Resources Commission sponsors two Harris Lake launch points: On Bartley Holleman Road off New Hill Road, south of the county park; and on Cross Point Road, off Christian Chapel Road in Chatham County on the lake's western shore. Motorboat access is allowed from those launches. For more, go to www.ncwildlife.org or call (919) 707-0010.

JORDAN LAKE
Apex
(919) 362-0586
www.ncparks.gov
Jordan Lake is a 14,000-acre body of water in eastern Chatham and western Wake counties, traversed by U.S. 64. The state parks system manages the lake and its recreation areas. Boat ramps at each of Jordan Lake's 11 developed recreation

areas allow access to the water. The ramps and docks at Ebenezer Church and Robeson Creek are open 24 hours per day. All others close when the park does. Most of the traffic is motorized—boats and jet-skis—but sailboats often leave from Vista Point, and windsurfers like Ebenezer Church. You can call (919) 387-5969 for temperature and wind speed information. Jordan Lake is a good place to cast for bass, crappie, catfish, and pan fish.

Privately owned Crosswinds Marina on the east shore of the lake rents fishing and pontoon boats and offers boat storage. The marina is at 555 Farrington Rd. For more information, call (919) 362-5391 or (919) 362-1615.

LAKE CRABTREE
1400 Aviation Parkway, Morrisville
(919) 460-3390
www.wakegov.com/parks/lakecrabtree
Lake Crabtree's 520 acres are open to sailboats, canoes, kayaks, rowboats, pedal boats, and boats with electric motors only. The park rents boats May through Labor Day. Fishermen can cast from a fishing platform, a pier, or the banks.

Fish Advisories

Studies have found high levels of PCBs in fish taken from Lake Crabtree, especially carp and catfish. The North Carolina Division of Public Health advises that no one eats these fish, and that consumption of other fish caught in Lake Crabtree be limited to one meal a month. The contamination is linked to the operations of an electric transformer company between 1964 and 1979. For more information on fish advisories, check with the **North Carolina Department of Health and Human Services** at (919) 707-5900 or www.rabies.ncdhhs.gov/epi/fish.

LAKE MICHIE
Durham
(919) 477-3906
www.durhamnc.gov/departments/parks
One of two reservoirs that supply Durham with water, Lake Michie (pronounced Mickey, like the Mouse) is in northern Durham County on Bahama Road off Roxboro Road, about 12 miles north of downtown. The Durham Parks and Recreation Department operates a boathouse there and sponsors programs such as fishing clinics for kids and stargazing. Fishermen appreciate its plentiful largemouth bass. Kayaks, canoes, and gas-powered motors are allowed on the 480-acre lake. Jon boats and canoes are available to rent. The lake is open mid-March through mid-November on Friday, Saturday, and Sunday. Call the Lake Michie Boathouse at the number above for more information.

LAKE WHEELER
6404 Lake Wheeler Rd., Raleigh
(919) 662-5704
www.raleigh-nc.org
Lake Wheeler is a secondary water source for Raleigh. The 650-acre lake is open to motorized and non-motor boats but not jet skis. The recreation area is 4½ miles west of I-40 in Wake County. Jon boats, canoes, and pedal boats are available for rent.

LITTLE RIVER LAKE
Durham
(919) 477-7889
www.durhamnc.gov/departments/parks
Like Lake Michie, Little River Lake supplies water for the city of Durham. It is on Orange Factory Road off Roxboro Road, about 10 miles from downtown. The 550-acre lake is open to fishermen but only boats rented by the Durham Parks and Recreation Department are allowed. Rowboats and electric motor boats are available to rent at the park. Little River Lake is open mid-March through mid-November, Friday through Sunday. Call the Little River Lake Boathouse at the number above for more information.

UNIVERSITY LAKE
Carrboro
(919) 942-8007
www.owasa.org

Just west of Carrboro, University Lake is a 213-acre body of water open late March through early November. Boating is limited to canoes, kayaks, rowboats, and boats with electric motors only. The lake is stocked with bass, crappie, catfish, bluegills, and sunfish. The recreation area is on University Lake Road south of Jones Ferry Road. If you cross the lake on Jones Ferry Road, you've missed the turn. Boats and motors are available for rent. UNC built the lake in 1932 as a reservoir for the school and towns.

Fishing License

To fish in North Carolina's Piedmont, you'll need an inland fishing license, which is different from the state's coastal fishing license. Fishing licenses are available for life, the length of the season, or for 10-day periods. Bait shops, sporting goods stores, marinas, and other places that sell fishing paraphernalia also sell licenses. To find a store that sells licenses or to buy a license online, go to **www.ncwildlife.org.** You can also buy a license over the phone by calling (888) 248-6834 weekdays, 8 a.m. to 5 p.m.

CANOEING AND KAYAKING

The Triangle lacks the class-five thrills that draw kayakers to North Carolina's mountains, but you can still find a range of great paddling within a half-hour's drive of the big cities. Mostly, the rivers here offer flat water interrupted by riffles and a few sets of class-two rapids. A few guided tours are available, and the Carolina Canoe Club (www .carolinacanoeclub.com) offers trips all over the state. The region offers a few spots with tougher rapids and tricky rock gardens to navigate. But around Raleigh and Durham, you'll mostly find a quiet paddle through a dense canopy of trees—an escape few residents ever get to see.

i Paul Ferguson's *Paddling Eastern North Carolina* offers a detailed guide to even the smallest navigable streams—a paddler's bible with maps. The book is updated frequently to reflect changes to roads and waterways. Find it at bookstores and outfitters.

ENO RIVER

Flowing through Orange and Durham counties, the Eno ranges from a quiet flatwater to churning class-three rapids pushing through a maze of rocks. Just 40 miles long, the Eno is extremely popular with kayakers and canoeists in the Triangle. Close to Durham and Raleigh, it offers a quick fix for paddlers and a chance to spot mountain laurel and rhododendrons on the banks as well as beavers or otters swimming past.

Before it joins the Flat and Little rivers, the Eno flows just north of downtown Durham, past several historic mill sites and through Eno River State Park and West Point on the Eno city park. The state park has backcountry campsites and excellent spots to fish for bluegill, largemouth bass, and crappie. But on any sunny day, you'll find company in colorful boats.

HAW RIVER

The Haw forms the southwest border of Orange County and flows through Chatham County to Jordan Lake. Eventually, the Haw joins the Deep River to form the Cape Fear, which flows to North Carolina's coast. But the stretch through northern Chatham County, just south of Chapel Hill, makes for some of the most exciting paddling in the Triangle.

The upper section at State Road 1545, aka Chicken Bridge Road, starts a nice run for novices with only a few tricky rapids, one of them ominously named Final Solution. This run ends at the dam at U.S. 15-501. But the lower Haw just above Jordan Lake is the most popular as the fall line creates numerous rapids. These waves can grow huge and dangerous at high water for inexperienced paddlers, earning the Haw its reputation as the area's top challenge.

NEUSE RIVER

The longest river entirely in North Carolina, the Neuse begins at the Falls Lake dam between Raleigh and Wake Forest, where it thunders down the spillway as a class-three rapid. This rapid is a popular spot for kayakers who want to practice their whitewater skills, but after the falls, the Neuse immediately turns into a slow-moving kitten of a waterway. Muddy year-round, the Neuse

snakes down Raleigh's eastern edge, interrupted only by the dam near U.S. 64.

You'll pass under several freeways, and one stretch below Buffalo Road offers little scenery. But for much of the ride through Raleigh, you'll see more wild turkeys and herons than people, and many large boulders beckon as picnic spots. Numerous take-outs offer options for a two- or three-hour paddle, but you can spend a day on the river without leaving Raleigh, or flow further down into Johnston County on the Neuse's path to the Pamlico Sound.

GOLF

While the Triangle is no Pinehurst, it does offer plenty of places where golfers can hone their skills in preparation for a tee time on that golf mecca an hour and a half to the south. With more than 50 courses in the area, a comprehensive list is beyond the scope of this guide. This list offers a few highlights of the Triangle's golf scene, ranging from the oldest course to some of the newest. All the listings are for public courses. Yardage is counted from the back tee, and pars are for men. Because winter weather is mild, courses are open year-round. Many offer rates on the lower end of the range between December and March, so it's good to call and check before heading out.

DUKE UNIVERSITY GOLF CLUB
3001 Cameron Blvd. at Science Dr.
(919) 490-0999
www.washingtondukeinn.com/golfclub.html
Set beside the stately Washington Duke Inn on the Duke campus, this course is a reviewer's darling. Renowned designer Robert Trent Jones laid the course out in 1957, and his son Reese revamped it in 1994. It hosted the NCAA Men's Golf Championship in 2001. The course is a 6,868-yard, par 72. Practice facilities include a driving range, putting and chipping greens, sand bunkers, and a target green. After the links, you can choose from fine dining at the Fairview Dining Room or more casual fare at the clubby Bull Durham bar in the Washington Duke Inn. Green fees are $30 to $100.

Outfitters

Frog Hollow
5435 Guess Rd., Durham
(919) 949-4315
www.froghollowoutdoors.com

Great Outdoor Provision Co.
2017 Cameron St., Raleigh
(919) 833-1741
800 East Franklin Street, Chapel Hill
(919) 933-6148
http://greatoutdoorprovision.com

Haw River Canoe & Kayak Co.
P.O. Box 22, Saxapahaw
(336) 260-6465
www.hawrivercanoe.com

Paddle Creek
9745 Fonville Rd., Wake Forest
(919) 866-1954
(888) 794-4459
www.paddlecreeknc.com

REI Store
www.rei.com
255 Crossroads Blvd, Cary
(919) 233-8444
6911 Fayetteville Road, Durham
(919) 806-3442
4291 The Circle at North Hills, Raleigh
(919) 571-5031

EAGLE RIDGE
565 Competition Rd., Garner
(919) 661-6300
www.playateagleridge.com
Opened in 2000 just south of Raleigh in Garner, Eagle Ridge's 6,904-yard, par-71 course was designed by the team of Tom Kite and Bob Cupp. It's a challenging course with six par 3s and five par 5s. The par-4 18th hole involves clearing a treacherous water hazard. The course is home to a beautiful clubhouse with a restaurant that serves casual sandwiches and more elegant dinner entrees. The course includes a driving range and putting green and private lessons are available. Green fees range from $30 to $59.

FALLS VILLAGE GOLF CLUB
115 Falls Village Dr., Durham
(919) 596-4653
www.fallsvillagegolf.com
In west Durham south of Falls Lake and north of I-540, Falls Village will one day be surrounded by the subdivisions planned to encircle it. For now it's a quiet haven for golfers and wildlife that's a short drive from I-40 and I-85. The 7,072-yard, par-72 course is straightforward but difficult, surrounded by thick stands of hardwood and dotted with 48 white sand bunkers. The clubhouse has a pro shop and bar that serves a casual menu. Private lessons are available. Green fees range from $40 to $59.

HEDINGHAM GOLF CLUB
4801 Harbour Town Dr., Raleigh
(919) 250-3030
www.hedingham.org
Along the banks of the Neuse River in northeast Raleigh, Hedingham makes beautiful use of its riverside terrain with tight fairways and quick greens. Course architect David Postlethwait put water hazards on eight holes of this 6,609-yard, par-71 course. Hedingham is semiprivate. Green fees range from $20 to $42. Instructors offer lessons and clinics.

THE HERITAGE
1250 Heritage Club Ave., Wake Forest
(919) 453-2020
www.playheritagegolf.com

The Heritage is the centerpiece golf course and club for the development that shares its name in Wake Forest. It sits at the center of a collection of 21 neighborhoods on what was once a dairy farm. Designed by Bob Moore, the semiprivate 6,929-yard, par-72 course features tree-lined fairways and fast greens. The club includes a putting green and driving range, a pro shop, and clubhouse. Private lessons are available from PGA instructors. Rates range from $40 to $62 in the off season, December through February, and from $48 to $84 March through November.

HILLANDALE
1600 Hillandale Rd., Durham
(919) 286-4211
www.hillandalegolf.com
Hillandale is the Triangle's oldest course and one of its best regarded. Donald Ross designed the original layout in 1911, but the course got a makeover from George Cobb when it was relocated in 1960. The 6,339-yard, par-71 course is in the middle of residential Durham. It features water hazards on nine holes. Its pro shop ranks among the best in the country with an extensive inventory. Pros offer private lessons and clinics and the course hosts many tournaments and charity events. Rates are $20 to $39.

LOCHMERE GOLF CLUB
2511 Kildaire Farm Rd., Cary
(919) 851-0611
www.lochmere.com
Lochmere is in south Cary adjacent to Hemlock Bluffs Nature Preserve in a residential setting. The surrounding trees and Swift Creek, which cuts through the 6,136-yard, par 71 course, help create an oasis. Designed by PGA great Gary Hamm, it makes great use of water hazards. Lochmere is a semiprivate course that includes a driving range, putting green, pro shop, and a restaurant. Green fees range from $20 to $49. Private lessons are available.

THE NEUSE GOLF CLUB
918 Birkdale Dr., Clayton
(919) 550–0550
www.neusegolf.com

The Neuse is one of the Triangle's mostly highly regarded courses, consistently earning top ratings for its design and condition. Designer John LaFoy laid out the 7,010-yard, par-72 course alongside the Neuse River, integrating the existing terrain. It will challenge golfers of all abilities. The semiprivate club includes a driving range, putting green, pro shop, and restaurant, The Links Grille. Clinics and private lessons are offered. Green fees range from $30 to $45.

THE PRESERVE AT JORDAN LAKE GOLF CLUB
840 The Preserve Trail, Chapel Hill
(919) 542-5501
www.thepreservegolf.com
East of Fearrington Village along Jordan Lake, the Preserve is in the midst of a residential area, but it retains the natural character of its wooded lakeside setting. It is a tough, 7,107-yard, par-72 course designed by North Carolina native Davis Love III. It features tight fairways and rolling greens. The club includes a pro shop, putting green, and driving range. PGA and LPGA staff offer private lessons. The Grille at the Preserve offers fine dining. Green fees are $28 to $68.

UNC FINLEY
Finley Golf Course Rd., Chapel Hill
(919) 962–2349
www.uncfinley.com
The University of North Carolina's golf course is open to the public and offers reduced rates for students, faculty, and alumni. The Tom Fazio–designed course is 6,231 yards and par 72, and offers challenges for golfers of differing abilities. Facilities include a driving range, putting green, pro shop, and a snack bar. Green fees are $35 to $62.

GYMS

Working out is a popular pastime in the Triangle, which usually rates high in those lists of "fittest cities," despite our Southern preference for fried food. As in most metros, the area is replete with locations of Gold's Gym, Curves, and Fitness Together, many of which are quite popular. This list offers a few well-regarded gyms that are particular to the area.

DUKE HEALTH & FITNESS CENTER
PepsiCo Fitness Center
3475 Erwin Rd., Durham
(919) 660-6660
www.dukehealth.org
At Duke you can take advantage of a highly educated staff of exercise physiologists, physical therapists, health psychologists, and dietitians who hold master's degrees or doctorates. The facility includes a heated indoor pool, indoor and outdoor tracks, weight machines and free weights, and a variety of treadmills, bikes, and cross-trainers. The 30,000-square-foot center is on the 26-acre Duke Center for Living Campus, home to some of the most renowned weight management programs in the world.

LIFESTYLE FAMILY FITNESS
601 E. Six Forks Rd., Raleigh, (919) 755-1706
6350 Plantation Center Dr., Raleigh, (919) 713-2275
1741 Walnut St., Cary, (919) 462-0823
1040 Vision Dr., Apex, (919) 387-3095
www.lff.com
Lifestyle is a Florida-based chain that offers only month-by-month memberships. That feature and some of the best class instructors in the Triangle make its four locations very popular. Each has cardiovascular and strength-training equipment, cycling studios, personal trainers, and tanning booths. Children play in the supervised Kids Club, with playground equipment and video games.

O2
2046 Renaissance Park Place, Cary, (919) 678-6302
300 Market St., Chapel Hill, (919) 942-6002
6118-F Fearrington Rd., Chapel Hill, (919) 354-3402
1920 Falls Valley Dr., Raleigh, (919) 846-5002
8111 Creedmoor Rd., Raleigh, (919) 676-5802
www.02fitnessclubs.com

O2 is a local chain of shiny, hip facilities accented with stylish touches like droplights and dramatic walls of glass. Its five Triangle locations are pretty places to work up a sweat. Each has more than 100 cardio machines, strength machines, and saunas and offers between 40 and 50 classes per week. Child care is provided.

PEAK FITNESS
1310 Broad St., Fuquay-Varina
(919) 567-9373

3900 Chapel Hill Blvd., Durham
(919) 489-2360
www.peakfitnessclubs.com
A regional chain with outposts in urban areas in North Carolina and South Carolina, Peak has two Triangle locations. Think of Peak as the Gap of gyms—affordable and nice. Gyms have cardio machines, free weights, and strength machines and offer a range of classes including yoga, Pilates, and martial arts. Personal trainers are available. Child care is provided.

TRIANGLE SPORTSPLEX
1 Dan Kidd Dr., Hillsborough
(919) 644-0339
With 80,000 square feet dedicated to an NHL-sized ice rink, a swimming center with three heated pools, weight and cardio fitness workout areas, a cafe, and a sports shop, Triangle Sportsplex is the largest sports center in the area. Outdoor facilities include basketball courts and a pond for canoeing. Many of the activities are organized classes or games, but the ice rinks are open to public skates as well. The Sportsplex offers after-school and day-camp programs for children.

UNC WELLNESS CENTER AT MEADOWMONT
100 Sprunt St., Chapel Hill
(919) 966-5500
www.uncwellness.com
The 52,000-square-foot facility is home to an indoor pool, indoor track, indoor basketball court, aerobics studios, cardiovascular and strength training equipment, and free weights. Center instructors lead a full slate of activities including weight training, aerobics classes, water workouts, cycling, and yoga for all ages. Nutrition and weight management, disease management, and rehabilitation programs are offered as well.

YMCAS
www.ymcatriangle.org
www.chcymca.org
Some of the most up-to-date workout centers with the most innovative classes in the Triangle are YMCAs. The YMCA of the Triangle has three fitness centers in Raleigh, three in Durham, one in Cary, one in Holly Springs, and one in Wake Forest. The Chapel Hill–Carrboro YMCA chapter includes two fitness centers in Chapel Hill. The Chatham YMCA's center is in Pittsboro. Their class instructors are highly regarded and most of the facilities are new or recently renovated.

YOGA STUDIOS

Dozens of yoga studios scattered throughout the Triangle mean it's easy to find a studio that suits your needs, whether that is a fitness-oriented take or a more meditative approach. These are a few of the better-known studios to help start your journey.

BLUE LOTUS
401 N. W. St., Raleigh
(919) 831-2583
www.bluelotusnc.com
Blue Lotus's new downtown space was built with an emphasis on energy efficiency and environmental consciousness evident in details like the cork flooring in the practice room and the soy candles. Classes include vinyasa or "low flow" yoga, flow and stretch, juicy flow, trance, and foundations of yoga. The studio also hosts touring yogis and community workshops.

i A couple of Raleigh parks host free outdoor yoga in warmer months. Early risers can find it at 7:30 a.m. on Sundays at Shelley Lake Park in North Raleigh. Fred Fletcher Park in downtown Raleigh offers free outdoor yoga at 9 a.m.

Recreation Leagues

Children and grown-ups with active inner children can find an array of organized sports to help them burn off calories and energy. Sports organized by area parks and recreation departments include traditional favorites like basketball, tennis, and flag football as well as trendier pastimes such as ultimate Frisbee, adult kickball, and dodge ball. Many towns have teams for the over-65 crowd as well. Find more information by contacting the city or county parks and recreation departments.

Apex
53 Hunter St., Apex
(919) 249-3402
www.apexnc.org

Carrboro
100 North Greensboro St., Carrboro
(919) 918-7364
www.ci.carrboro.nc.us

Cary
316 North Academy St., Cary
(919) 469-4062
www.townofcary.org

Chapel Hill
200 Plant Rd., Chapel Hill
(919) 968-2784
www.townofchapelhill.org

Chatham County
90 East St., Pittsboro
(919) 545-8555
www.chathamnc.org

Clayton
715 Amelia Church Rd., Clayton
(919) 553-1550
www.townofclaytonnc.org

Durham
400 Cleveland St., Durham
(919) 560-4355
www.durhamnc.gov

Holly Springs
128 South Main St., Holly Springs
(919) 552-6221
www.hollyspringsnc.us

Garner
Seventh Ave., Garner
(919) 772-4688
www.ci.garner.nc.us

Knightdale
950 Steeple Square Court, Knightdale
(919) 217-2233
www.knightdalenc.gov

Morrisville
240 Town Hall Dr., Morrisville
(919) 463-7110
www.ci.morrisville.nc.us

Orange County
300 West Tryon St., Hillsborough
(919) 732-8181
www.co.orange.nc.us

Raleigh
2401 Wade Ave., Raleigh
(919) 831-6836
www.raleighnc.gov

Wake Forest
401 Elm Ave., Wake Forest
(919) 554-6180, (919) 554-6183
www.wakeforestnc.gov

Wendell
601 West Third St., Wendell
(919) 366-2266
www.townofwendell.com

Zebulon
202 East Vance St., Zebulon
(919) 269-7455
www.ci.zebulon.nc.us

TRIANGLE PILATES & CARY YOGA CENTER
202 Ledgestone Way, Cary
(919) 466-9989

2425 Kildaire Farm Rd., Suite 103, Cary
(919) 851-7221
www.trianglepilates.com
The experienced instructors at Triangle Pilates do a good job of laying the groundwork for new students, helping them understand the philosophies behind Pilates and yoga while they get acquainted with the techniques. The studios offer a range of classes, from beginning to advanced, including barre work. The instruction is very personalized with an emphasis on form.

YOGA PRACTICE CENTER
Executive Office Park
1920 N.C. 54, Suite 230, Durham
(919) 484-9200
Kundalini, Journey through the Chakras, Asana Liberation, and Power Yoga are among the classes taught at the Yoga Practice Center, a small studio in south Durham. The instructors are experienced and include faculty members from UNC and Duke. Massage services are also provided at the center.

BOWLING

THE ALLEY
2512 Hillsborough St., Raleigh
(919) 832-3533
www.bowlthealley.com
A well-preserved relic of another time, the Alley is an old-school bowling alley all done up in mid-century tones of turquoise, lemon yellow, and sunburst orange. Until 2008, it was home to Western Lanes, a bowling alley and diner that served North Carolina State students for more than 50 years. New management changed the name and added some flat-screen TVs, but retained the vintage look of the place and the laid-back vibe. It's popular with undergrads and families as well. Rare Brunswick equipment still refreshes the pins, and players must mark their own score cards—no electronic machines here. The bar has 20 beers on tap and the restaurant

now offers a menu of burgers, salads, and hearty bar fare. If you look for it, you can still see a groove worn in the linoleum top by the former longtime bartender, who was famous for sliding beer cans across the counter to customers.

AMF
Capital Lanes
1827 Capital Blvd., Raleigh
(919) 832-3747

Durham Lanes
4508 Durham–Chapel Hill Blvd., Durham
(919) 489-9154

Pleasant Valley Lanes
5501 Commercial Ave., Raleigh
(919) 783-0080

S. Hills Lanes
301 Nottingham Dr., Cary
(919) 467-2411
www.amf.com
The national chain has four locations in the Triangle where bowlers can roll on scores of lanes. For those who like bowling in the dark, the alley turns down the lights and pumps up the music for Xtreme Bowling at night. AMF sponsors teams and leagues, offering bowlers a range of competitive and casual group opportunities. Groups are available for children, teens and adults of all ages. Frequent specials include all-you-can-eat pizza and bowling for $14.99 per person.

BUFFALOE LANES
151 High House Rd., Cary
(919) 468-8684

5900 Oak Forest Dr., Raleigh,
(919) 876-5681

6701 Fayetteville Rd., Raleigh, NC 27603
(919) 779-1888
www.buffaloelanes.com
Buffaloe Lanes is a locally owned chain with three alleys in the Triangle. The facilities are modern with 40 or more lanes, electronic scoreboards, arcades, and pool tables. Buffaloe throws parties and organizes a variety of other group events.

The snack bar is open for breakfast and has specialties like fried okra and yam sticks on the menu. Buffaloe serves no alcohol, so don't look for those pin-shaped bottles of suds here.

ROCK CLIMBING

NORTH CARY PARK
1100 Norwell Blvd., Cary
(919) 460-4964
The park's distinguishing feature is a pair of 8-foot climbing boulders. The structures offer challenges for veteran climbers and opportunities for novices to practice the basics. Admission is free.

TRIANGLE ROCK CLUB
102 Pheasant Wood Court, Morrisville
(919) 463-7625
www.trianglerockclub.com
Triangle Rock Club has more than 9,000 square feet of climbing walls, more than 100 lead and top-rope routes, a 14-foot top-out boulder with 3,000 square feet of climbing area, a lead cave, and more than 100 boulder problems. Also on site are a gym with cardio machines and strength-training equipment, a lounge, and a viewing deck. The club offers camps for ages as young as seven and a range of courses for adults as well.

VERTICAL EDGE CLIMBING CENTER
2422 U.S. 70, Durham
(919) 596-6910
www.verticaledgeclimbing.com
The Vertical Edge has 8,500 feet of climbable surfaces, including 60 top-rope climbs that go as high as 24 feet, a bouldering cave, a leadable cave, and 20 leadable routes. Group or one-on-one classes are available for beginners ages 14 and older. Equipment is available for rent, and climbers who need belay partners can schedule them in advance. Supervised climbing parties can be arranged for children of all ages.

MOUNTAIN BIKING

The Triangle has a great mountain biking scene. The hilly terrain offers plenty of challenges for every skill level. An active biking club, Triangle Off-Road Cyclists (TORC) often pitches in with work on the trails on public land. Good tracks for beginners are at Umstead State Park, Lake Crabtree, and Harris Lake. More advanced riders should try trails near the Beaverdam recreational area at Falls Lake or the Newlight trails, also at Falls Lake. Clayton's Legend Park, Garner Rec Park, Little River Regional Park, and Chapel Hill's Adam Preserve and Carolina North Forest are also favorites. TORC's Web site, www.trianglemtb.com, offers reviews, updates on trail changes, rules of use, and notice of when trails are closed due to weather.

TENNIS

Several local affiliates of the United States Tennis Association work in Triangle communities to promote the sport and organize competition. Racquet clubs and swim-and-tennis neighborhoods abound throughout the area, and most county and city recreation and parks departments run programs and leagues as well. Courts are located throughout the Triangle. Here we've listed the tennis associations and the larger public tennis facilities.

DURHAM ORANGE COUNTY TENNIS ASSOCIATION
www.docta.org

RALEIGH TENNIS ASSOCIATION
www.raleightennis.com

THE WAKE FOREST AREA TENNIS ASSOCIATION (WFATA)
www.wakeforesttennis.com

WESTERN WAKE TENNIS ASSOCIATION
www.network.usta.com

CARY TENNIS PARK
2727 Louis Stephens Dr., Cary
(919) 469-4062
www.townofcary.org
The Cary Tennis Park is a city-run facility with 30 courts, including one stadium court and one

Swimming

The cities of Raleigh, Durham, Cary, Morrisville, Wake Forest, and Chapel Hill operate public pools, indoor and outdoor. The premiere facilities are the Pullen Aquatics Center in Raleigh, with an indoor Olympic-size pool, and the Triangle Aquatic Center in Cary with a 50-meter competition pool and a 25-yard program pool. Indoor pools and aquatic centers are open year-round. Outdoor pools are open seasonally.

Cary
Indoor
Triangle Aquatics Center
275 Convention Dr.
(919) 459-4045
www.triangleaquatics.org

Chapel Hill
Indoor
A. D. Clark Pool
216 North Roberson St.
(919) 968-2784

Community Center Pool
120 South Estes Dr.
(919) 968-2790

Hargraves Community Park
216 North Roberson St.
(919) 968-2794

Homestead Aquatic Center
300 Northern Park Dr.
(919) 968-2799

Durham
Indoor
Campus Hills Pool
2000 South Alston Ave.
(919) 560-4781

Edison Johnson Aquatic Center
600 West Murray Ave.
(919) 560-4265

Outdoor
Hillside
1300 South Roxboro St.
(919) 560-4783

Long Meadow Pool
917 Liberty St.
(919) 560-4202

Morrisville
Indoor
Morrisville Aquatics and Fitness Center
301 Morrisville Parkway
(919) 463-6900

Raleigh
Indoor
Millbrook Exchange Pool
1905 Spring Forest Rd.
(919) 872-4130

Optimist Pool
5902 Whittier Dr.
(919) 870-2882

Pullen Aquatics Center
410 Ashe Ave.
(919) 831-6197

Outdoor
Biltmore Pool
701 Crown Crossing Lane
(919) 831-6736

Chavis Pool
720 Chavis Way
(919) 831-6565

Lake Johnson Pool
1416 Athens Dr.
(919) 233-2111

Longview Pool
321 Bertie Dr.
(919) 831-6343

Ridge Road Pool
1709 Ridge Rd.
(919) 420-2322

Wake Forest
Outdoor
Holding Park Pool
133 West Owen Ave.
(919) 554-6180.

specially designed for teaching, a ball machine, and a double-sided backboard. A pro shop, locker rooms, and snack bar are also on the premises. The tennis center hosts local and regional tournaments and other competitions.

MILLBROOK EXCHANGE TENNIS CENTER
1905 Spring Forest Rd., Raleigh
(919) 872-4128
www.raleighnc.gov
Millbrook is a city-run facility with 23 courts, four backboards, two ball machines, and a covered observation deck. Also on site are locker rooms with showers and a pro shop where players can have rackets restrung or grips replaced and buy balls. The city has 112 courts at 25 locations, where lessons and league play take place. Millbrook is the central location for most of the instructional programming and the site of most citywide tournament play.

HOCKEY AND ICE SKATING

POLAR ICE HOUSE
1410 Buck Jones Rd., Cary
(919) 460-2756

The Factory
1839 S. Main St., Wake Forest
(919) 453-1500

103 New Rand Rd., Garner
(919) 861-7465
www.polaricehouse.com
Three locations offer skate lessons for ages 3 to adult including figure skating instruction and hockey classes for beginners of all ages. The rinks run day camps for ages 5 to 12 and hold public skate sessions. Parents who aren't skating can watch from the Wi-Fi zone. On-site amenities include snack bars and pro shops.

RALEIGH ICEPLEX
2601 Raleigh Blvd., Raleigh
(919) 878-9002
www.iceplex.com
Kids and adults can find league hockey play on Raleigh IcePlex's Olympic-size sheet of ice. The rink also offers public ice skating sessions with skate rental available for all sizes. Figure skating classes are available in group and private sessions.

RECZONE
912 W. Hodges St., Raleigh
(919) 754-0441
www.reczone.net
When the Carolina Hurricanes aren't practicing here, young National Hockey League hopefuls and aspiring Olympic figure skaters take over. Classes are offered for ages as young as three, and instruction ranges from basics for beginners to multi-day, intense hockey clinics. League play is organized for kids and adults. RecZone is also the home ice for the N.C. State University hockey team. Check the calendar for public skate sessions and pick-up games.

CRICKET

DURHAM CRICKET CLUB
www.durhamcricketclub.net
The Durham Cricket Club plays in the Mid-Atlantic Cricket Conference against teams from North Carolina, South Carolina, and Virginia. Founded in 1999, the team draws players from all areas of the Triangle. The season runs April through September. Home turf is at Luther Green Park on Barbee Road in Morrisville.

GREENWAYS

One of the Triangle's most attractive assets is that just about anywhere you go, there's a great place to take a walk. This is due to the area's extensive greenway network. Cities, towns, and counties, along with citizen greenway support organizations and multi-jurisdictional groups, maintain hundreds of miles of paved paths where residents can walk, run, bike, roller blade, pogo-stick, or do just about anything but drive a motorized vehicle. Many of the greenways connect parks within or between cities, and some connect one city to another.

In smaller communities like Chapel Hill and Carrboro, commuters can get to and from work using greenways and bike paths exclusively. Raleigh's system, while vast, doesn't offer this level of convenience, as most commutes would need to include city streets shared with vehicle traffic. But with a little planning, Raleigh's greenways can be incorporated into a bike path to and from work.

More often, the area's greenways serve as an off-hours escape within the city limits, a narrow ribbon of parkland running through the urban environment. On a bike, with the wind rushing past, you travel through a tunnel of trees and shrubs to emerge at a familiar busy street that you usually see only through the windshield of your car. Exploring the city by greenway offers a fresh perspective on the place, serving to remind us that before we developed the land, nature flourished in the creeks and on the hills that now lend their names to subdivisions and shopping centers. It helps us remember that the natural world isn't a destination at the end of a long drive. It is where we live.

Most greenways ask that riders and walkers follow similar rules. No motorized vehicles are allowed. Dogs must be kept on leashes, and owners must clean up after them. Most greenways are open dawn to dusk, but some sections honor longer hours for commuters. In addition, it is recommended that greenway users follow accepted etiquette and precautions. When passing someone from behind, tell them you're coming and on which side. Bikers should slow down when approaching horses or walkers. Pick up trash and fallen sticks. Bring water with you. Even if the stretch of greenway you choose to travel passes through a developed area, water may not be readily available near the trail. And, of course, smile and say hello when you pass a stranger.

This chapter aims to offer readers an overview of the area's greenways. Because the Triangle includes many different systems that are maintained by many different groups, a comprehensive map of the network remains elusive. Trails are constantly being improved and expanded, as well. The disparate groups offer maps that are most often available online for download. The most comprehensive collection of these is at www.bikewalkdurham.org/dost/. Another good site to check is www.getgoingnc.com, written by Joe Miller, the former outdoors writer for the *News & Observer* of Raleigh. He does a good job of keeping readers up to date on changes to the greenways systems. The trails mentioned here are good places to start an exploration.

AMERICAN TOBACCO TRAIL

The American Tobacco Trail stretches for more than 22 miles, following the paths of former rail beds. Much of the trail is paved, though some are crushed gravel or other rough surface. It runs from northern Wake County, west of Apex near the Chatham County line, north into downtown Durham. Along the way, the trail skirts the towns of Cary and Apex. It offers a range of scenery, from inner-city development to neighborhoods to relatively undisturbed wetlands and forests. Connecting trails offer access to north Durham and to the woodlands surrounding Jordan Lake, where cyclists should keep their eyes out for sightings of bald eagles. The Triangle Rails to Trails Conservancy manages the American Tobacco Trail. The non-profit was established to preserve the area's abandoned railroad corridors, and it is the best source of information on the ATT and its many ongoing projects. For more information and frequently updated maps, go to www.triangletrails.org.

CARY

The town of Cary has 34 miles of greenway trails and bicycle routes throughout the city that link neighborhoods and commercial districts and provide lovely riding tours of the area. Routes range from moderate to strenuous and cover a wide variety of scenery. The town offers a number of suggested routes for those who would like to get familiar with the system. The 5½-mile Park Central Loop takes cyclists through some of Cary's oldest and prettiest neighborhoods on a gentle course, while the 6-mile Three Lakes Loop offers more challenging terrain and the impressive scenery of the MacGregor Downs golf community and the tony Kildaire Farms neighborhood. Cyclists can follow bike paths through Hemlock Bluffs Nature Preserve, dense with wildlife, to Regency Park and the Koka Booth Amphitheatre. The Black Creek Greenway links Lake Crabtree in north Cary with Umstead State Park. Plans are in the works to connect this stretch with the American Tobacco Trail on the western edge of town. That would make it possible for healthy cyclists to travel between Cary and downtown Durham without mixing with vehicular traffic, which would make for a much different sort of commute than the I-40 slog.

CHAPEL HILL AND CARRBORO

In Chapel Hill, the town maintains half a dozen short greenways that offer cyclists access to key community sites, including parks, the UNC campus, and Chapel Hill High School. In Carrboro, the Libba Cotten Bikeway connects downtown Carrboro with the UNC campus. In addition, both towns offer many miles of roadside bike lanes that give cyclists increased safety when traveling alongside motorized traffic and off-road paths that help them avoid high-traffic areas. Find downloadable maps of the greenways and bike path system at www.townofchapelhill.org.

DURHAM/DUKE TRAILS

More than 15 miles of paved greenways snake through Durham, including more than 7 miles of the American Tobacco Trail. The city maintains a series of greenways that begins near West Point on the Eno city park in north Durham, along Warren Creek. The route takes bikers past the Duke Homestead State Historic Site and the Museum of Life and Science into downtown Durham. There it takes travelers through Durham's Central Park, past both the Historic Durham Bulls Athletic Park and the new Durham Bulls Athletic Park where it connects with the American Tobacco Trail at N.C. 147. The Durham Open Space and Trails Commission, an advisory board to Durham's county and city government, maintains a Web site with a comprehensive collection of maps of Triangle area greenways. The site also provides updates on greenway construction projects and master plans for greenway systems. Find it at www.bikewalkdurham.org/dost.

MOUNTAINS-TO-SEA TRAIL

The Mountains-to-Sea Trail is an ambitious effort to link Clingman's Dome in North Carolina's Great Smoky Mountains with Jockey's Ridge on the Outer Banks via a 1,000-mile trail. It's meant as a unifying celebration of North Carolina's natural and cultural beauty. The path is unsurfaced and narrow, more appropriate for hiking than biking in most places, but bikers use it as well. More than 100 miles of the trail will cut through the Triangle when the trail is completed, and more than half of those sections are ready for walkers. In the Triangle, the trail stretches from northern Orange County near Occoneechee Mountain State Natural Area east, through the Eno River State Park and Durham's West Point on the Eno Park to Falls Lake. There, 37 miles of trail will wind around the hills and woods surrounding the water. From Falls Lake, the trail follows the Neuse River to the Johnston County line.

Local members of the Friends of the Mountains-to-Sea Trail continue to work on the trail through the Triangle. Find out more on trail construction and what sections are ready to hike at www.ncmst.org.

RALEIGH

Raleigh's Capital Area Greenway system includes 63 miles of trails on 3,000 acres, spread throughout the city. The paths connect neighborhoods with city parks and Umstead State Park, provide access to the N.C. State campus from the neighborhoods surrounding it, and allow residents to view the urban development from a different vantage point. Most of the greenway within the city is paved.

One of the longest stretches of the Capital Area Greenway begins in southeast Raleigh, near WakeMed hospital, and moves northwest parallel to Crabtree Creek through the city. It goes under the busy thoroughfares of Capital Boulevard, Atlantic Avenue, and Wake Forest Road and passes through quiet residential areas before running alongside the commercial sprawl of Crabtree Valley Mall. Along the way, bikers cross wetlands on a wooden boardwalk, pass miles of backyards, and can stop at Lassiter Falls. A millstone and a historical marker recall centuries past when the falls powered a number of mills that stood at the spot, and when city dwellers found a pastoral escape along Crabtree Creek's banks. Today, Lassiter Falls is smack in the middle of the city it once offered escape from.

One of the most challenging sections takes bikers from N.C. State's main campus, through Meredith College's campus onto the grounds of the North Carolina Museum of Art. Along the way, bikers ride a 12-foot-wide, triple-arched bridge across eight lanes of I-440 traffic, then ride past the museum's giant sculptures, all while conquering steep hills that leave most riders breathless.

The city Web site has a comprehensive map of the system under its Parks and Facilities tab. Go to www.raleigh-nc.org.

SPECTATOR SPORTS

As you may have heard, college basketball is a big deal in the Triangle. That's been the case the past half century, and should remain so for the next. The area's longstanding passion for college ball is born of a couple of factors. One is the continuing excellence of the Triangle's teams and the passionate rivalries that burn between them, particularly Duke and UNC. The other is that professional sports are fairly new to the state. Lacking a major city for most of the 20th century, there was no major league franchise to inspire passion. NBA basketball didn't arrive in Charlotte until the Hornets, now in New Orleans, played their inaugural season in 1988. The NFL expanded its franchise with the Carolina Panthers, based in Charlotte, in 1993. And when the owner of the Hartford Whalers, Peter Karmanos, announced that he was moving his National Hockey League team south, skepticism was the primary response. Given that the average winter low in North Carolina's Piedmont hovers around 40 degrees, few natives grow up practicing their slapshots on frozen ponds.

Despite early doubts, hockey has caught on big in the Triangle, as proved by the red-and-white flags flying from the windows of countless minivans along the I-40 corridor. But if neither hockey nor basketball is your thing, there are other diversions to keep you cheering. Roller derby at Dorton Arena, a pair of minor league baseball teams that play in first-class stadiums, and some old-school car racing might be the ticket. Those tickets would be much easier to come by than passes to college basketball games, anyway. As you may have also heard, these are the hottest seats in town December through March.

Price Code

The Price Code includes the cost of one, regularly priced adult ticket. Most venues offer group discounts, discounted tickets for children 12 and younger, deals on multi-event passes, and admissions specials. Call ahead to see what specials may apply to members of your party.

$.....................Under $5
$$ ....$5 to $10
$$$ ....$11 to $15
$$$$ ....Over $15

AUTO RACING

ORANGE COUNTY SPEEDWAY $$
9740 N.C. 57, Rougemont
www.ocstrack.com
(336) 365-1222

Called the fastest ³/₈-mile track in the country, Orange County Speedway nurtured some of NASCAR's biggest stars in their early days: Jimmy Johnson, Bobby Labonte, and both Jeff and Ward Burton. Built in the early 1960s, the speedway started as a dirt track before being paved. The speedway sits in northeastern Orange County near Rougemont, about 15 miles north of Durham. OCS now features drivers in the late model, limited sportsman, grand stock, and pure stock class, and for its size, there's really not a bad seat in the house.

BASEBALL

CAROLINA MUDCATS $–$$
Five County Stadium
1501 N.C. 39, Zebulon
(919) 269-2287
www.gomudcats.com

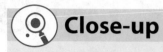

Close-up

Occoneechee Speedway

Fifty years ago, kids would climb the trees near Occoneechee Speedway to watch the races for free—a chance to see the checkered flag fall behind legends like Junior Johnson, an early titan of NASCAR who cut his driving teeth running moonshine. Racing has come a long way since anybody with a name like Fireball Roberts got behind a wheel. Now a system of trails, the Speedway sits in the woods of Hillsborough, and the roar of engines has been absent there for 30 years. One of three racetracks on the National Register of Historic Places, it is the only loop remaining from NASCAR's inaugural 1949 season.

Today, you can walk a pair of trails along the Eno River and recall when small North Carolina towns defined stock car racing. Now that the big-time series of races has abandoned its roots in Wilkesboro and Rockingham, favoring larger and more urban tracks and courting an audience of suburban dads, it is worth a trip to contemplate the days when racing was truly wild. The mile-long track drew 17,000 screaming fans in 1949, and at the time was one of less than a handful of mile-long tracks. It is fitting that the final flag in 1968 fell on Richard Petty, one of the last vestiges of racing's audacious past. The speedway, at 320 Elizabeth Brady Rd. in Hillsborough, is open and free to the public. Check www.enoriver.org/eno/parks/occspdwy.htm for details.

To hear the purists tell it, this is the spot for baseball fans most interested in watching the game. In Durham, fans may be toting children off to the climbing wall beyond the right field stands. But in Zebulon, they're paying attention to the score. Set at the eastern edge of Wake County, Five County Stadium gives fans a rural treeline beyond the outfield wall instead of a city skyline. Here, the mascot is Muddy the Mudcat, who sports foot-long whiskers off his fishy face. The ballpark's flavor is decidedly less influenced by the Triangle, giving off more of a country vibe. The town of Lizard Lick sits a few miles down the road. You'll see as many fans munching barbecue sandwiches with slaw and Texas Pete as eating hot dogs. The stadium is also home to Cattails Restaurant, a fancy white-tablecloth skybox space where the menu includes shrimp and grits and Southern style crab cake Napoleon.

The most famous Mudcat of recent years is Dontrelle Willis, the 2003 National League Rookie of the Year who helped the Florida Marlins beat the New York Yankees for the World Series title. Despite this, the place still feels like the middle of nowhere, which contributes to its appeal.

DURHAM BULLS $$-$$$
Durham Bulls Athletic Park
409 Blackwell St., Durham
(919) 956-2855
www.dbulls.com

It is hard to spend a finer summer evening in the Triangle than in the stands of Durham Bulls Athletic Park, where the highlight is seeing the enormous bovine beast on the left field wall spout smoke from its nostrils every time a batter smacks a home run. It's a snug stadium, but it's nearly always full. Even if you don't care for baseball, you can always wait for mascot Wool E. Bull to race a toddler around the bases—losing every time—or to race around the outfield warning track in a souped-up miniature car.

In 1902, this team took the field as the Durham Tobacconists—perhaps the least interesting tidbit from the storied franchise history. In 1926, baseball Commissioner Kenesaw Mountain Landis—the same man who banned Shoeless Joe Jackson from professional baseball following the Black Sox Scandal in 1918—rode onto the Durham park atop a live bull. In 2003, pop idol and Triangle native Clay Aiken sang the National

Anthem to a sold-out crowd. Throughout its history, Major League stars Joe Morgan, Greg Luzinski, and Evan Longoria have all gotten their starts in the Bull City.

But the Bulls are forever linked to the 1988 movie that shares the team's name. Even though the club no longer plays inside the park where Kevin Costner played Crash Davis to Tim Robbins's Nuke LaLoosh, it is impossible to sit in the stands without thinking of lines from *Bull Durham*. Seasoned fans can tell you where scenes from the film were shot around the Triangle. Watch the Bulls put on a subpar show and you'll finding yourself saying, "You lollygag around the infield . . ."

i There isn't a bad seat in the house at Durham Bulls Athletic Park, but the more expensive seats between first and third bases cut out glare and rain.

HOCKEY

CAROLINA HURRICANES $$$
RBC Center
1400 Edwards Mill Rd., Raleigh
(919) 467-7825
www.rbccenter.com
When the Hartford Whalers migrated south in 1997, few thought a sport played on ice skates, mostly by Canadians, could catch on in the land of barbecue and basketball. But within a few years, once Raleigh found its home team vying for the Stanley Cup, the Canes found a Southern-fried crowd crazy for hockey.

The Canes spent their first few seasons in Greensboro, about an hour outside the Triangle, until Raleigh built the RBC Center, which draws an average of 15,000 to 17,000 fans. Along with the on-ice action, Canes games offer Stormy, the team's ice-skating hog mascot—a nod to the state's pork industry and its turbulent coastal weather—and professional wrestler Ric Flair, whose wild-eyed holler of "Woo!" on the Jumbotron in celebration of Carolina goals inspires countless imitations. Off the ice, handsome player Eric Staal has developed an almost cult-like following among females, who post Eric Staal-at-Target sightings on his Facebook page.

The Canes missed the Cup in 2002, but won it in 2006. The team paraded through downtown Raleigh, and soon the red-and-white spiral insignia could be spotted on thousands of drivers' rear windows, and middle-schoolers everywhere were sporting heavy red jerseys. In a region that has feuded for decades over the three-way rivalry in college sports, the Triangle now has a team for everyone.

Ticket prices vary, but are cheapest when purchased at least a week in advance. Bought early, they range from $9.99 for upper deck seats to $200 for the front row. Many season and group ticket offers are available at http://hurricanes.nhl .com, along with a fans' ticket exchange.

ROLLER DERBY

CAROLINA ROLLERGIRLS $-$$
Dorton Arena, State Fairgrounds
1025 Blue Ridge Rd., Raleigh
www.carolinarollergirls.com
If your idea of entertainment is a dozen women zooming past on urethane wheels, all of them bruised, broken, and crashing into each other, the Rollergirls provide a few hours of intense and cringe-inducing fun. Officially, they're skating in circles, passing each other, elbowing for position, but few of the fans really understand the rules. They're here to watch Penelope Bruz or Kelly Clocks'em smash teeth.

The pack of skaters whiz around a circular track inside the butterfly-shaped Dorton Arena on the N.C. State Fairgrounds, making a hum like a hornets' nest. They combine rugby-style pileups with a gritty playfulness, and to see their intensity on wheels is to love them. You'll be glad they skate in Raleigh, and you'll take pride when they frighten teams from bigger cities.

SOCCER

CAROLINA RAILHAWKS $$-$$$
101 Soccer Park Dr., Cary
Off E. Chatham St.
(919) 859-5425
www.carolinarailhawks.com

In 2007, more than 6,000 people watched the birth of Cary's first professional sports team when the Railhawks debuted at WakeMed Soccer Park. The team gave a huge boost to the Triangle and Cary. Christened for a fictitious bird, the Railhawks' name hints at the town's birth as a depot on a regional rail line. Soon after the team's start, it won the Southern Derby Cup and on the last day of the season, earned its way into the USL First Division playoffs. In the 2009 season, the team announced it would form and seek sanctioning for the new North American Soccer League starting play in 2010, along with teams in Atlanta, Miami, St. Louis, Minnesota, Montreal, and Vancouver.

COLLEGE SPORTS

The Triangle's Big Three

For the past 50 years, a three-way feud has raged across the Triangle, a rivalry fierce enough to pit husband against wife. It is common to see two, or even three, flags flying off a front porch: red for the N.C. State Wolfpack, royal blue for Duke Blue Devils, and sky blue for the Tar Heels of UNC. College sports fever burns all year, but reaches red-hot intensity in the winter basketball season. And for a few weeks in March, time stops. No one gets any serious work done during the Atlantic Coast Conference Tournament, and if your team goes deep into March Madness, it's hard to remember to eat meals. Many businesses shut their doors, and at the few workplaces pretending it's a normal day, you'll find the crowds huddled around the office television. The Duke–UNC rivalry is often called the best in the nation, more volatile than a Red Sox–Yankees contest, and the most rewarding for any fan. It is the rare sourpuss who can keep from getting caught up in the fervor. Even if you think you'll never care about college basketball, you'll wind up calling one of these teams yours.

UNIVERSITY OF NORTH CAROLINA AT CHAPEL HILL
http://tarheelblue.cstv.com

The Heels, as they are affectionately nicknamed, sport a turquoise shade called Carolina Blue. Their mascot is an ornery ram, and their fans consider their seasons a yearly struggle for all that is right in the world. The women's basketball and soccer teams are consistently excellent and the baseball team vies for national honors regularly, but the men's basketball team inspires worship. Longtime men's coach Dean Smith retired in 1997, but his presence still hangs over Chapel Hill like a holy spirit. And since his former assistant Roy Williams returned in 2003 from a long stint at the University of Kansas, the Heels have taken two national titles. Expectations run high every year, and if you score tickets to the "Dean Dome," the best of which go to alumni and hardcore student fans, expect a crush of Carolina blue madness. The 20,000-seat dome can seem too quiet at times, especially compared to the thunderous noise of Duke's Cameron Indoor Stadium, but when the crowd comes to life, they know how to make some noise.

DUKE UNIVERSITY
www.goduke.com

Fans of Duke's consistently excellent men's basketball team go by the name "Cameron Crazies," and they are the most fearsome, dedicated crowd anywhere. In Durham, players themselves consider the fans a sixth man on the court, good for an extra 10 points. The noise inside tiny Cameron Indoor Stadium is deafening, and the blue-painted fans stand almost in arm's reach of the opposing team, taunting them with well-researched personal jabs. Coached by Mike Krzyzewski, who also led the U.S. Olympic team, Duke has four national titles. The bad news for fans is tickets are nearly impossible to get. Students themselves camp out for an entire semester to score them, living in a tent city known as Krzyzewskiville. Duke's football team is a perpetual struggler, but its golf, women's basketball, and many other teams excel nationally.

N.C. STATE UNIVERSITY
www.gopack.com

In Raleigh, the Wolfpack plays with a storied tradition and a loyal fan base. Everett Case, who

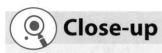

Close-up

Duke's Krzyzewskiville

Just after Christmas, the first tents start to arrive, colorful affairs stuffed with undergraduates with their mittens, raincoats, and laptops. By the day of the big game, the lot outside Cameron Indoor Stadium is crowded with 100 tents—all of its campers painted blue and driven to frenzy by the cold and their fanatic fandom. This is Krzyzewskiville, or K-ville for short, named for the fiery Duke University coach who put the Blue Devils on a national stage.

Every college with a winning sports team can boast stories of fanatic fans willing to stand in line overnight. But in 1986, 15 Duke students took devotion a step further. They arrived outside Cameron on Thursday for a Saturday game, sharing four tents until game time. And with that, Krzyzewskiville was founded. Now, the annual tent city that sprouts up on campus is rigidly regulated and inspected to make sure enough students are actually staying in the tents. You can get your tent kicked out of K-ville for failing to maintain an adequate population of campers. And with a sleeping bag, not to mention the Ethernet ports and Wi-Fi access Duke provides, a Dukie can stay comfortable, keep up with studies, and bond with other zealots. Coach K has been known to buy pizza for the tents.

coached the team in the 1950s when it played on the central campus at Reynolds Coliseum, is largely credited with sparking the craze for ACC basketball in what had been football territory. In 1983, Jim Valvano led the underdog "Cardiac Pack" to a national title, and when he died from cancer a decade later, he left the spirit of Jimmy V in Raleigh forever. Today the Pack's men's hoops squad plays in the RBC Center. At Reynolds, the women's team recently lost Coach Kay Yow—just as beloved a fighter as Valvano—to cancer. The football team plays across from the RBC dome at Carter-Finley Stadium, and its tailgate parties are nearly daylong affairs. Like its rivals in Durham and Chapel Hill, the Pack has struggled on the gridiron, but it draws devoted fans.

Jimmy V Celebrity Golf Classic

Since the death of Jim Valvano, this tribute to the much-beloved Wolfpack coach has raised more than $13 million for cancer research. More than 15 years after his death, the irreverent, exuberant Jim Valvano's urging to "Don't give up . . . don't ever give up" endures. Returned to Raleigh in 2009, the golf tournament attracts hundreds of film and sports stars that have included Arnold Palmer, Charles Barkley, Branford Marsalis, and Meat Loaf. The tournament is the centerpiece of

a weekend of fundraising events, with proceeds going to the V Foundation for Cancer Research. For more information, see www.golfclassic.org.

Bull City Gridiron Classic

A few miles apart, Duke and N.C. Central universities serve widely different student bodies. A private school costing roughly $50,000 per year, Duke is considered "Southern Ivy League." A public and historically black school where tuition, room, and board come closer to $7,000 a year, Central draws mostly students from North Carolina.

So when Duke and Central played in their first football game in 2009, it was more than a sporting gesture. The idea was to unite black and white Durham. The match was inspired in part by the 2006 Duke lacrosse incident, in which three Duke players were wrongly accused of raping a part-time Central student who was hired as a stripper at a team party. The players were proven innocent and the district attorney was disbarred in shame, but the sting of racial and social unrest lingered.

Duke came away from the first match-up in 2009 with a 49-14 win, and a new rivalry was born.

ATTRACTIONS

The Triangle sits between North Carolina's beautiful mountains and its spectacular coast, just where the coastal plain begins its rise into Piedmont. This geographic situation does not create many awe-inspiring views, but rather an unbroken string of beautiful but subtle rises and falls that those who live here appreciate daily. When we get the chance to sit for a moment to gaze across the lawn at the North Carolina Museum of Art Park or the terrace garden at Sarah P. Duke Gardens, we remember what a privilege it is to call such a lovely place home. Likewise, the cultural opportunities that draw visitors from out of town are often part of everyday life in the Triangle. Classes and lectures at the Morehead Planetarium or the North Carolina Museum of Natural Sciences are routine, as are trips to the Carrboro Farmers' Market. It's commonplace for visitors who come to see friends in the Triangle to be struck by how many "attractions" are part of daily life.

This is by no means a comprehensive list of everything there is to see in the Triangle. Other points of interest include the state parks and natural areas that showcase the natural beauty of the area. Those are covered in detail in the Parks and Greenways chapters. Other attractions include sporting events such as the Carolina Hurricanes and the Durham Bulls, which you can find in the Spectator Sports chapter. And there are plenty of options outlined in our Kidstuff chapter for the younger set.

Price Code

Code includes one regularly priced ticket for admission for one adult. Many sites offer discounts for children and seniors. Call ahead to see if discounts apply to members of your party.

$	$5 and Under
$$	$6 to $10
$$	$11 to $15
$$$	Over $15

AMERICAN TOBACCO CAMPUS
318 Blackwell St., Durham
www.americantobaccohistoricdistrict.com
The most impressive of downtown Durham's revitalization projects, the American Tobacco Campus was once part of the Duke family's cigarette empire, founded in the late 1800s. The soaring water tower painted with the Lucky Strike logo remains the iconic symbol of the complex, but today the elegantly aged brick bays are home to an advertising agency, a YMCA, software companies, five restaurants, loft apartments, and studios of public radio station WUNC. A man-made stream gurgles and falls through the middle of the complex, creating the feel of a natural oasis. Free concerts are presented on the lawn beneath the water tower during warm months and the annual lighting of the Lucky Strike tower in December has become a holiday tradition. Across Blackwell Street is the Durham Bulls Athletic Park, which means American Tobacco eateries like Mellow Mushroom and Tyler's Tap Room fill up before and after games. It's a lovely place to have a meal and marvel at the powers of restoration. Admission to the complex is free.

AVA GARDNER MUSEUM $$
325 E. Market St., Smithfield
(919) 934-5830
www.avagardner.org
Screen legend Ava Gardner, one of the most beautiful women of her time, was born not far from

Smithfield in the community of Grabtown. She lived in various places around North Carolina and Virginia while growing up, but retained family ties to Smithfield, and is buried there. The Ava Gardner Museum features a collection of 40 portraits of Gardner by Dutch painter Bert Pfeiffer, clothing and costumes Gardner wore, gowns, movie posters, and other memorabilia. The museum holds a film festival once a year to celebrate her life. For more on the Ava Gardner film festival, see the Annual Events section of the book.

BENNETT PLACE STATE HISTORIC SITE
4409 Bennett Place Memorial Rd., Durham
(919) 383-4345
www.nchistoricsites.org/bennett/bennett.htm
As the Civil War ground to a halt in the spring of 1865, Confederate General Joseph Johnston and Union General William T. Sherman met at farmhouse near Durham Station to work out the details of peace. The matter in question was the surrender of 90,000 Confederate soldiers. The generals came to an agreement about the fate of these men, their weapons, and horses at the home of James and Nancy Bennitt. (History mangled the spelling.) The surrender meant that most of North Carolina escaped the destruction that General Sherman's army had wreaked on Georgia and South Carolina.

Today, visitors can see a short historical film; tour the restored farmhouse, kitchen, and smokehouse; and read the story of the Bennitt family and the role the surrender at their farm played in history. Bennett Place stages a historical re-enactment with volunteers in period clothing every year on the last weekend in April to commemorate the surrender. (Find more details about the surrender re-enactment in the Annual Events chapter.) Other, smaller re-enactments are staged throughout the year. The site also has a picnic area and a gift shop. Admission to site is free.

BENTONVILLE BATTLEFIELD
5466 Harper House Rd., Four Oaks
(910) 594-0789
www.nchistoricsites.org/bentonvi/bentonvi .htm

U.S. General William T. Sherman faced his last significant challenge from the Confederate army in March 1865 at Bentonville, a small crossroads community about 50 miles southeast of Raleigh. Today, the Bentonville Battlefield is a National Historic Landmark that serves as a monument to the lives lost and a lesson in Civil War history.

Visitors can see the restored and furnished farmhouse of John and Amy Harper, which was turned into a hospital during the battle, a Confederate mass grave, miles of earthworks that soldiers dug during the fight, and artifacts collected from the battlefield. Monuments built in the decades after the war dot the landscape. Inside the visitors' center, an interactive fiber-optic map exhibit provides visual and audio explanation of the first day of the battle. Every five years, re-enactors commemorate the battle with a two-day re-creation of the fight and other period events, involving hundreds of volunteers and antique munitions. The last re-enactment marked the 145th anniversary of the battle in March 2010. Other smaller re-enactments are held throughout the year. Admission to the site is free.

CAROLINA BASKETBALL MUSEUM
450 Skipper Bowles Dr., UNC campus,
Chapel Hill
(919) 843-9921
http://tarheelblue.cstv.com/museum
College basketball fans can immerse themselves in one of the sports most legendary programs at the Carolina Basketball Museum. The 8,000-square-foot space is next to the Tar Heel's home court, the Dean E. Smith Center, aka the "Dean Dome" on the southern edge of campus. Visitors can watch several video tributes and displays, featuring interviews with Michael Jordan, James Worthy, and Phil Ford, as well as recaps of some of Carolina's greatest games. Memorabilia includes national championship trophies, game balls, nets, old uniforms, shoes, and a letter from Duke coach Mike Krzyzewski to a high school player named Michael Jordan, regretting Jordan's lack of interest in the Blue Devils. Parking here, as with everywhere else at UNC, is scarce. It's best

not to plan a visit on a game day during football or basketball season. Admission is free.

CARRBORO FARMERS' MARKET
301 W. Main St. on the Town Commons, Carrboro
(919) 280-3326
www.carrborofarmersmarket.com
After more than three decades in operation, the Carrboro Farmers' Market is the oldest and most renowned of the Triangle's many markets. A meeting point for local farmers and customers, it has helped them build relationships that are key to the area's thriving sustainable agriculture movement and its farm-to-table dining scene. The market's home is on the Carrboro commons beneath a series of pergolas and tin roofs, where about 75 farmers, cheese makers, bakers, jelly makers, flower growers, potters, weavers, and craft workers of other stripes present their wares. A co-op of vendors runs the market and ensures that everything presented is locally grown or made by the seller. On a sunny morning, nothing beats picking up tomatoes for Saturday night dinner while making a breakfast of bread and cheese bought fresh from their makers.

The market is open Saturday mornings year-round, and crowds are heaviest between 8 and 10 a.m. It's advisable to bring your own bags for produce, and the vendors will smile at you if you pay them in small bills. During the growing season, the Carrboro Market is open on Wednesday afternoons, and Carrboro Market vendors also sell in Southern Village on Thursday afternoons.

DUKE HOMESTEAD STATE HISTORIC SITE
2828 Duke Homestead Rd., Durham
(919) 477-5498
www.nchistoricsites.org/duke/duke.htm
In the aftermath of the Civil War, Washington Duke was a poor farmer who changed his luck. Just as he switched from growing cotton to cultivating bright-leaf tobacco, the small town of Durham near his farm was gaining a reputation as a tobacco manufacturing center. The company Duke and his sons founded went on to perfect the mechanized production of cigarettes in the 1880s and became the largest tobacco company in the country, the American Tobacco Company, by 1890.

Visitors to the Duke Homestead can see where the enterprise, which eventually endowed and renamed Duke University, began. The plain white farmhouse that Washington Duke built in 1850 still stands, alongside a smokehouse and grape arbors, and barns and outbuildings where tobacco was stored and processed by the Duke family. Also on site are displays explaining the agricultural process of growing and curing tobacco. The Homestead presents a Harvest and Hornworm Festival every September, where costumed interpreters demonstrate agricultural practices and an auctioneer calls out tobacco prices. Other events are scheduled throughout the year. Admission to the site and events is free.

DUKE UNIVERSITY CHAPEL
1 Chapel Dr., Duke University, Durham
(919) 681-9414
www.chapel.duke.edu
Approaching Duke Chapel for the first, or even the 50th, time can be truly breathtaking. As you turn onto Chapel Drive, your eyes fill with the Gothic façade, and its 210-foot spires seem to reach for heaven. The interior is just as grand. Stone statues gaze down from the carved portal. Light filters through the stained-glass faces of Biblical figures on 77 brilliantly colored windows. Three separate pipe organs fill the cathedral with sound. Three members of the Duke family are entombed in Duke Chapel: James B. Duke, Washington Duke, and Benjamin Duke. Memorial plaques honor members of the Duke family who passed more recently, including Doris Duke.

Constructed between 1930 and 1935 at a cost of $2.3 million, Duke Chapel was the last building completed on the university's West Campus. Its designer was Philadelphia architect Julian Abele, among the first renowned African-American architects. He took inspiration for the neo-Gothic chapel from English cathedrals and other American university chapels.

Sunday worship services at 11 a.m. are open to the public, as are the Thursday evening vespers services held at 5:15 p.m. during the school year.

The Duke Chapel Choir's annual presentations of Handel's *Messiah* offer a chance to experience the cathedral in all its grandeur. (See the Performing Arts chapter for more on the Duke Chapel Choir.) Otherwise, the chapel is open to visitors daily with no admission cost. Make sure to call ahead to see if a wedding is scheduled, especially on the weekends. The chapel is a popular wedding site, and visitors are not allowed into private events.

Triangle Modernist Houses Tour

The Triangle has the third-largest concentration of mid-century Modernist houses outside of Los Angeles and Chicago. This wealth of arresting architecture is the legacy of the College of Design at North Carolina State University. In 1948, the school hired Henry Kamphoefner to lead the school, and he brought some of the most progressive architects in the country to join the faculty. They designed homes throughout Raleigh and the Triangle that feature the Modernist movement's sleek lines, parabolic roofs, and strategic use of windows to bring the outside in.

Triangle Modernist Houses, a group dedicated to highlighting and preserving this heritage, offers frequent tours of these modernist homes as well as notice of their sales and potential endangerment. The Web site www.trianglemodernist houses.com is a treasure trove of history on the local movement and the architects behind it.

EXECUTIVE MANSION
200 N. Blount St., Raleigh
(919) 807-7950
www.nchistoricsites.org/capitol

A study in Queen Anne stateliness, the Executive Mansion has served as home to North Carolina's governors since its completion in 1891. It is the third structure in Raleigh to serve as official home to the governor. The mansion sits on the edge of downtown's government buildings district, a few blocks from the legislative building. Inside the brick-and-wrought-iron walls surrounding the mansion are a small rose garden, massive oaks and magnolias, azaleas, camellias, and rhododendrons as well as a formal Victorian garden and a kitchen garden. Large works by North Carolina artists, including chainsaw carver Clyde Jones, accent the grounds. The mansion's 28 rooms include a ballroom, library, grand hall, and separate gentlemen's and ladies' parlors, still named thus despite the 2008 election of the state's first female governor, Beverly Perdue. Decor includes carpets adorned with oak leaves, the symbol of the city of Raleigh, as well rare 19th-century furniture and portraits of former governors and first ladies. The first floor of the mansion is open for tours by appointment. Call the Capital Area Visitor Services to make arrangements at least two weeks prior to visiting. Admission is free.

i For a more casual look at the grounds, drop by the mansion on Halloween, when the outdoors are done up in a haunted house theme to welcome trick-or-treaters.

HISTORIC STAGVILLE
5828 Old Oxford Hwy., Durham
(919) 620-0120
www.stagville.org

What's most interesting about the Historic Stagville plantation is not that at the start of the Civil War its owner was deemed to be the richest man in North Carolina, with family holdings of 30,000 acres and 900 slaves. What's most interesting is that, unlike most other plantation sites, Historic Stagville offers glimpses of what the lives of those slaves were like. Most historic sites bear no trace of the slave quarters. At Historic Stagville, a collection of 71 acres divided into three tracts, visitors can see not only the 19th-century home of the Bennehan family plantation, but also four two-story, four-room buildings where the enslaved lived, and a giant timber-framed barn that bears witness to the craftsmanship of enslaved labor. In December, re-enactors stage a re-creation of holiday life in the plantation house and the slave quarters.

The Bennehan-Cameron family that owned the Stagville land for most of two centuries left behind many historic papers that have helped historians create vivid pictures of life there, which inform the tour guides. The plantation is open Tuesday through Saturday. Call ahead to see what times tours will be offered each day. Admission is free.

i Historic Stagville is an isolated spot, so it's a good idea to bring water and maybe a picnic because no concessions are sold on site.

J.C. RAULSTON ARBORETUM
4415 Beryl Rd., Raleigh
(919) 515-3132
www.ncsu.edu/jcraulstonarboretum
Operated by the Department of Horticulture Science at N.C. State University, the eight-acre arboretum sits just off busy Hillsborough Street and not far from I-440. It offers an oasis for strolling as well as countless opportunities for learning about what grows in North Carolina's piedmont soil. The arboretum has one of the Southeast's largest collections of landscape plants, so it serves as a font of inspiration for gardeners. Within the arboretum are several gardens, including a formal white garden inspired by English tradition, a Japanese garden, a rose garden, a mixed border and a perennial border, and a butterfly garden. A learning center gives a home to classes and events. A rooftop terrace and water gardens offer spots for contemplation.

The arboretum sponsors frequent free lectures and tours on matters of horticulture as well as more intense workshops that require fees. Once a year, arboretum members can participate in a giveaway of rare plants that sees thousands of specimens snatched up in minutes on a Saturday morning, usually in early October. The arboretum also schedules group tours to other gardens of note. Admission and parking are free.

MARBLES KIDS MUSEUM $
201 E. Hargett St., Raleigh
(919) 834-4040
www.marbleskidsmuseum.org
A temple to children's creativity, Marbles has just about everything kids 12 and under could want. It's not really a museum but more like a two-story, 84,000-square-foot playroom. The museum and adjacent IMAX Theater occupy most of a city block. The best thing for kids is the sense of freedom and exploration they have as they run from one activity to another. The best thing for parents to do is to find a bench and watch them go. For more on the Marble Kids Museum, see our Kidstuff chapter.

MOREHEAD PLANETARIUM
AND SCIENCE CENTER $$
250 E. Franklin St., Chapel Hill
(919) 962-1236
www.moreheadplanetarium.org
A state-of-the-art digital video projection system fills the 68-foot dome ceiling of the Morehead Planetarium with a brilliant re-creation of the night sky. The planetarium serves as a classroom for UNC students and as a theater for learning and entertainment for visitors. Along with star shows, the planetarium presents educational films about astronomy and weather and laser shows set to Led Zeppelin and U2. Renamed to include the phrase "Science Center" in 2002, the planetarium has recently expanded its mission to offer programs about developments in sciences other than astronomy. Visitors can watch a star show, attend a forum on a current scientific issue, or hear a lecture by a visiting expert. Much of the planetarium's programming is geared to children, who can take part in the science camps and workshops. The planetarium also sponsors off-site star viewing at Jordan Lake. The Morehead Planetarium is easy to find on Franklin Street—just look for the 35-foot sundial out front.

One Giant Leap

From 1959 to 1975, the Morehead Planetarium trained NASA astronauts, including moonwalkers Neil Armstrong and Buzz Aldrin, in celestial navigation. The astronauts needed to be able to navigate using the stars in case their computer navigation systems failed. A memorable example of such a failure was the *Apollo 13* mission, during which an explosion debilitated the spacecraft's navigation system. As computers became more reliable in the 1970s and NASA began using shuttles, the celestial navigation program ended.

MUSEUM OF LIFE + SCIENCE $$-$$$
433 W. Murray Ave., Durham
(919) 220-5429
www.ncmls.org
Best known for its enchanting tropical butterfly house with its 30-foot conservatory, the Museum of Life + Science also devotes acres of land to other forms of life, thriving and extinct. The museum, supported by Durham County and the state of North Carolina, aims its educational programs at children, but adults never cease to learn something when they tag along. From watching the keepers feed poison dart frogs to traipsing through a wooded trail with dinosaur replicas on either side, the museum offers a wide variety of ways to experience the natural world. For more about the Museum of Life + Science, see our Kidstuff chapter.

NORTH CAROLINA BOTANICAL GARDEN
Totten Center, Old Mason Farm Rd.,
Chapel Hill
(919) 962-0522
The Botanical Garden is the University of North Carolina's center for native plant conservation. Native southeastern plants decorate the landscaped areas surrounding the Totten Education Center offering ideas for gardeners who want to make the most of the climate's attributes and work within its limitations. Display gardens include a native plant border, water gardens, carnivorous plants, an herb garden, a fern collection, and a horticultural therapy garden. Every fall, a new set of outdoor sculptures is installed throughout the garden for a two-month exhibition. The garden offers lectures on botany and horticulture and children's programs. Admission is free.

NORTH CAROLINA MUSEUM OF ART
2110 Blue Ridge Rd., Raleigh
(919) 839-6262
www.ncartmuseum.org
The North Carolina Museum of Art Park makes it possible to expose children to more than half a dozen works of art without stepping foot indoors. A 35-foot whirligig topped with a bicycle wheel and propellers, among other reused objects, acts a greeter, leading to a series of three giant arches that train the gaze skyward. A cloud chamber, hidden like a hobbit's house, and a sculpture made of several tons of newspapers called "To see Jennie smile" await in the wooded area. It's all on the way to a pedestrian bridge that spans I-440. Interpretive signs throughout explain and guide.

Indoors, the museum also offers educational programs for children of all ages, from scavenger-hunt explorations of the permanent collection to art camps for kids. The museum's amphitheater is a great place for family concerts, and the summer movie series always includes programming for children. For more on the art museum, see the Museums chapter. Admission to the park and museum is free. Special exhibits charge an entry fee.

NORTH CAROLINA MUSEUM OF HISTORY
5 E. Edenton St., Raleigh
(919) 807-7900
www.ncmuseumofhistory.org
The North Carolina Museum of History shares a downtown plaza with the North Carolina

Museum of Natural Sciences, between the Capitol and the Legislative Building. The museum covers the state's history from American Indian tribes to the Elizabethan-era pirates who prowled the coast, to NASCAR's beginnings in the western Piedmont. A separate gallery on the third floor, the North Carolina Sports Hall of Fame, is devoted to accomplishments of the state's athletes. Among the museum's most popular exhibits are a pair of No. 3 Chevrolets, one driven by early NASCAR legend Junior Johnson, the other by Dale Earnhardt Sr.; driver Richard Petty's racecar; and an exhibit on the life of weapons inventor David Marshall "Carbine" Williams.

The museum aims to serve all ages, and the best exhibits, like the recent look at piracy, provide historical context for adults along with interactive learning opportunities for children. The museum sponsors lectures related to current exhibits and performances that showcase North Carolina's cultural heritage, including bluegrass, jazz, blues, and folk music. Its annual events include an African-American Cultural Celebration in January, Farm Fresh Family Day celebration of agriculture in September, and an American Indian Heritage Celebration in November. Admission to the museum is free, but an entry fee is charged for some exhibits and programs. A museum shop is on the ground floor.

NORTH CAROLINA MUSEUM OF NATURAL SCIENCES
11 W. Jones St., Raleigh
(919) 733-7450
www.naturalsciences.org

Opposite the downtown plaza from the state history museum stands the North Carolina Museum of Natural Sciences. It is a four-story catalog of natural history and evolving ecology with a focus on North Carolina and the Southeast. Its collections include the skeleton of a 55-foot-long sperm whale, nicknamed "Trouble," that washed ashore along the North Carolina coast in 1928 as well as a 110-million-year-old Acrocanthosaurus skeleton. That carnivorous dinosaur is the only fossil of its kind on display in the world. You can see it from the outside through the museum's

glass tower, and inside as part of the dinosaur exhibit "Terror of the South." Less vicious native animals, both live and stuffed, are also on view. Fish swim in the first-floor aquariums, while insects crawl and fly in glass cases on the fourth floor, and nearby a three-toed sloth lounges in a tropical conservatory.

The museum hosts frequent traveling exhibits that in recent seasons have included an exposition of the Dead Sea Scrolls and a look at the role chocolate has played in economic and social history. During First Friday gallery crawls, the museum presents a film, usually camp or vintage horror, in its auditorium. Its biggest program is BugFest, the daylong celebration of all things creepy crawly. (For more on BugFest, see the Annual Events chapter.) Both adults and children can avail themselves of the many educational opportunities the museum offers, from learning to propagate plants to following a museum educator on a two-day birding trip through Eastern North Carolina. (For more on programs for children, see the Kidstuff chapter.)

A fourth-floor cafe serves sandwiches, fries, and the like. The museum gift shop is on the first floor. Museum admission is free, but traveling exhibits, programs, and workshops charge a fee.

OAKWOOD HISTORIC DISTRICT
N. Person St. to Linden Ave., E. Edenton to Franklin St.
Downtown Raleigh
www.historicoakwood.org

OAKWOOD CEMETERY
701 Oakwood Ave., Raleigh
(919) 832-6077
www.historicoakwoodcemetery.com

Oakwood is a neighborhood of restored late 19th-century and early 20th-century homes that grew up just east of downtown after the Civil War. It thrived as an important white middle-class community until the 1940s. Stroll along the tree-covered sidewalks today and you can take in a variety of architectural influences, including Second Empire, Queen Anne, and neoclassical, seen nowhere else in the city. This beautiful area had fallen into decay after the rise of streetcars and automobiles fostered suburban growth. By the mid-1970s the city eyed it for destruction. A revival ensued and the neighborhood was named a historic district by the National Register of Historic Places. Today the homes are among the most prized in the city. Oakwood residents open their doors during an annual holiday Candlelight Tour in December, and welcome visitors to their gardens during the annual Garden Tour and Tea in May. Admission is charged for the tours.

On the edge of the Oakwood neighborhood sits Oakwood Cemetery, a beautiful expanse of green lawns and towering hardwoods that is a lovely place for a walk. The cemetery was founded after the Civil War when Federal troops vowed to rid the Federal cemetery of any Confederate dead. The locals had a few days to find a place for their dead before the U.S. troops tossed the bodies into the street. Henry Mordecai, who owned the land that was to become the neighborhood and the cemetery, donated a grove of trees on a hill. Today, rows of white tombstones mark the Confederate cemetery and a charming stone House of Memory recounts the exploits of all the North Carolinian lost to war. Ramble along the hilly, paved paths, and you'll encounter the markers of other interesting lives, including that of former U.S. Senator Jesse Helms and N.C. State basketball coach Jim Valvano as well as generals, governors, educators, and scoundrels key to Raleigh and North Carolina history. A series of plays produced by Burning Coal Theatre each spring and set in the cemetery recounts the colorful lives of many of Oakwood's dead. (See the sidebar about the Oakwood plays in the Performing Arts chapter.)

i If a powerfully sweet aroma of sugar and baking yeast hits you as you're wandering through Oakwood's streets, you can follow your nose to the Krispy Kreme doughnuts store at the corner of Person and Peace streets.

SARAH P. DUKE GARDENS
426 Anderson St., Duke University, Durham
(919) 684-3698
www.hr.duke.edu/dukegardens
Hundreds of thousands of visitors come to Duke Gardens every year to enjoy the vast array of plants found in its meticulously designed, well-tended 55 acres. Five miles of paths wind through three separate gardens, beneath pergolas and past fountains; under the shade of pines and magnolias; alongside rhododendron, irises, roses, and water lilies; and at the edges of ponds. Thousands of species of plants are collected in the H.L. Blomquist Garden of Native Plants, the Williams L. Culberson Asiatic Arboretum, and the original Terrace Gardens. The gardens were designed by Ellen Shipman, a famed early 20th-century landscape designer, and are among the only surviving examples of her work.

Duke Gardens presents a calendar full of performances, classes, and workshops, including tours led by horticulturalists, bird walks, musical events, craft sales, and nature camps and programs for children. A terrace cafe near the entrance serves lunch, and the Doris Duke Center near the entrance also houses a garden shop and horticultural library. Admission to the garden is free, but visitors must pay for parking during peak hours. Parking rates are about $2 per hour.

STATE CAPITOL
1 E. Edenton St., Raleigh
(919) 733-4994, (919) 807-7950
www.nchistoricsites.org/capitol
Completed in 1840 after the original state house burned, the State Capitol was designed by renowned New York architects Ithiel Town and Alexander Jackson Davis. It is among the best remaining examples of 19th-century Greek Revival style, with its dome rotunda, symmetrical cross-shaped floor plan, exterior Doric columns, and interior Corinthian and Ionic columns. The statue of George Washington dressed as a Roman general in the middle of the rotunda is a copy of the Antonio Canova statue destroyed in the first state house fire. Plaques commemorating historical figures and events ring the rotunda.

North Carolina's legislature has not con-ducted official business in the State Capitol build-ing since 1963, when both chambers of the General Assembly moved two blocks away to the Legislative Building. The governor and lieutenant governor retain offices in the capitol. At the cen-ter of downtown, the capitol grounds serve as a public space where crowds gather to watch the Christmas parade turn from Hillsborough Street on its way to Fayetteville Street. Monuments to war veterans and governors dot the lawn, includ-ing a towering Civil War obelisk.

The capitol is open to tourists on weekdays, and guided tours are available on weekends. Call ahead for hours. The governor's lighting of the capitol Christmas tree is a great time to see the building and grounds illuminated. It is usually the first or second Wednesday of December. Admission is free.

STATE FARMERS' MARKET
1201 Agriculture St., Raleigh
(919) 733-7417
www.ncagr.gov
At the State Farmers' Market you can buy every-thing from wine to sod, but most people come for the produce. Saturday mornings in the spring and summer are the market's liveliest days, when thousands show up to buy fresh tomatoes and peppers or live herbs and bedding plants from scores of vendors in the long outdoor shed. At the indoor stalls, you'll find local honey, locally raised meats and cheese, crafts, and candy. A sea-food restaurant sells fried North Carolina shrimp and oysters, and the Famers' Market Restaurant is known for its down-home specialties like fried okra and sweet potato pie. Most vendors take cash or checks only. There's an ATM machine between the two sheds. The market is off Lake Wheeler Road. Just follow the signs.

KIDSTUFF

The Triangle's national reputation for high quality of life relies in part on how high that quality is for children. Good public schools are part of the equation, but places to learn and play outside the classroom also contribute to the picture. Just about every cultural organization in the area offers ways for children to get involved, from specially designed tours of the North Carolina Museum of Art to historical re-enactments at sites such as Historic Stagwell and Duke Homestead that spur children's imaginations.

Among the possibilities too numerous to catalog here are the many public libraries and bookstores that present frequent story times for children. Also worth considering are seasonal activities such as berry picking in the spring and corn mazes in the fall. The large number of farms located close to the Triangle's urban centers mean there's usually one within a half-hour's drive.

Scheduled activities abound at area sports centers and skating rinks, but the Triangle also offers an abundance of places where kids can run around and just be kids. Every neighborhood, it seems, has its own playground, but for special occasions we've listed a couple of "destination playgrounds" that have memorable features. We've singled out a few pools for their kid-friendly "spraygrounds." Find a more complete list of public pools in the Recreation chapter.

No matter where you take your child for an outing, it's a safe bet you'll find adult companionship in the form of other parents. Just leave some space on that butterfly-shaped park bench and ask if they need an extra juice box.

Price Code

Price codes refers to the cost of admission for one child. Admission to some attractions can vary based on which activities the child plans to participate in and the child's age. Call ahead to verify prices for your party and activity.

$	Under $5
$$	$5 to $10
$$$	$11 to $15
$$$$	Over $15

GOLF, GAMES, AND GO-KARTS

ADVENTURE LANDING $$-$$$
3311 Capital Blvd., Raleigh
(919) 872-1688

Three 18-hole miniature gold courses, laser tag for beginners and advanced players, a 100-game arcade, a quarter-mile go-kart track, and nine batting cages should keep the kids busy for a while. Adventure Landing offers frequent specials, like family night deals that include a pizza with admission, and special events including overnight lock-ins.

FRANKIE'S FUN PARK & RESTAURANT $-$$
11190 Fun Park Dr., Raleigh
(919) 433-7888
www.frankiesfunpark.com

Off Southern Parkway in northwest Raleigh, Frankie's is near the Brier Creek shopping district and I-540. On site are three go-karts tracks, including one for the younger set, three 18-hole miniature golf courses, bumper boats, a laser tag arcade with a viewing area, two climbable fun houses, batting cages, a plummet ride, and an arcade. A full-service restaurant serves a menu of burgers, wrap sandwiches, pizza, and entrees like chicken marsala and grilled salmon. Package prices are available for groups of 10 or more.

PUTT-PUTT OF RALEIGH $$
4020 Tryon Rd., Raleigh
(919) 832-2228
www.puttputtfuncenters.com

The original miniature golf course, Putt Putt's branch in Raleigh offers 18 holes, a go-kart track, a climbable fun house, a batting cage, miniature rides for younger kids, an arcade, and a stuff-your-own bear station. On the edge of Raleigh, it is convenient to Cary as well.

SPLASH

SILVER LAKE $$–$$$
5300 Tryon Rd., Raleigh
(919) 851-1683
www.silverlakeraleigh.com

A five-story waterslide, nicknamed "the Beast," is the highlight of this man-made lake park. Silver Lake also has a shallow kiddie area, bumper boats, floating-walk obstacle paths, several smaller waterslides, a playground, pedal boats, volleyball courts, horseshoe pits, and a shaded picnic area. Because it is a lake, and not a cement-bottomed pool, Silver Lake has a more rustic feel than the mega-water parks found in most metro areas. Concessions are available on site or you can bring your own food. Picnic areas have charcoal grills.

SKATING AND SUCH

THE FACTORY
1839 S. Main St., Wake Forest
(919) 453 1839
www.eatshopplay.com

The Factory is one-stop shopping for kid activities, which makes it a meeting point for parents and children. The complex includes: Delicious Skate Board Shop and Park, which has a 25,000-square-foot skate park; South Main Speedway, with an 18-hole miniature golf course and go-karts; Jumpin' Beans, a bounce-house center with inflatables plus an espresso bar with free Wi-Fi for parents; the Polar Ice House skating rink; MVP Sports Factory, an indoor soccer facility; the Fac-

tory Ballpark, which has six baseball and softball fields and a field house; and a YMCA location. Shops and restaurants within the complex or an easy walk away mean parents can browse or eat if they have downtime while the kids are playing.

JELLYBEANS SUPER SKATE CENTERS
1120 Buck Jones Rd., Raleigh
(919) 467-5238

10701 Common Oaks Dr., Raleigh
(919) 562-2326
www.skatejellybeans.com

Popular with tween-age inline skaters and roller skaters, both rinks offer camps and day-off-school programs for children in fifth grade and under. Children as young as three years old can participate in skate classes. Both rinks have snack bars and no outside food and drink are allowed. Parents who aren't skating pay no admission.

SKATE RANCH OF RALEIGH $–$$
2901 Trawick Rd., Raleigh
(919) 790-3808
www.skateranchofraleigh.com

Skate Ranch of Raleigh believes you're never too old to roller skate. Weekly specials include a family night, a Saturday morning free-skate for parents with children, a teen night, and an 18-and-older night hosted by local radio disc jockeys. The Ranch also offers after-school programs and summer camps.

TAKE AIM

GOTCHA PAINTBALL $–$$$
Store: 3029 Capital Blvd., Raleigh
Field: 176 Darius Pearce Rd., Youngsville
(919) 501-7770

Gotcha Paintball is the largest paintball field in Raleigh. You buy the paint from the Gotcha store on Capital Boulevard, then play in the field in Youngsville, north of Raleigh in Franklin County. Referees monitor the action. The facility includes a woods course and Hyperball and X-Ball courses. Equipment is for rent at the store along with the paintballs. The action is for ages 10 and older.

HANDS-ON FUN

KIDZU KIDS MUSEUM $
105 E. Franklin St., Chapel Hill
(919) 933-1455
www.kidzuchildrensmuseum.org

Geared toward children eight and younger, Kidzu offers play stations and programs that work to get young ones exploring the world and using their brains. Children can experiment with the power of gravity with an oversized plastic maze, manipulate 6-foot foam noodles to create semipermanent works of art, try on hard hats and vests in the construction zone, sell faux produce at the market, or make music on a giant xylophone. Traveling and curated exhibits change three or four times a year and have included a life-size recreation of Mister Rogers' neighborhood, a look at medieval castles, and lessons in tolerance taught through picture books. Programs include presentations by storytellers and do-it-yourself art projects. The museum's home is a storefront on Franklin Street.

MARBLES KIDS MUSEUM $
201 E. Hargett St., Raleigh
(919) 834-4040
www.marbleskidsmuseum.org

Marbles is a museum where kids can touch, and in some cases tumble through or bounce on, everything they see. Start with the cab of a city bus that children can drive, then head for the replicas of fire trucks, ambulances, and mail trucks. A store, a stage with costumes, a three-story pirate ship, indoor and outdoor splash stations, an "underwater" room lit by disco lights, and a science activity center finish out the first level. On the second level, kids can build their own cars and race them down an incline, play with oversized building blocks, design outfits using scraps of material, and paint and hammer. An international room holds a piece of the Berlin wall, a Moroccan tea set, a video of drum-dancers at Rio de Janeiro's Carnival, and holes where kids can play at ice fishing. One wing of the upper level is reserved for rotating exhibits, which can include Mr. Potato Head–themed trips around the world or obstacle courses and climbing walls.

The building itself is eye candy for adults. The two-story, 84,000-square-foot space occupies half a city block. Its open indoor courtyard provides a view of the suspension bridge that connects two parts of the second level. On the second floor, kids can peer out at Moore Square from a glassed-in overlook or look down at the courtyard. Museum workers regularly move the 2-foot chess pieces aside and lead hokey pokey in the courtyard. Outside there's a garden, a sand box, and a courtyard with a stream running through it. The museum includes a snack bar and gift shop, and an IMAX movie theater is next door.

MUSEUM OF LIFE + SCIENCE $$–$$$
433 W. Murray Ave., Durham
(919) 220-5429
www.ncmls.org

With 65,000 square feet of indoor space and 13 acres outside, the Museum of Life + Science is a learning playground. Indoors, kids can get in a real Apollo Space Capsule or, if it's feeding time, watch keepers give the poison dart frogs a snack. In all, the museum is home to more than 75 species of animals. Some of the more beautiful are the flittering residents of the East Coast's largest butterfly conservatory, the Magic Wings butterfly house. While these might hold kids' attention for a while, before long they'll want to head outside for the Dinosaur Trail, where towering replicas of the late Cretaceous age await along a wooded trail. A nature park offers glimpses of live bears, wolves, lemurs, barred owls, woodchucks, possums, young alligators, and snakes. In the farmyard, kids can pet sheep, pigs, a donkey, a steer, a rabbit, a turkey, a duck, and goats.

Children can operate radio-controlled sailboats on a pond; take a ride in an ornithopter, a winged flying machine; or launch giant seed pods from a tower. Among the most popular activities is the Ellerbee Creek Railway's miniature train, which takes visitors through the park. It is especially popular at Christmastime when Santa rides along. Educational programs offer plenty of ways for kids to get involved, and events like the

Butterfly Bash in April, which celebrates insects in many forms, draw big crowds.

NEW HOPE VALLEY RAILWAY $
5121 Daisy St., New Hill
(919) 362-5416
www.nhvry.org
On the western edge of Wake County, you can board a train and take a one-hour round trip between New Hill and Bonsal. The New Hope Valley Railway owns several diesel engines and one steam engine, and the track runs through a wooded, sparsely populated area that has not seen commercial service since 1981. For any child or adult bitten by the train bug, this is a day to remember. Not only can you ride the train, but visitors can also see the North Carolina Railway Museum's historic railroad equipment and the garden-scale replica railroad, which includes a Thomas the Tank Engine. Admission to the museum and scale railroad is free. Tickets are required to ride the railway. Christmastime rides feature Santa and are very popular, so it's advisable to buy tickets long in advance via the Web. The railroad cars are covered but open to the elements, so dress for the weather.

NORTH CAROLINA MUSEUM OF
NATURAL SCIENCES   FREE
11 W. Jones St., Raleigh
(919) 733-7450
www.naturalsciences.org
Just taking in everything the Museum of Natural Sciences has on display is enough to keep first-time visitors entertained for an afternoon. Wandering through the displays of living fish, insects, snakes, and frogs; seeing the three-toed sloth; and gazing at the towering skeleton of the 110-million-year-old Acrocanthosaurus are good ways to start. In the Discovery Room, kids can do some hands-on learning when they touch fossils and bird wings, watch as bees fly from outside the museum into a glass-covered hive, and try on insect costumes.

BugFest in September is the museum's marquee festival, but programs throughout the year offer opportunities for children to get acquainted with the sciences. The museum is open late during every First Friday gallery walk and after special downtown events like the governor's tree lighting ceremony at the State Capitol and First Night Raleigh New Year's Eve events. Astronomy Days in January, Reptile and Amphibian Day in March, Earth Day in April, and the Groundhog Day appearance of the museum's prognosticating marmot, Sir Walter Wally, are big events. Admission to the museum and to most events is free.

RDU OBSERVATION PARK   FREE
RDU International Airport
www.rdu.com
Sometimes all your little guy—or maybe your big guy—wants to do is watch powerful machines in motion. At RDU International, they've set aside an elevated observation deck just for them. It overlooks RDU's longest runway, and gives you the full sonic and visual experience of watching plane after plane take off into the sky. You can listen to the conversations between the pilots and the air traffic controllers in the tower nearby. You can bring a picnic and eat at one of the tables near the playground or buy lunch at the Crosswinds Cafe. The park is near the general aviation terminal. No security check is required for entry.

TALK TO THE ANIMALS

CAROLINA TIGER RESCUE $–$$$
1940 Hanks Chapel Rd., Pittsboro
(919) 542-4684
www.carolinatigerrescue.org
Carolina Tiger Rescue is a wildlife sanctuary that has 72 animals—tigers, caracals, servals, ocelots, binturongs, and kinkajous. The preserve is about 3½ miles east of Pittsboro on 55 acres. All the preserve's cats have been abandoned by previous owners or are unable to survive in the wild due to physical impairment or prolonged captivity. The group opposes keeping wildcats in captivity as pets or entertainment. Part of its mission is to educate visitors about the perils of keeping wildcats.

Guided tours are offered by advance reservation during the day on Saturday and Sunday, and in cooler months at twilight on Saturday. The twilight tours are the best time to catch the creatures while they are active. Participation in the twilight tours is for ages 13 and older only.

DUKE LEMUR CENTER $-$$
3705 Erwin Rd., Durham
(919) 489-3364
www.lemur.duke.edu
With more than 200 lemurs on site, the Duke Lemur Center is the only facility in the world dedicated to the study of these close human relatives. The center is dedicated to better understanding prosimians and their habitat and to educating the public about the need to protect these creatures. Lithe and playful, lemurs charm with their humanlike mannerisms and their dark, soulful eyes. Watching them interact with their keepers and one another is a rare treat for nature lovers. The public is admitted on guided tours, by appointment only. The center is open to all ages, but tours may be too advanced for toddlers. Tours book up quickly during the spring and summer, so call at least two weeks in advance to secure reservations during warmer months. Off Duke's West Campus, the center can be a bit hard to find. Specific directions are available via a hidden link on the Web site. Get the link by calling the center for reservations.

PLAY

KIDS TOGETHER PLAYGROUND AT
MARLA DORREL PARK
111 Thurston Dr., Cary
www.kidstogethercary.org
The centerpiece of this park inspires its nickname, the "Dragon Park." A giant, multi-piece dragon sculpture seems to poke out of the ground, inviting children to climb aboard. Climbing structures, water and sand areas, playhouses, picnic shelters, and a fenced area for preschoolers cover the rest of the two-acre park. The playground is cleverly set amid the trees and shrubs to foster children's interaction with the natural environment. Much of the playground equipment is accessible to children with physical impairments.

PULLEN PARK
408 Ashe Ave., Raleigh
(919) 831-6468
www.raleigh-nc.org
The first public park in North Carolina, Pullen has been entertaining children and giving adults breathing room since 1887. It is adjacent to N.C. State's main campus off Western Boulevard. The centerpiece is an early 1900s Dentzel Carousel, one of 14 still operating on this continent. A designated site on the National Register of Historic Places, the carousel has 52 carved animals and two chariots that rotate around gilded mirrors to the sounds of a Wurlitzer organ. The park is also home to an historic miniature train that laps the park regularly, an electronic miniature boat track, and a pond where paddleboats are for rent. You can also find swings, slides, picnic areas, and an old full-size caboose. Also in the park is an aquatics center with an indoor pool, the home of Theatre in the Park, an arts center, and tennis courts. Park admission is free, but rides require tickets. The annual Santa Train Express, which features visits from St. Nick and the holiday lights of the park is a popular tradition, and advanced tickets are suggested. Buy them at the park's ticket office or online at reclink.raleighnc.gov.

YOUTH SPORTS LEAGUES

Parks and recreation departments in towns and counties throughout the Triangle organize an array of sports for children and adults. Leagues exist to cover everything from basketball and tennis to swimming and gymnastics. For more on youth sports see the Recreation chapter.

ANNUAL EVENTS

While street festivals dominate the Triangle's cultural calendar in warmer months, there's much more to the scene than that. Film festivals that draw cultural icons, literary events, living history presentations, and explorations of the area's cultural and architectural heritage help create a well-rounded slate of events. A weekend rarely passes when some happening doesn't draw residents out of their homes in large numbers. January may be the lone exception, a time when the holidays have left everyone spent and the weather is usually at its worst. August can also be a slow time, when the heat of the North Carolina summer makes outdoor activities seem like a chore rather than a joy and the beaches and mountains beckon.

This list aims to provide a look at the best-attended community events and some that are unique or distinguishing, but it is far from comprehensive. Parks and cultural centers put on smaller-scale festivals with regularity, and some of the more engaged neighborhoods stage their own parades and street parties when volunteers find the time. Community music festivals are common, too. Many weekends in the spring and summer, you may find yourself wishing that it wasn't so hard to choose between events.

Events are continually evolving, so consult the Web site or phone number to make sure venues and prices have remained constant.

JANUARY

**MARTING LUTHER KING JR. DAY
OF SERVICE**
United Way of the Triangle
2400 Perimeter Park Dr., Suite 150,
Morrisville
(919) 460-8687
www.unitedwaytriangle.org
In the past two decades, the Martin Luther King Jr. holiday has morphed from a day dedicated solely to remembrance into a day dedicated also to service. In communities across the Triangle, thousands turn out on the third Monday in January to volunteer their time for others, with the goal of realizing one of King's guiding principals: "Everyone can be great, because everyone can serve." The United Way of the Greater Triangle, which includes Durham, Johnston, Orange and Wake counties, organizes service projects throughout the communities it serves. Volunteers might spend the day doing anything from collecting goods for the needy overseas, to repairing homes in impoverished neighborhoods, to assembling care packages for members of the military.

JANUARY/FEBRUARY

CHINESE NEW YEAR FESTIVAL
Triangle Area Chinese American Society
of N. Carolina
P.O. Box 1041, Cary 27512
www.nctacas.org
Thousands show up at the N.C. State Fairgrounds to usher in the Chinese New Year with food, music, and displays of Chinese folk art, including drum performances, martial arts, and yo-yo. The sponsoring organization, the Triangle Area Chinese American Society, seeks to merge its festival of tradition with community customs. At a recent celebration of the year of the bull, Wool E. Bull, mascot for the minor league Durham Bulls Baseball team, was a guest of honor. Because the Chinese community in the Triangle has no geographic home, such as the Chinatowns in

larger metro areas, the association's events provide a moving cultural locus. The festival also gives Chinese food lovers a chance to taste more authentic versions of their restaurant favorites, including salt and pepper chicken, egg rolls, sticky rice, sushi, dim-sum, and North Carolina pork barbecue prepared Chinese style. Admission is $5 to $8. Children six and younger get in free. (Chinese New York fluctuates according to the lunar calendar.)

FEBRUARY

REVOLUTIONARY WAR LIVING HISTORY DAY
Alexander Dickson House
150 E. King St., Hillsborough
(877) 732-7748

Hillsborough is one of the Triangle's oldest towns and thus one of the few places where Colonial history is celebrated. By the late 18th century, the town was well established, and the state legislature met there during the American Revolution. In February of 1781, after fierce fighting along the Virginia–North Carolina border, British General Charles Cornwallis encamped his army in Hillsborough to prepare for the Battle of Guilford Courthouse, about 25 miles west. The town recalls its Revolutionary-era life with a re-enactment of camp life complete with musket fire by costumed Red Coats and Revolutionaries and camp-food cooking demonstrations. History buffs can also take a guided tour of the Revolutionary-era sites in the historic district. Viewing the re-enactment is free. The tour is $5.

FEARRINGTON FOLK ART SHOW
The Fearrington Barn
Fearrington Village, Pittsboro
(919) 542-2121
www.fearrington.com/village/folkart.asp

A barn full of folk art helps take the chill out of a cold winter's day, especially if the barn is snuggled amid the green hills of Fearrington Village, a dairy farm turned exclusive retirement community and fashionable inn and restaurant (see the Accommodations and Restaurants chapters).

Some of the Southeast's favorite folk artists are included in the invitation-only show, and all participants are outsider artists, meaning none has received classical artistic training. Offerings can include bold, colorful paintings of barnyard creatures, animal sculptures crafted from machine parts, pottery jugs shaped to resemble faces, decorative cars, and the work of local celebrity and outsider artist Clyde Jones. His medium is cedar logs, which he carves to resemble alligators, pigs, porcupines, and other familiar fauna using a chainsaw. Admission is $5.

HAYTI HERITAGE FILM FESTIVAL
The Hayti Heritage Center
804 Olde Fayetteville St., Durham
(919) 683-1709
www.hayti.org/hayti-film-festival

Formerly the Black Diaspora Film Festival, the event features films by African-American directors as well as lectures and discussions featuring African-American filmmakers and actors. Filmmakers can enter full-length features or short films in competitive categories. In revamping the 15-year-old festival, organizers have put an emphasis on giving undiscovered filmmakers an opportunity to grab the spotlight. Passes to the three-day festival are $50. One-day passes are $25. Admission to blocks of film screenings are $8 each.

MARCH

ST. PATRICK'S DAY PARADE AND FESTIVAL
Downtown Raleigh and Moore Square,
corner of Blount and Hargett streets
www.raleighstpats.org

Traditional Irish dancers, bagpipers and drummers, floats both traditional and humorous, horses, marching bands, Renaissance fair enthusiasts, and the occasional Irish wolf hound owner take to the streets of downtown Raleigh on the Saturday closest to March 17 for the wearing o' the green. Organized by the Raleigh St. Patrick's Day Committee, an independent consortium of Irish pride groups, the parade draws more than 3,000 participants. A festival featuring some of the marching musicians and dancers follows the parade at its end point, Moore Square, a public park conveniently located across from Tir Na Nog, one of the city's largest Irish-themed bars. Admission is free.

RALEIGH SPY CONFERENCE
N.C. Museum of History
5 E. Edenton St., Raleigh
(919) 831-0999
www.raleighspyconference.com
Staged by local conservative columnist and publisher Bernie Reeves, who puts out the Triangle's *Metro* magazine, the Raleigh Spy Conference draws speakers from around the world to discuss espionage and international politics. In its six-year run the conference has examined the role of women spies in espionage, the future of the CIA, Fidel Castro's legacy, and why the United States should continue to fear Russia's KGB. Guests have included former CIA and KGB operatives as well as authors and journalists. The conference also includes an opening reception and closing gala. Attendance is $250.

APRIL

PIEDMONT FARM TOUR
Western Triangle, various locations
(919) 542-2402
www.carolinafarmstewards.org
The Carolina Farm Stewardship Association organizes the tour, now into its second decade. It's essentially a giant open house to showcase the efforts of small independent farmers who practice sustainable agriculture in rural Alamance, Chatham, Orange, and Durham counties in the western Triangle. Customers get a chance to see where their food is grown, as many of the farmers sell at the Triangle's urban markets. Participants can get a closer look at lambs, pigs, and chickens being raised for meat; cows and goats on dairy farms; small-scale production of organic vegetables, herbs, berries, and flowers; and vineyards. Children can gather eggs and pet the livestock. Several thousand people turn out. The cost is $30 per car for access to any of the 35 farms, or $10 per car per farm.

FULL FRAME DOCUMENTARY FILM FESTIVAL
Carolina Theatre
309 W. Morgan St. and other downtown locations , Durham
(919) 687-4100
www.fullframefest.org
Topics covered at this well-known festival can range from weighty matters of global political importance to lighthearted takes on everyday subjects to fascinating glimpses into unfamiliar corners of our culture. The four-day event draws established masters of the documentary genre as well as newcomers aiming to establish their reputations. The films screen at various locations around Durham, including the historic Carolina Theatre, which means the thousands in attendance effectively take over downtown for the weekend.

Celebrities and cult figures often attend. Filmmakers Ken Burns, Martin Scorsese, and Sydney Pollack; actors Joan Allen and Danny DeVito; actor-turned-politician Senator Al Franken; author Walter Mosley; and activist Wavy Gravy have turned up at Full Frame in years past. The festival culminates with an awards ceremony and barbecue on Sunday afternoon. Festival passes range in price from $100 for admission to 15 films to $500 for admittance to all festival films and activities. Tickets to individual films are $10.

BENNETT PLACE RE-ENACTMENT
Bennett Place
4409 Bennett Place Memorial Rd., Durham
(919) 383-4345
www.nchistoricsites.org/bennett/bennett.htm
On April 26, 1865, two weeks after Confederate General Robert E. Lee surrendered his troops at Appomattox, U.S. General William T. Sherman accepted Confederate General Joseph Johnston's surrender of about 90,000 troops at the Bennett family farm. It was the largest troop surrender of the war, and the details had been worked out at the family's farmhouse. Costumed re-enactors set up camp at the historic site to re-create life as it was during the Civil War, including cooking

over open fires and practicing musket fire. Many of the re-enactors sleep out overnight beneath cloth tents or under the stars to recall the lives of the era's soldiers.

WORLD BEER FESTIVAL—RALEIGH
Moore Square
Corner of Blount and Hargett streets, Raleigh
(800) 977-2337
www.allaboutbeer.com/wbf

Tickets go fast to these days of drinking, eating, and music, so beer lovers should watch the Web to see when they go on sale. As the date nears, flyers also show up tucked inside six packs of craft brews sold at local stores. The spring festival is held in Raleigh while the fall version takes place in Durham. Ticketholders can taste more than 300 beers, including regional craft brews and suds from around the world. Organized by *All About Beer* magazine, headquartered in Durham, the day is divided into two drinking sessions, noon to 4 p.m. and 6 to 10 p.m. Local reggae, bluegrass, and dance bands provide entertainment. General admission is $40, and VIP tickets, which include free food and access to exclusive beers, are $75.

CLYDE FEST
Bynum Ballpark
173 Bynum Hill Rd., Bynum
(919) 542-0394
www.chathamarts.org

Local folk artist Clyde Jones loves kids, so the day the community organizes in his honor focuses squarely on them. Jones's chainsaw-carved cedar log critters—giraffes, pigs, deer—ignite the imagination with their chunky forms and whimsical paint jobs. The highlight of Clyde Fest is a chance to watch Jones pare down a hunk of wood into an animal. Other activities include games such a beanbag toss into old tires decorated like flowers, face painting, art projects for children, music, magicians, and clowns. Hungry Clyde fans can buy cookies shaped like the artist's critters as well as ice cream and barbecue from local vendors. Admission is $5, $2 for ages 2 to 12.

Clyde Jones

Hands down Bynum's most famous resident, folk artist Clyde Jones is known nationally and internationally for his chainsaw-carved critters. A retired mill worker, Jones began creating his critters in 1982. Since then, a colorful herd of them has graced his zany-looking yard in Bynum. A Clyde Jones critter adorns the lawn of the Executive Mansion in Raleigh, one is in the Smithsonian, and one is rumored to have made it to the Great Wall of China. The rough-hewn angles and clumsy proportions of his wooden animals are complemented by the finishing touches—a coat of pink paint or polka dots, a tennis ball for a nose, or plastic reflectors for eyes. Jones remains an unassuming man. He doesn't sell his works, but gives them away, and gawkers are welcome to slow down and look at his front yard art collection.

GREAT GRAPES WINE, ARTS & FOOD FESTIVAL
Koka Booth Amphitheatre, Cary
www.uncorkthefun.com/

About 20 wineries—most from North Carolina—artists, and crafts makers from around the Southeast and local musicians gather to offer samples and sell their wares at this daylong fete. Attendees can also see cooking demonstrations, get tips on wine tasting and winemaking, and hear speakers on regional cuisines. Kids are welcome, and can work off some energy in the bounce house while parents sip. Admission and a tasting glass are $18. Designated drivers are admitted for $10. Kids 12 and younger are free.

NORTH CAROLINA RENAISSANCE FAIRE
Wake Forest Golf Course
13239 Capital Blvd., Wake Forest
(919) 755-8004
www.ncrenfaire.com

Jousting, juggling, and the trappings of another era mark this celebration of all things Elizabethan. The event runs for three consecutive weekends. Three jousting bouts are staged daily. Costumed interpreters and vendors demonstrate medieval crafts, court dancing, acrobatics, dance, puppetry, and theater of the era on seven stages. The festival itself is a large bit of theater, as courtesans, gypsies, pirates, and peasants populate the streets, acting out the storyline of the day. Food vendors sell turkey legs meant to recall the appetites of kings alongside modern (read deep-fat-fried) fair food. Between 4,000 and 5,000 attendees show up to watch the drama and comedy unfold. Admission is $12 for adults, $6 for children and seniors.

SHAKORI HILLS SPRING FESTIVAL
Shakori Hills festival grounds
1439 Henderson Tanyard Rd., Pittsboro
(919) 542-8142
www.shakorihills.org

Once in the spring and once in the fall, the fields and woods of the Shakori Hills grounds near Silk Hope, in Chatham County, fill with hundreds of campers, music lovers, and enthusiastic environmentalists for this four-day festival. The lineup of more than 60 performers can include such diverse acts as pop stars Arrested Development, alt-country pickers Chatham County Line, and jam band Donna the Buffalo. If the event had an aura, it would definitely be green. At the Sustainability Pavilion, festival-goers can hear speakers talk about such topics as eco-friendly building practices, composting techniques, and public transportation initiatives. There's a hippie vibe but it's very family friendly, with a number of bands and performers geared to children. Kids can participate in activities in the Kids Zone, including face painting, art projects, storytelling, and learning wilderness survival skills. Local vendors sell coffee and a variety of food, from

curried rice to crepes. A biodiesel-fueled shuttle ferries folks who choose not to camp to and from stops in Carrboro, Chapel Hill, and Durham. Admission ranges from $95 for a four-day adult pass to between $22 and $36 for one-day passes, depending on the day. A four-day pass for ages 13 to 15 is $45, with one-day passes ranging from $11 to $18. Children 12 and younger get in free. Vehicle camping is $60 per day.

MAY

ARTSPLOSURE
Downtown Raleigh
(919) 832-8699
www.artsplosure.org

The city closes off six blocks downtown for two days to make room for scores of artists and artisans to fill the streets with booths of paintings, pottery, jewelry, photographs, woodcraft, blown glass, and the like. Party musicians like Buckwheat Zydeco provide music for thousands to shop by. Kids can experiment with musical instruments, dress up like rock stars, play chess on a life-size board, or make puppets with members of the Paperhand Puppet Intervention, a giant puppet performance troupe. Acrobats perform and artists create a mammoth sand sculpture in Moore Square to commemorate the festivities. Downtown residents stage a home tour to coincide with Artsplosure and downtown restaurants offer special prix fixe menus. Admission to the festival is free but attendees should bring money for parking, food, and, of course, art.

HEN-SIDE THE BELTLINE TOUR D'COOP
Raleigh, private homes inside the Beltline
hensidethebeltline.blogspot.com

Like many progressive urban areas, Raleigh is awash in backyard chicken keepers. This tour of stylish and creative residential henhouses is one of the city's newer traditions, but a very popular and growing one that draws hundreds each year. Participants traipse through strangers' yards in the same way that flower lovers take a garden tour, but it's the Araucanas and Sebrights and their coops they've come to see.

Henhouses range from innovative structures created with salvaged materials to miniature versions of their human keepers' homes painted to match. Attendees include fellow chicken keepers seeking inspiration for their own flocks' digs as well as aspiring poultry collectors and the simply curious. Tickets go on sale the day of the tour at a number of businesses around the city. Admission is a non-perishable food item or cash donation to Urban Ministries of Wake County.

GOT TO BE NC FESTIVAL
N.C. State Fairgrounds
1025 Blue Ridge Rd., Raleigh
(919) 733-7887 ext. 265
www.ncagfest.com

This relatively new three-day event is a scaled-down version of the N.C. State Fair, held annually in October. Carnival rides and game hawkers crowd the midway alongside petting zoos and fried food vendors. Because the festival is smaller and less well-attended, it's easier to navigate than the fall fair. Regional beach, bluegrass, and country bands play, but no big-name entertainers grab the headlines, so antique tractor pulls and farm equipment displays take center stage. Food and wine lovers can get a taste of North Carolina's bounty. Unlike the State Fair, the Got to Be NC Festival allows wine sales. Vendors offer sips of wine and dollops of salsas, dips, and specialty sauces and foods made with produce grown in state. Admission is $5, but ride tickets and entry to special events like tractor pulls are extra.

JUNE

HILLSBOROUGH HOG DAY
Cameron Park, corner of E. King St. and
St. Mary's Rd., Hillsborough
(919) 732-8156

If the aroma of three dozen pigs sizzling on giant gas grills makes your mouth water, you'll want to be in Hillsborough the third weekend in June. The town's festival pays homage to the state's most prolific mammal and the only meat North Carolinians call barbecue—pork. Don't waste your time looking for beef brisket or ribs. About

---

Free Concerts

Free music is a given across the Triangle. Two of the best-attended series are in downtown Raleigh and Durham.

In Raleigh, the Downtown Live Series brings acts to Moore Square every other Saturday from Memorial Day to Labor Day. The lineup usually focuses on the retro circuit and in recent years has included classic rocker Joan Jett and pop stars Arrested Development. The shows begin in the afternoon and last until 11 p.m., and it's easy to come and go.

In Durham, Music on the Lawn at the American Tobacco Campus brings local and regional performers in many genres—blues, jazz, acoustic, salsa, traditional, and new folk among them—to the greenspace in the center of the campus. The series runs May to October and concerts are held on Thursday, Friday, Saturday, or Sunday.

---

three dozen cooking teams fire up their grills on Friday night and roast whole pigs, hoping their 'cue will win over a slate of local celebrity judges. Festival attendees can purchase what the judges don't eat in the form of sandwiches or take-home pints. While you're waiting for the pig to cook, browse the arts and crafts, check out a car show featuring hot rods and vintage autos, and listen to musical entertainment. Country, alt-country, pop, and beach music, that uniquely Carolinian form of blue-eyed R&B, tend to dominate. Admission is $5. Children 12 and younger are admitted free. Park in the Eno River Public Parking Deck near Weaver Street Market for $3 all day or take a shuttle from an outlying stop into downtown.

AMERICAN DANCE FESTIVAL
Durham Performing Arts Center
123 Vivian St., Durham
Duke University, various locations
(919) 684-6402

Hundreds of modern dancers and dance aficio-nados from around the world make their way to Durham every summer for six and a half weeks of performances, workshops, and celebrations of their art. The festival, which began in Bennington, Vermont, in 1934, relocated to Duke University in 1977. Many of the country's most avant-garde and renowned dance troupes—Pilobolus and Paul Taylor Dance Company among them—make regular appearances. Choreographers stage works commissioned expressly for the festival. In addition to a constant program of stage performances, the festival offers a series of youth classes and community programs designed to introduce young people to modern dance. Tickets to individual performances range from $22 to $43. Admission for most community programs is free.

JULY

FESTIVAL FOR THE ENO
W. Point on the Eno River City Park
5101 N. Roxboro Rd., Durham
(919) 620-9099 ext. 207
www.enoriver.org

West Point on the Eno River is Durham's favorite city park, so every Fourth of July thousands gather to celebrate independence and the river with three days of singing, dancing, and cooling off in the shallows beneath the trees. More than 80 acts are on the bill, including gospel groups, local alt-pop bands, bluegrass pickers, singer-songwriter strummers, cloggers, traditional danc-ers, and rockers who sing songs just for kids. The event seeks to raise awareness of the waterway's role in the ecosystem, so along with the music are booths and displays devoted to sustainability issues like beekeeping and composting and vari-ous non-profit organizations. About 100 crafts-men and artisans show up to sell their wares. Playing in the river, whether in canoes or not,

is encouraged, and naturalists offer workshops and tours. Food is sold on site, and coolers are allowed but no alcohol. Admission is $15 per day or $35 for a three-day pass. Shuttles take festival-goers from downtown Durham to the park.

AUGUST

NORTH CAROLINA GAY AND LESBIAN FILM FESTIVAL—DURHAM
Carolina Theatre
301 W. Morgan St., Durham
(919) 560-3030

The four-day film festival showcases works that explore and celebrate issues related to gay, lesbian, bisexual, and transgendered life. The schedule includes short films, documentaries, and feature-length movies with a good mix of the comic and the consciousness-raising. Com-munity organizations attend to get the word out about gay-friendly groups, social clubs, and volunteer opportunities. Admission is $8.50 to individual screenings or $70 for a 10-movie pass.

LAZY DAYS ARTS & CRAFTS FESTIVAL
Academy and Chatham streets, Cary
(919) 469-4061

This celebration of local and regional artists draws tens of thousands to Academy Street in down-town Cary. The juried event highlights a local artist as featured artist of the festival and awards prizes in various artistic categories. Hundreds of arts and crafts booths line the streets selling pottery, textiles, hats, candles, soap, paintings, furniture, baskets, blown glass, stained glass, and dulcimers. Vendors sell requisite fair food, includ-ing Polish sausage, funnel cakes, and kettle corn, and a beer garden offers brews domestic and imported. Area groups have a chance to shine as performances by high-school bands, youth musi-cal groups, town bands, and local magicians and puppeteers are among the perennial favorites. Admission is free.

LA FIESTA DEL PUEBLO
N.C. State Fairgrounds, Raleigh
(919) 835-1525

Sponsored by the Raleigh-based Latino advocacy group El Pueblo, the event brings thousands of Hispanic residents of the Triangle together for two days of celebration, cultural exposition, and community outreach and organization. Four stages of entertainment present popular and traditional music and dance from Central and South America and the Caribbean. In fact, the entertainment aspect of the event has become so popular that organizers are working to return to the emphasis on the youth and adult soccer tournaments that gave La Fiesta its start. Crafters and food vendors round out the festival picture. The variety of Hispanic dishes offered is impressive, so if you've never had to choose between pupusas and empanadas, get ready for a difficult decision. Admission is $5 to the festival, $7 to the festival and soccer tournament. Children 12 and younger are admitted free.

SEPTEMBER

BUGFEST
N. Carolina Museum of Natural Sciences
11 W. Jones St., Raleigh
(919) 733-7450
For a festival that might seem to be aimed squarely at third-grade boys, this insectapalooza winds up having something for anyone who's ever wondered what that thing buzzing in his ear was. During the day, the festival draws thousands of school age kids for a wide variety of bug-themed activities. Crowds fill the commons between the science and history museums and much of the capitol lawn. Participants can watch as cockroaches compete in speed races. They can make origami butterflies. They can taste bug ice cream or crunch on fried crickets. Dance troupes perform bug-related numbers and bands sing odes to insects. Along with the more frivolous activities, the museum offers classes on beekeeping and short lectures and displays on the important role bugs play in the natural world. In the evening, a more grown-up version of the day's events lures adults to contemplate our creepy crawly friends while they listen to music and drink beer. Admission to BugFest is free, but some classes require fees.

EASTERN TRIANGLE FARM TOUR
Various locations in Chatham, Durham,
Franklin, Granville, and Wake counties
(919) 542-2402
www.carolinafarmstewardship.org
Organized by the Carolina Farm Stewardship Association, this two-day tour is similar to the longer-running version that showcases farms in the western Triangle, the Piedmont Farm Tour in April. Passes are $30 per car for access to any of 20 farms or $10 per car per farm.

NORTH CAROLINA LITERARY FESTIVAL
University of N. Carolina at Chapel Hill
Various venues on campus
www.ncliteraryfestival.org
The four-day event celebrates authors from the state and throughout the South with appearances by more than 100 writers and thousands of readers. Past keynote speakers have included John Grisham, Anna Deavere Smith, and Elizabeth Strout. Organizers often tap the bestselling authors who live in the Triangle—Lee Smith, Jill McCorkle, Daniel Wallace, and Alan Gurganus among them—to participate. A children's area offers entertainment for readers 12 and younger. Writers read stories, and kids can create illustrations for their favorite books or tales of their own, watch puppet shows, and meet costumed characters like Clifford the Big Red Dog and the Durham Bull's Wool E. Bull. Admission is free but some events require tickets.

BULL DURHAM BLUES FESTIVAL
Historic Durham Athletic Park
428 Morris St., Durham
(919) 683-1709
The Bull City celebrates the Blues, and the Piedmont Blues style in particular, in this two-day concert. The Piedmont Blues sound, which originated in central North Carolina, relies more heavily on finger picking and recalls ragtime more than the better-known Delta Blues style. St. Joseph's Historic Foundation stages an evening of Blues at the Hayti Heritage Center before the noon-to-midnight outdoor festival packs the Historic Durham Athletic Park. Past performers have

included Bobby Blue Bland, Koko Taylor, Aaron Neville, and Ruth Baker. Plan on a side of barbecue and a cold brew to help the blues go down easy. Kids can play in area just for them, and arts and crafts vendors are on hand with souvenirs of the blues. Tickets are $55 for the Saturday show. Tickets to the Friday night concert are $45. Children ages 2 to 12 get in for $5.

SPARKCON CREATIVE FESTIVAL OF THE SOUTH
Various locations, downtown Raleigh
www.sparkcon.com

Sparkcon is a four-day schedule of events that aims to show off the talents of the Triangle's young creative types and entrepreneurs. Thousands of performers show up to put on an outdoor fashion show featuring designs of local artists, poetry readings, musical performances, video game displays, dance performances, and a cocktail making contest, among others. Art is showcased in galleries as well as in interactive outdoor displays including street-chalking, sculpture, and digital presentations. Discussions and workshops that address topical issues such as urban development and building networks between creative types are also part of the program. The action takes place in various venues from Fayetteville Street to Moore Square, and downtown restaurants offer menus and specials for attendees. It's a growing festival and organizers are making it up as they go along, so anyone who went last year can expect something different this year. Admission to most events is free, but musical performances at clubs usually charge between $10 and $20 for tickets.

CARRBORO MUSIC FESTIVAL
Various venues in Carrboro
(919) 918-7367
www.carrboromusicfestival.com

More than 150 musicians and musical groups play at more than 20 venues, indoors or outside, throughout Carrboro for this daylong festival. Attendees can hear blues and Americana outside the locally owned grocery, take in hip-hop and electronica upstairs from a Mexican restaurant,

or dance in the middle of Main Street to ska and reggae-infused rock. And since Carrboro is rife with fabulous restaurants, tasty fuel for attendees is always close at hand. Food vendors are plentiful as well. A biodiesel-powered shuttle bus runs from the Carrboro Plaza Park and Ride lot to music sites. The festival is free.

RAY PRICE CAPITAL CITY BIKE FEST
Fayetteville St., downtown Raleigh
(919) 832-2261
http://capitalcitybikefest.com

Wheels of steel rumble to Raleigh for this annual celebration of motorcycle culture that fills downtown with the scent of well-oiled leather and the roar of gunning engines. Tribute bands honoring acts that range from the Eagles to Motley Crüe to Alice in Chains and adult magicians are on the entertainment bill. But the real draw is the bikes. Bike owners can enter their machines in 20 competitive classes in hopes that their chrome will win some first-place trophy brass. The event draws thousands. Admission is free.

CENTERFEST
Across from Durham Central Park
534 Foster St., Durham
(919) 560-2722

A jury of respected artists chooses more than 100 artists and artisans to display and sell their works at this two-day event. Mediums include painting, pottery, photography, blown glass, wood, jewelry, fibers, stained glass, and metal. A range of performers, from choral singers to steel drum bands and cloggers to jump rope teams, keep three stages busy. Kids can paint pictures and make masks, magnets, and musical instruments. The festival sponsor, the Durham Arts Council, asks for a $4 per person donation or $12 for families of four or more.

OCTOBER

INTERNATIONAL FESTIVAL OF RALEIGH
Raleigh Convention Center
500 S. Salisbury St., Raleigh
(919) 832-4331
www.internationalfestival.org

A United Nations–like roster of 40 ethnic groups shows up for this event to show off the traditional songs, culture, and food of their homelands. A dance stage features groups from Japan, China, India, Venezuela, Mexico, and the Middle East, to name a few, while singers in the biergarten represent Brazil, France, Ireland, and Portugal. Kids can enjoy storytelling by international exchange students, acrobats, and limbo contests. Adults can watch cooking lessons or try their hips at hula and belly dancing. That would be a great way to work off the food. The array of amazing international cuisine available for tasting impresses even food critics. Arts and crafts from around the world offer something for those looking for longer lasting remembrances of the day. Admission is $6 per day for adults or $15 for a weekend pass. Children 12 and younger get in free.

AVA GARDNER FESTIVAL
Ava Gardner Museum
325 E. Market St., Smithfield
(919) 934-5830
www.avagardner.org
Smithfield's most famous native is without a doubt screen legend Ava Gardner, who was born near the town and is buried there. The Ava Gardner Museum preserves her film legacy and once a year celebrates her life with a film festival. Past themes have explored Gardner's interest in independent films and her relationship with Ernest Hemingway, who penned the novels on which some of her best-known films were based. Activities include screenings of Gardner films, tours of the area focused on sites of significance in Gardner's life, and a gala. Tickets to the two-day festival are $99 per pair. The movie screenings are free, and tour tickets are $10 per person.

WORLD BEER FESTIVAL—DURHAM
Historic Durham Athletic Park
Durham
(800) 977-2337
www.allaboutbeer.com/wbf
Tickets sell out fast to these days of drinking, so beer lovers should watch the Web to see when they go on sale. They can also check six packs of craft brews sold at local stores, because organizers usually stick festival flyers inside as the date nears. Ticketholders can taste more than 300 beers, including regional craft brews and beers from as far away as Europe and the Pacific. Organized by *All About Beer* magazine, headquartered in Durham, the day is divided into two drinking sessions, noon to 4 p.m. and 6 to 10 p.m. Local reggae, bluegrass, and dance bands provide the music.

The magazine sponsors two World Beer Festivals in the Triangle, one in the fall and the other in the spring. The fall event is preferred for its venue, the Historic Durham Athletic Park. It was home to the minor league Durham Bulls baseball team until the new park was built in the early 1990s, and had a starring role in *Bull Durham* alongside Susan Sarandon and Kevin Costner.

NORTH CAROLINA STATE FAIR
N.C. State Fairgrounds
1025 Blue Ridge Rd., Raleigh
(919) 828-9478
www.ncstatefair.org
Tens of thousands of people from all over the state pour into Raleigh for this nine-day celebration of agriculture, commerce, and deep fat frying. Single-day attendance on some Saturdays in years past has topped 118,000. It's fairly common for Triangle residents to catch the "fair flu" and play hooky from work so they can enjoy a weekday trip to the fair with only 50,000 or so of their fellow North Carolinians. Midway rides and games are big draws as are the food booths, where fare runs the gamut from traditional favorites like chicken, pastries, barbecue, cotton candy, and corn dogs to more innovative food-on-a-stick creations like whole cheeseburgers breaded and fried. A lineup of mostly country and contemporary Christian acts performs in Dorton Arena, the parabolic concert hall on the grounds. Past headliners have included Montgomery Gentry, Kellie Pickler, and Third Day. In addition to the traditional displays of farm animals and preserved agricultural products, visitors can check out exhibits on green technology, landscape architecture, and the farm-to-table movement.

A fireworks display lights up the sky nightly at 9:45. Admission is $7. Children ages 2 to 12 get in for $2. Ride tickets are $1 each, and rides require between two and six tickets. Get free admission on the second Thursday of the fair by bringing four cans of food to donate to the hungry.

SHAKORI HILLS FALL FESTIVAL
Shakori Hills festival grounds
1439 Henderson Tanyard Rd., Pittsboro
(919) 542-8142
www.shakorihills.org

This fall version of the Shakori Hills festival is much like the spring event (see April). Admission ranges from $95 for a four-day adult pass to between $22 and $36 for one-day passes, depending on the day. A four-day pass for ages 13 to 15 is $45, with one-day passes ranging from $11 to $18. Children 12 and younger get in free. Vehicle camping is $60 per day.

CITY OF OAKS MARATHON
Start and end at N.C. State's Centennial Campus
www.cityofoaksmarathon.com

Raleigh is not a flat city, which makes its marathon tough. The course does have its rewards, though. The scenery is varied, ranging from the N.C. State University's new Centennial campus to Raleigh's refurbished downtown to the wooded trails of Umstead State Park. Relatively new to the running calendar, the race has drawn thousands in recent years. Runners can do the whole 26.2-mile course or the half-marathon. The race is a qualifier for the Boston Marathon, and time limits of 3½ hours for the half marathon and 6 hours for the marathon are imposed. A health expo featuring 40 vendors runs on Friday and Saturday at N.C. State's McKimmon Center. The entry fee is $80 for the marathon and $75 for the half.

RALEIGH WIDE OPEN
City Plaza, Fayetteville St.
(919) 996-8500

A funny thing happened when Raleigh cut the ribbon on its makeover of Fayetteville Street in 2006. Thousands of people crammed into a couple of blocks downtown to see what it looked like. Once a centerpiece and requisite parade route for events of statewide significance, the stretch of Fayetteville Street between the State Capitol and Memorial Auditorium was closed to traffic in the 1970s to become a pedestrian walkway. The experiment was deemed a failure by the turn of the century, and reopening Fayetteville Street to vehicle traffic was part of downtown revitalization efforts. Since the reopening, the city has marked the anniversary of the celebration with a street festival and concert attended by thousands. For some suburbanites, it's the only time they venture into the heart of the city. The event is free.

HALLOWEEN ON FRANKLIN STREET
Franklin St. between Columbia St. and Rosemary St., Chapel Hill

Tens of thousands of costumed partiers turn out on Franklin Street in Chapel Hill on Halloween night. It's a see-and-be-shocked costume show that has grown from a UNC student tradition to a major, unofficial festival. Adult revelers fill the closed street, stopping at the bars that line either side for grown-up treats. Estimates have put the party at 80,000 people in recent years. The town, which must control the crowd and clean up after it, has sought to limit the attendees, but without much success.

NOVEMBER

CARY BAND DAY
Downtown Cary and Cary High School
www.caryband.org/band_day/cbd.shtml

For five decades, high school bands have come to Cary to bang their drums and toot their horns as they compete for the coveted Heart of Cary award in one of the longest-running high school band competitions in the country. Between 25 and 40 bands from schools in North Carolina and surrounding states regularly attend. Residents line the streets to watch the bands march from downtown, beginning at 10 a.m., down Walnut Street to Cary High School for the competition. Tickets to the stadium competition are $6 for adults, $3 for ages 65 and older, and free for those 10 and younger.

VEGETARIAN SOCIETY OF THE TRIANGLE THANKSGIVING FEAST
Cafe Parizade
2200 W. Main St., Durham
www.trianglevegsociety.org

Organizers say it is the largest vegetarian Thanksgiving Day event in the country. It draws as many as 600 people, all of whom prefer tofu to turkey and long for kinship on a day traditionally spent devouring meat. Diners come from the Triangle's healthy vegetarian communities and from other states as well. The buffet menu includes gourmet vegan dishes such as cardamom pickled beets, seared seitan with peppercorns and fig glaze, and carpaccio vegetale—vegetables sliced paper thin. There are two seatings to accommodate the crowds. The cost is $26.50 for adults, $7 for children ages 5 to 10, and free for those 4 and younger. Ticket sales are in advance only.

DECEMBER

CHATHAM STUDIO TOUR
Chatham County
http://chathamstudiotour.com

For two weekends in December, the artists and crafts makers who work in the studios scattered throughout rural Chatham County welcome visitors and shoppers to come in and peruse their creations. About 50 artists participate, including painters, potters, weavers, sculptors, jewelers, and furniture makers. The Chatham Artists Guild prints maps of participating studios that are available at the General Store Cafe in Pittsboro, the ArtsCenter in Carrboro, and other arts organizations and supporting businesses in the area.

THEATRE IN THE PARK'S
A CHRISTMAS CAROL
Memorial Auditorium
Progress Energy Center
2 E. S. St., Raleigh
(919) 831-6058

If Charles Dickens had written musical comedies—well, the world would be a different place, wouldn't it? But if you like your Victorian morality plays set to song, Theatre in the Park's A Christmas Carol is your holiday ticket. Since 1974, thousands of fans have returned year after year to see Ira David Wood III as Scrooge in the lighthearted adaptation of Dickens that he wrote and stars in. The quality of the production is high, with lavish costumes and sets, and past cast members include Michael C. Hall, Lauren Kennedy, Frankie Muniz, and Evan Rachel Wood, daughter of Ira. The play runs for a week, with 11 stagings. Tickets range from $21 to $77.

RALEIGH LITTLE THEATRE'S CINDERELLA
A.J. Fletcher Theatre
Progress Energy Center
2 E. S. St., Raleigh
(919) 821-3111

Most of the audience will tell you they return to see this comic production of the fairy tale not so much for the beautiful heroine but for her two unattractive tormentors, Henrietta and Gertrude, the Ugly Step-Sisters. In an embrace of the English tradition of holiday pantomime, the sisters are played by men. And the female personas of these men, Dennis Poole and Tim Cherry, make Walter Mathau and Jack Lemmon in Some Like It Hot seem like supermodels. It's a funny show and has drawn thousands for more than 25 years. Cinderella runs for nine stagings over 10 days. Tickets are $16 to $26.

CAROLINA BALLET'S NUTCRACKER
Memorial Auditorium
Progress Energy Center
2 E. S. St., Raleigh
(919) 719-0900

Renowned choreographer Robert Weiss, the ballet's artistic director, meets Tchaikovsky's romantic music with his own interpretation for this holiday tradition. Sugarplum fairies, mouse kings, marzipan—it's all there. A young company, with a little more than a decade under its tutu, the Carolina Ballet is well respected for its talent and for Weiss's vision. Triangle's Nutcracker lovers are fortunate to have such a top-notch version of the classic within their reach, and they show their love by turning out appreciatively. There are 14 stagings of the ballet, with a few after Christmas Day. Tickets are $20 to $100.

TINSEL TOWN
Koka Booth Amphitheatre
8003 Regency Parkway, Cary
(919) 462-2025

Most Southerners have never seen a white Christmas or glided hand-in-hand across an icy pond. But as more transplants make the Triangle home, a collective longing for cold sets in during the darkest days of winter. To oblige, Booth Amphitheatre sets up an outdoor skating rink, surrounded by trees dressed in white lights. Santa visits on the weekends. Holiday music plays. Hot cocoa is served. Sometime the weather even cooperates and Jack Frost show up to nip at skaters' noses. Admission for skaters Monday through Thursday is $6, or $4 for ages 3 to 12. Admission Friday through Sunday is $8 for adults, $6 for children. Skate rentals are $2, free for those younger than 2. For those who just want to walk around and take in the winter, admission is free.

FIRST NIGHT RALEIGH
Fayetteville St. and various locations,
downtown Raleigh
(919) 832-8699

First Night Raleigh began in 1990, and has gained momentum ever since. The party involves musicians in genres from opera to gospel to rock, dance performances, sleigh rides, poetry readings, and juggling comedians performing in venues spread across downtown. A separate roster of activities aims to entertain children. At the heart of the celebration is the dropping of the acorn. Inspired by New York City's New Year's Eve ball drop, Raleigh, the City of Oaks, commissioned a bronze acorn the size of a Buick, which it drops twice on December 31. One drop occurs at 6 p.m. for families with children, and the other is at midnight. Before each, a parade, which anyone can join simply by getting in line, marches down Fayetteville Street to the drop site. Paperhand Puppet Intervention's giant creations are always part of the procession. The parade is free. Admission to other First Night Activities requires the purchase of a button. Buttons are $12, $10 for ages 6 to 12. Children five and younger get in free with an adult wearing a button.

SHOPPING

The Triangle is home to a plethora of shopping malls, most of which are dominated by the expected big-box stores. In recent years, the number of smaller specialty boutiques has begun to grow as well.

A couple of areas offer a concentration of these boutiques and independently owned stores, where shoppers could spend an hour or two browsing, going from store to store, stopping in between for a coffee or snack. Cameron Village, in central Raleigh, is one of the Triangle's most established shopping districts. The first suburban shopping center in Raleigh, it has been drawing shoppers from around the region and the state since the 1950s and '60s. Today Cameron Village is home to national chains of women's clothing stores as well as uber-chic women's boutiques that feature designer clothing and accessories, art galleries, craft shops, children's stores, and gift shops. Another well-established, boutique-heavy area is North Hills. The shopping center underwent a massive upgrade in recent years and is today home to several women's boutiques, children's stores, art galleries, and upscale restaurants in addition to a movie theater, a day spa, and a hotel.

For antiques and gifts, shoppers can head to historic downtown Pittsboro. Well-preserved 19th- and early 20th-century buildings populate the blocks surrounding the center of town. Shoppers can find antiques, jewelry, pottery, art, garden goods, and a thrift store.

A local co-op grocery and a cafe are also near the square. Historic downtown Hillsborough is similarly equipped to entertain shoppers, with antiques, art, a wine store, and several restaurants.

If you're looking for something in particular, you may be able to find it at some of the disparate, independently owned stores and shops scattered throughout the Triangle. This chapter aims to bring some of the more obscure merchants to light, from a nationally known mid-century modern antiques dealer to every Raleigh woman's favorite handbag designer.

ANTIQUES

Durham

THE CLOCK DEPOT
3750 Chapel Hill Blvd., Durham
(919) 402-8714
www.theclockdepot.com
A local family owns this shop, which specializes in nothing but stately timepieces for the home—grandfather clocks, mantel clocks, wall clocks, weather clocks, cuckoo clocks, atomic clocks. Designs range from antique standing grandfathers to funky wall clocks inspired by the aesthetic of Frank Lloyd Wright. It's a nostalgic departure from big-box stores, where clocks are but one among thousands of items in the inventory.

Pittsboro

FRENCH CONNECTIONS
178 Hillsboro St., Pittsboro
(919) 545-9296
Antiques from France, art from Senegal, and baskets from half a dozen African countries are among the treasures you'll find at French Connections. The shop also carries a range of hard-to-find fabrics, including French florals and African batiks. The owners are a married couple. He is a South African–born Frenchman, and she is from North Carolina. Their shop, housed in a turn-of-the-20th-century house in downtown Pittsboro, reflects their travels and passions.

Cameron Antiques District

Cameron sits off U.S. 1, about an hour south of Raleigh and about 15 miles north of Southern Pines. Reach the historic district by taking N.C. 24/27 from U.S. 1. For antiques hunters, it's a worthy daytrip in its own right. It's also a fun stop on a tour of the Pinehurst and Southern Pines area. The town has made its name with Carthage Street (N.C. 24/27), flanked by a dozen antique shops housed in turn-of-the-century homes. The range of wares is impressive, with vintage quilts, 19th-century armoires, stained glass, and mid-century kitsch hiding in the nooks of the old houses and galleries. For lunch, try the **Dewberry Deli and Soda Fountain** in the basement of the Old Hardware Building at 485 Carthage St. for sandwiches and chocolate malts served in a retro setting. There's also **Miss Belle's Tea Room,** at 562 Carthage St., for a more refined repast.

Cameron Antiques District
Carthage St. (N.C. 24/27)
(910) 245-3055
www.antiquesofcameron.com

Raleigh

FATHER AND SON
107 W. Hargett St., Raleigh
(919) 832-3030
www.swankarama.com
Your first glance around Father and Son might not convince you that a mid-century modern treasure awaits inside, but once your eyes adjust to the jumbled inventory, you'll realize you've come to the right place. Sleek retro pieces that look as if they came from the set of *Bewitched*, vintage album covers and signs, local artwork, and oddities galore compete for space in the store's two-levels. Upstairs is vintage clothing. The shop's owner is nationally renowned as a dealer in mid-century modern pieces and his clients have included actress Hilary Swank. The inventory changes frequently, so there's always a reason to pop in.

PIRATE'S CHEST ANTIQUES
2050 Clark Ave., Cameron Village
Raleigh
(919) 833-1230
With more than 20,000 square feet of retail space and more than 30 vendors, Pirate's Chest offers a wide variety of merchandise, from stately to quirky. It's easy to spend an hour or two perusing the merchandise before you stop and wonder where the time went. It's especially good hunting ground for antique jewelry.

BOOKSTORES

BARNES & NOBLE
Cary Commons
760 SouthE. Maynard Rd., Cary
(919) 467-3866

New Hope Commons
5400 New Hope Commons, Durham
(919) 489-3012

The Streets at Southpoint
8030 Renaissance Parkway, Suite 855,
Durham
(919) 806-1930

Brier Creek
8431 Brier Creek Parkway, Raleigh
(919) 484-9903

Crabtree Valley Mall
4325 Glenwood Ave., Raleigh
(919) 782-0030

Triangle Town Center
5959 Triangle Town Blvd., Raleigh
(919) 792-2140
www.barnesandnoble.com

The chain has six stores in the Triangle. Each offers a range of programs, including storytime activities for preschoolers and older children and appearances by local and national authors. Wi-Fi is available throughout the Barnes & Noble stores in the Triangle, which makes their open, airy cafes popular spots for work and study. The stores' large, colorful children's areas include mini-theaters with kid-size benches where young readers can get comfortable in settings made just for them. Customer service is uniformly reliable with booksellers who are readily available. The stores' music sections include listening stations. Programming is especially strong at the Cary Commons, Brier Creek, Streets at Southpoint and New Hope Commons stores, which organize several themed book groups for adults and host frequent author events.

THE BOOKSHOP
400 W. Franklin St., Chapel Hill
(919) 942- 5178
www.internationalistbooks.org
The Bookshop specializes in rare and used books, and has an inventory of more than 100,000 titles. Specialties include humanities, social sciences, foreign languages, and North Carolina and Southern history and literature. The shop has been in operation for more than 25 years, and has recently changed hands.

BORDERS
1541 Beaver Creek Commons Dr., Apex
(919) 363-8446

1751 Walnut St., Cary
(919) 469-1930

1807 Fordham Blvd., Chapel Hill
(919) 929-8332

404-101 E. Six Forks Rd., Raleigh
(919) 755-9424

8825 N. Six Forks Rd., Raleigh
(919) 845-1154

Raleigh-Durham International Airport
Terminal 1, near Gate A17
(919) 840-1155
www.borders.com

The Triangle is home to six outposts of the national chain, including one in RDU airport. Free Wi-Fi in Borders' cafes keeps the coffee-and-keyboard set happy. The central Raleigh location on Six Forks Road has a patio and is an easy walk or bike ride from the city's greenway. The North Raleigh outpost boasts an extensive travel section, and Cary customers are enjoying the recent renovations made at the Borders on Walnut Street. The Chapel Hill location, set just off Interstate 40 between UNC and Duke, offers a wide selection of contemporary literature and arts and sciences books. Programming at Triangle Borders' stores is aimed at movie lovers as well as readers and includes midnight release parties for books and DVDs. The RDU location is a boon for readers who left home without tucking a paperback in their carry-on.

INTERNATIONALIST BOOKS
405 W. Franklin St., Chapel Hill
(919) 942-1740
www.internationalistbooks.org
Internationalist Books is dedicated to activist literature, independent and alternative publishers and hard-to-find titles. Founded in the 1980s as a source of information for the anti-apartheid movement, the store today serves as a meeting place for a number of progressive causes. A co-op owns Internationalist Books, and members volunteer their time working in the store.

MCINTYRE'S FINE BOOKS
2000 Fearrington Village Center, Pittsboro
(919) 542-3030
www.fearrington.com
In keeping with the aesthetic of the carefully tended village that surrounds it, McIntyre's is the picture-book ideal of a bookshop. Follow the red-brick path to the front door, step inside, and find your way to in a wingback chair by the fire where you can settle in with a prospective purchase. The shop carries a good selection of young adult and children's books and a strong collection of mystery fiction, among other genres. The shop is a frequent stop for national and local authors.

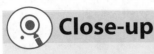

Close-up

Farmers' Markets

In addition to the nationally known Carrboro Farmers' Market and the large State Farmers' Market in Raleigh, both of which are profiled in the book's Attractions chapter, the Triangle enjoys dozens more. And it seems another crop of markets pops up every season. Many are growers-only markets, which means market managers ensure that vendors who sell produce or meat had a hand in raising it and that it came from nearby fields and farms. Settings can range from a half-dozen tents set up in a suburban parking lot to a row of vendors spread out beneath the trees in a downtown square.

Most farmers' markets run April through November, though a few are year-round. Most meet on Saturday mornings, and some offer a mid-week session as well. The Chatham County Cooperative Extension Agency's Web site hosts a useful guide to Triangle markets, updated by Extension Agent Debbie Roos. The site offers lists of markets in eight counties, including Chatham, Durham, Orange, and Wake. It also presents farmer profiles and links to other resources related to the area's farm-to-table scene. Find it at www.ces.ncsu.edu/chatham/ag/sustag. Details are subject to change from season to season so check the Web site for updated information.

CHATHAM

Carolina Brewery Farmers' Market
Carolina Brewery Brewpub & Restaurant
120 Lowes Dr., Suite 100, Pittsboro
8 a.m. to noon Saturday

Fearrington Farmers' Market
Fearrington Village
East Camden, Pittsboro
4 p.m. to early evening Tuesday

Pittsboro Farmers' Market
Chatham County Fairgrounds
Dr. Martin Luther King, Jr. Drive, Pittsboro
3:30 to 6:30 p.m. Thursday

DURHAM

Durham Farmers' Market
Durham Central Park
501 Foster St., Durham

8 a.m. to noon Saturday April through November
10:00 a.m. to noon December through March
3:30 to 6:30 p.m. Wednesday, starting in May

ORANGE

Carrboro Farmers' Market
301 West Main St., Carrboro
7 a.m. to noon Saturday, 9 a.m. to noon winter
3:30 to 6:30 p.m. Wednesday April through October

Eno River Farmers' Market
Public Market House in Downtown Hillsborough
120 East Margaret Lane, Hillsborough
8 a.m. to noon Saturday, April through November
10 a.m. to 1 p.m. first and third Saturdays, December through March

---

The store's programming includes storytime for preschoolers and open mic night for readers and writers.

QUAIL RIDGE BOOKS AND MUSIC
3522 Wade Ave., Raleigh
(919) 828-1588
www.quailridgebooks.com

In Raleigh's Quail Ridge Shopping Center, the independently owned bookstore has been a Raleigh favorite since 1984. The shelves hold a wide variety of titles, including the best selection of local and Southern authors in the Triangle. The stores hosts three or four authors per week, ranging from celebrities to local favorites. Program-

Hillsborough Farmers' Market
Home Depot parking lot at the intersection
of NC 86 and I-40
Hillsborough
8 a.m. to noon Saturday year-round
4 to 7 p.m. Wednesday, starting in April

South Estes Farmers' Market
Parking lot at A Southern Season
201 South Estes Dr., Chapel Hill
8 a.m. to noon Saturday, April through
November
9 a.m. to noon first and third Saturday
inside University Mall, December through
March

Southern Village Farmers' Market
Market Street in Southern Village,
Chapel Hill
4 to 7 p.m. Thursday

WAKE

Apex Farmers' Market
Downtown Apex Depot
220 North Salem St., Apex
9 a.m. to 2 p.m. Saturday

Cary Downtown Farmers' Market
Chatham Square, 744 East Chatham St., Cary
8 a.m. to 12:30 p.m. Saturday
3 to 6 p.m. Tuesday

Holly Springs Farmers' Market
Town Hall Parking Lot
128 South Main St., Holly Springs
8 a.m. to noon Saturday

Raleigh Downtown Farmers' Market
City Plaza, Downtown Raleigh
Fayetteville Street, Raleigh
10 a.m. to 2 p.m. Wednesday

Midtown Farmers' Market
The Commons at North Hills
4160 Main at North Hills St., Raleigh
8 a.m. to noon Saturday

North Raleigh Farmers' Market
Falls River Town Center
3900 Merton Dr., Raleigh
8 a.m. to noon Saturday
4 to 7 p.m. Wednesday

State Farmers' Market
1201 Agriculture St., Raleigh
5 a.m. to 6 p.m. Monday through Saturday
8 a.m. to 6 p.m. Sunday
Open year-round

Wake Forest Farmers' Market
Historic downtown Wake Forest
150 South White St., Wake Forest
8 a.m. to noon Saturday

Western Wake Farmers' Market
Carpenter Village Marketplace, Cary
Morrisville-Carpenter Rd., between NC 55
and Davis Drive
8 a.m. to noon

ming also includes musical performances, book club events, and events for teens and children.

THE REGULATOR BOOKSHOP
720 Ninth St., Durham
(919) 286-2700
www.regulatorbookshop.com

The Regulator has been a staple on Ninth Street, beside Duke's campus, since 1976. The independently owned shop has hosted the likes of former President Jimmy Carter, *A Year in Provence* author Peter Mayle, and *Goosebumps* scribe R. L. Stine. Its selection is wide and varied, and programming aims at a wide variety of readers. Events include "Peter's Pajama Party," which involves local songwriter Peter Holsapple singing songs and telling stories in his PJs.

GARDEN SHOPS

ATLANTIC AVENUE ORCHID AND GARDEN
5217 Atlantic Ave., Raleigh
(919) 878-8877
www.atlanticavenuegarden.com
The North Raleigh store has been in the orchid and gardening business for more than a dozen years. Atlantic Avenue has a vast selection of plants and gardening paraphernalia. Inventory includes bird supplies, irrigation supplies, and the store's own brand of fescue. They have a large selection of orchids and orchid supplies as well as tropicals and topiaries. Their selection of shrubs, trees, perennials, and container gardening plants is impressive as well.

LOGAN TRADING CO.
707 Semart Dr., Raleigh
(919) 828-5337
www.logantrd.com
Downtown in the Shops at Seaboard Station, Logan's has a knowledgeable staff that takes a lot of the guesswork out of buying plants. The business began as a vendor booth at the State Farmers' Market in 1965 and moved to the old Seaboard Rail Station downtown in 1991. Logan's selection of perennials, annuals, vegetables, trees, and shrubs is vast, and they offer ideas to suit particular gardening situations. Inside the store is a good selection of tropicals, orchids, bird supplies, pots, and, when in season, some fresh local produce. Logan's is also home to the Seaboard Cafe, which serves lunch six days a week. Logan's is closed on Sunday.

STONE BROTHERS DURHAM
700 Washington St., Durham
(919) 682-1311
www.stonebrothers.com
A small shop in downtown Durham near the Historic Durham Athletic Park has a great selection of plants and garden products, including some things you're not likely to find elsewhere. Their selection of tomato and vegetable stakes alone is impressive, going far beyond the usual cages to offer more attractive alternatives. The store also offers classes and operates a great online catalog at its Web site.

GOURMET SHOPS AND GROCERIES

Chapel Hill and Carrboro

3 CUPS
227 S. Elliott Rd., Chapel Hill
(919) 968-8993
www.3cups.com
This store sells wine, tea, coffee, and chocolate for consumers with discriminating palates who care about where their drinks come from. Wines are sourced from small estates, coffees come from small farmers, and the people who work at 3 Cups can tell you all about them. The shop also carries locally made cheeses and jams. The cafe serves foods from local restaurants and bakers and wine, tea, and coffee by the cup or glass. But don't go in and rattle off an order for a grande latte with soy milk to go. No espresso drinks are offered, just French press coffee made while you wait.

A SOUTHERN SEASON
201 S. Estes Dr., Chapel Hill
(919) 929-9466
www.southernseason.com
The Zabar's of the South, A Southern Season is a 60,000-square-foot food and cooking store packed with cookware, cookbooks, cooking machines, spices, hard-to-find ingredients, a cheese and meat counter, a wine shop, and a demonstration kitchen. It is a mecca for foodies of all stripes, Southern and otherwise. The store hosts events featuring regional and national names in food and offers a full slate of cooking lessons that range from purveyors' lectures on tea to instructional sessions on how to cook fish or make empanadas. Instructional wine tastings are held on Friday nights. Also on site is the Weathervane, a cafe where chefs make use of the store's bounty of ingredients.

WEAVER STREET
101 E. Weaver St., Carrboro
(919) 929-0010

228 S. Churton St., Hillsborough
(919) 245-5050

716 Market St. in Southern Village, Chapel Hill
(919) 929-2009

Weaver Street is Carrboro's landmark co-op grocery, specializing in locally grown and made food, fair trade goods, and environmentally sound products. The market bakes its own bread and pastries and sells vitamins and herbal supplements, antibiotic- and hormone-free meats, locally grown produce, and prepared foods made on site. Opened in 1988, the market now has three locations and operates Panzanella, a Mediterranean-style restaurant in nearby Carr Mill Mall. The large lawn and patio serve as a meeting place for crowds of Carrboro residents on most any warm day.

Durham

FOSTER'S MARKET
2694 Chapel Hill Blvd., Durham
(919) 489-3944

750 Martin Luther King Jr. Blvd., Chapel Hill
(919) 967-3663
www.fostersmarket.com

A former caterer for and cookbook collaborator with Martha Stewart, Sarah Foster opened her market in Durham in 1990. The cozy shop is part cafe, part prepared foods counter, part gourmet provisioner. The prepared foods are made with seasonal ingredients, and the grocery items include locally roasted coffee, good wines, and rare confections. Foster opened her second market in Chapel Hill in 1998. The Durham market is a popular lunch spot, especially when weather permits sitting on the Adirondack chairs out front.

PARKER AND OTIS
112 S. Duke St., Durham
(919) 683-3200
www.parkerandotis.com

In downtown Durham near Brightleaf Square, Parker and Otis is a coffee shop and sandwich counter surrounded by an interesting selection of wines, gourmet goods, greeting cards, and sweets. The store has a selection of specialty candies, shining like gems in old apothecary jars, used to fill the store's custom-made gift baskets. The cafe serves breakfast and lunch and offers prepared foods as well as sandwiches.

Morrisville

CAPRIFLAVORS
1012 Morrisville Parkway, Morrisville
(919) 462-9255
www.capriflavors.com

Owners Costanzo and Titina Vuottoare are an Italian couple who spent much of their lives on the island of Capri, where, it is said, Titina's mother invented the caprese salad. Today the couple runs a thriving Italian food import business that provides pastas, flours, sparkling sodas, ceramics, and a host of other culinary products from their Italian homeland. Titina teaches cooking lessons on site, imparting secrets of Italian culinary arts.

CLOTHING BOUTIQUES

Children's

DILLY DALLY/OH, BABY!
4209-108 Lassiter Mill Rd., Raleigh
(919) 844-7557
www.dillydally.net

Dilly Dally, which has a store in Charlotte as well, specializes in upscale furniture and accessories for nurseries and childrens' rooms. Recently merged with Oh, Baby!, the North Hills site now offers upscale clothing as well. Loyal patrons love the attentive staff and the unique selections. A play kitchen helps keep children entertained while parents peruse the inventory.

MOXIE KIDS
2026 Cameron St., Cameron Village, Raleigh
(919) 821-3348
www.moxiekidsonline.com

Serving the eight and younger crowd, this shop is where to find stylish baby shower gifts, from bibs to high chairs. The inventory includes a large selection of shoes and modern nursery decor. The clothes tend to be less frilly and more hip, in a range of colors that go far beyond pink and baby blue.

SILLY GOOSE
1839-104 S. Main St., Wake Forest
(919) 453-1900
www.shopsillygoose.com
In the Factory in Wake Forest, Silly Goose carries a wide range of nationally known children's clothing designers for girls age 10 and younger and boys under age 7. Amanda Remembered, Cach-Cach Clothing, Jack and Lily, Baby Nay et al, Royal Child, Sarah Louise, Sweet Potatoes, Victoria Kids, Viva la Fête, WeeOnes, Will'beth, and Zutano are among the shop's best-known labels. The staff's pretty gift wrapping is renowned, which makes Silly Goose a great place to pick up a shower or birthday gift.

Men's

CHOCKEY'S MEN'S DESIGNER FASHION
6325-A Falls of Neuse, Raleigh
(919) 872-3166
www.chockeysmensfashion.com
In North Raleigh, Chockey's carries a wide range of suits and men's wear and specializes in custom fitting. The inventory ranges from suits to jeans and includes accessories and shoes as well. The owners stay on top of fashion trends while continuing to serve their more conservative clients who prefer traditional looks. The store carries a range of designers including Canali and Tommy Bahama. *Esquire* magazine named Chockey's one of the top 100 men's clothing stores in the country.

NORMAN STOCKTON
107 Meadowmont Village Circle, Chapel Hill
(919) 945-0800
A nationally respected North Carolina men's clothier and tailor that has been around since

Holly Aiken Bags

Take a look around any Raleigh restaurant or party and you'll no doubt see a few Holly Aiken bags. The bags have clean lines and Aiken's signature minimal stitch line-and-circle detailing. Their sturdy, made-in-the-USA construction and distinctive style have made them wildly popular. Color schemes include retro combinations such as mustard and parchment, gunmetal and tomato, and avocado and olive. Aiken also joins forces with local artists to incorporate oddball cartoonish art in some designs. A graduate of N.C. State's School of Design, Aiken sells bags from her downtown shop, Stitch, at 20 East Hargett St. and online at www.hollyaiken.com, or call (919) 833-8770.

1909, Norman Stockton carries labels including Canali, Burberry, Zanella, Robert Talbott, and Gitman. The store is known for its tailoring and top-notch customer service. Norman Stockton, which has a second location in Winston-Salem, is among the top 100 men's clothing stores in the country, according to *Esquire* magazine.

Women's

BEANIE + CECIL OF RALEIGH
412 Daniels St., Cameron Village, Raleigh
(919) 821-5455
www.beanieandcecil.com
In Cameron Village, the boutique carries clothing from designers not found elsewhere in the Triangle and pieces from well-known lines like DVF and Nicole Miller. Fashionistas appreciate Beanie + Cecil's minimalist aesthetic, which lets the clothes speak for themselves without interference from overwrought displays. It's a go-to place

for special-occasion dresses. The Kate Spade bags are in the back—make sure to check and see if any are on sale!

GALATEA BOUTIQUE
10 W. Franklin St., Shops at Seaboard Station, Raleigh
(919) 833-8565
www.galateaboutique.com
Find designer clothes from Barbara Lesser and 2 Star Dog as well as accessories from local jewelry makers and handbags from Hobo Intl. at this hip but laid-back boutique in the Shops at Seaboard Station. The hat selection is extensive. Galatea's sales staff is low-pressure yet helpful. The store stocks a range of sizes—quite refreshing for a boutique.

SCOUT & MOLLY'S
4421-103B Six Forks Rd., N. Hills Mall, Raleigh
(919) 881-0303

105 Meadowmont Village Circle, Chapel Hill
(919) 969-8886
www.scoutandmollys.com
Nanette Lepore, BCBG, and MBLEM by Mandy Moore are among the labels on the racks at Scout and Molly's boutiques in North Hills mall and Chapel Hill's Meadowmont. The stores are cozy and comfortable, and the sales staffs are helpful. It's a great place to find everything from jeans to a flirty party dress. Next door to the North Hills store is WALK, a Scout & Molly's shoe boutique carrying designers including Marc Jacobs and Michael Kors and bags by BCBG, Heather Hawkins, and Joe's Jeans, to name a few. Scout & Molly's offers its own private label jewelry as well as pieces by local designers. The shop is named for the owner's beloved Labrador retrievers, who can sometimes be found lolling about on the boutique floor.

CRAFTS

THE COLLECTORS GALLERY
443 Fayetteville St., Raleigh
(919) 828-6500
www.thecollectorsgallery.com
In a gleaming new space on Raleigh's downtown plaza, the Collectors Gallery offers stylish works by a range of North Carolina artisans and crafts workers. Mediums include blown glass, pottery, and woodworks, with a leaning toward contemporary styles.

NORTH CAROLINA CRAFTS GALLERY
212 W. Main St., Carrboro
(919) 942-4048
www.nccraftsgallery.com
Find artisanal works by North Carolina craftsmen and craftswomen at this Carrboro gallery. Selections include traditional and modern pottery, blown glass, turned woodworks, jewelry, garden art, and folk art. More than 500 artists from across the state contribute to the inventory. The gallery hosts two shows per month and artisans are often on site for receptions held during the community's Second Friday Art Walk.

SEAGROVE POTTERY
443 B Daniels St., Cameron Village
(919) 831-9696
www.seagrovepotterygallery.com
The Seagrove area of North Carolina, southwest of the Triangle, has been known for its pottery for more than 200 years. Today, a couple of hundred potters have studios in the countryside in and around Asheboro, comprising the largest pottery community in the country. This gallery in Cameron Village collects a range of Seagrove works, from traditional utilitarian bowls and platters to unique decorative pieces.

DAY TRIPS AND WEEKEND GETAWAYS

Living in the Triangle puts you within a few hours' drive of some of the most beautiful scenery in the country. I-40, the main artery through the region, provides access to the Blue Ridge Mountains to the west and the beaches of the Cape Fear Coast to the east. The internationally renowned golf courses of the Pinehurst and Southern Pines area are little more than an hour away. A three-hour drive can put you in the middle of Charlotte's glittery downtown or standing on a quiet stretch of sand in the shadow of a 19th-century lighthouse, watching wild horses run in the wind. While the make-your-friends-jealous destinations abound, the state also holds hidden gems that await along less-traveled roads, like the potteries of Seagrove and the tiny antiques village of Cameron. As more people have discovered the charms of North Carolina's getaways in recent years, the quality of the food and levels of service have risen to the challenge, meaning you can find an interesting meal in just about any corner of the state. And if avoiding high-season crowds at the beach or the mountains is your aim, it's easy to take advantage of low-season deals. You may find that the solitude of an empty tourist town has a calming effect.

DAY TRIPS

Wilmington and Wrightsville Beach

Downtown Wilmington and Wrightsville Beach sit 10 miles apart on opposite sides of a narrow peninsula bounded by the Cape Fear River to the west and the Atlantic Ocean to the east. Between them, they offer the architecture and history of the antebellum South, great dining and shopping, and the lighthearted fun of a day at the beach. A straight shot down I-40 from the Triangle, getting there takes between 2½ and 3 hours. Both destinations are best explored on foot, as parking is scarce downtown and at the beach.

Downtown Wilmington

Wilmington sits on the Cape Fear River, and for much of the 19th century its prowess as a shipping center made it among the most prominent towns in North Carolina. Its historic waterfront recalls the days when ships docked here to take on the cotton crop from nearby plantations, and slaves found means of escape on those seagoing vessels. The riverfront along Water Street and the surrounding historic district are now among the state's most charming tourist destinations. In recent years, the well-weathered blocks have served as backdrops for stars including Katie Holmes of *Dawson's Creek*, Sophia Bush of *One Tree Hill*, and Danny McBride of *East Bound and Down*, all filmed in Wilmington. A stroll along the **Riverwalk,** which parallels Water Street from Nun Street to the riverfront Hilton, offers a chance to watch ospreys lighting on the treetops of undeveloped islands and see the **USS North Carolina,** a World War II–era battleship open for tours. Above the water the historic district's well-preserved late 19th-century and early 20th-century homes and B&Bs sit surrounded by live oaks draped with Spanish moss. Several restaurants along the Riverwalk have decks and balconies where you can sip a drink riverside. And docked along the Riverwalk is the **Henrietta III,** a steamboat replica that offers sightseeing and sunset cruises. At the intersection of Market and Water Streets are stations for horse-drawn carriage tours of the historic district. Among the sites to see is the **Bellamy Mansion Museum** at 503 Market St., an imposing example of urban antebellum design guarded by rows of white columns and formal gardens and topped by a belvedere. The grounds include a spartan red-brick building where slaves once lived, one of the most intact remains of urban slave quarters in the South. Nearby, two of downtown's favorite restaurants sit side by side in the 100 block of Market Street, **Deluxe,** which offers an internationally inspired menu in a white-tablecloth atmosphere, and **Dixie Grill,** which serves up diner fare with Southern flare.

Opposite the Cape Fear River from the Hilton sits the 36,000-ton, 728-foot **USS *North Carolina*** at 1 Battleship Rd. Northeast, (910) 251-5797, www.battleshipnc.com. Built in 1937, the battleship carried 2,500 or so sailors and marines into battle in the Pacific theater in World War II. Since it was dedicated a historic site and positioned permanently at Wilmington in the 1960s, the ship has become a memorial and museum to the men who served on her. Visitors can inspect the bridge and gun turrets, tour the tiny living quarters below decks, and see memorabilia and oral histories that tell how the ship's sailors and marines lived and fought on board. The self-guided tour takes about two hours. Admission is $12 for adults, $6 for children six and older, free for five and younger.

More than 350 films, TV shows, and commercials have been produced at **EUE Screen Gems Studios** in Wilmington, 1223 North 23rd St., (910) 343-3433, www.screengemstudios.com, beginning in 1982 when *Firestarter* with Drew Barrymore came to the area. The most recent big-screen projects were *Nights in Rodanthe* and *The Secret Life of Bees.* Visitors can tour the studios, including the sets for *One Tree Hill,* on weekends. Admission is $12 for adults, $8 for ages 5 to 12, and free for children 4 and younger.

If you decide to turn your daytrip into an overnight stay, the historic district is home to about a dozen bed-and-breakfasts and the **Hilton Wilmington Riverside,** at 301 North Water St., (910) 763-5900, which offers lovely waterfront rooms.

Travel information: www.wilmington downtown.com.

Wrightsville Beach

From the waterfront, take Market Street (U.S. 17) through Wilmington east to the intersection with Eastwood Road (U.S. 74). Just before Eastwood Road crosses the Intracoastal Waterway is **Lumina Station,** 1900 Eastwood Rd., a shopping center named for the early 20th-century pavilion where beachgoers danced. Offerings include boutiques for women's and children's goods and eateries, including a French bistro, a steakhouse, and a martini bar. Just before the bridge over the Intracoastal is the turn for Airlie Road, a curving strip of asphalt that passes beautiful homes and well-preserved landscapes on its way to **Airlie Gardens,** 300 Airlie Rd. Once part of the estate of Gilded Age industrialist Pembroke Jones, the garden was designed by German landscape architect Rudolf Topel and was said to hold half a million azaleas and 5,000 camellias at its peak in the 1920s. Many of those plants remain on the 67 acres that comprise the public gardens today. Among the many beautiful spots in the garden is the **Minnie Evans Sculpture Garden and Bottle Chapel,** a multicolored glass monument to the garden's one-time gatekeeper, Minnie Evans, who became a celebrated outsider artist after her dream-inspired paintings and drawings were discovered by New York art lovers. Admission to the gardens is $5 for adults, $3 for children 6 to 12.

Once across the waterway, the task is to find parking at the beach. Lumina Avenue is the main beach drag. High-end travelers can find dining and drinks by the pool at the beachfront **Blockade Runner Resort,** 275 Waynick Blvd. Other beach hangouts include **Johnny Mercer's Pier,** 23 East Salisbury St., a popular spot for fishing and people-watching since the 1930s, and **Trolley Stop Hot Dogs,** 1 North Lumina Ave., a beach landmark that serves wieners a dozen different ways and wins vegetarians with its veggie dogs.

Travel information: (800) 650-9106, www .visitwrightsville.com.

Carolina Beach

South of Wilmington and Wrightsville Beach is Carolina Beach, accessible from Wilmington via College Road (N.C. 132) and Carolina Beach Road (U.S. 421). Historically a more affordable beach destination than Wrightsville, Carolina Beach retains its blue-collar charm even as brightly colored new cottages sprout up all over the island. A walk along its boardwalk, between Harper Avenue and Cape Fear Boulevard, is pure nostalgia, and during the summer must include a stop at **Britt's Donuts.** Open since 1939, the doughnuts are a magical cross between a beignet and a Krispy Kreme glazed. And glazed is the only variety, so don't ask for cream-filled. The best way to get around the island is by bikes, single seat or six-seat, available at several Carolina Beach rental companies. Along with the beach, nature lovers can explore several ecosystems at once with a trip to **Carolina Beach State Park,** 1010 State Park Rd. Trails meander through tidal marshes, stands of longleaf pines, and tall sand dunes, offering glimpses of fiddler crabs and Venus flytraps. The park offers campsites as well. Overnighters seeking more creature comforts should check out the **Courtyard by Marriott Carolina Beach,** 100 Charlotte Ave., (800) 321-2211.

Travel information: (910) 341-4030, www.carolinabeachgetaway.com.

Fort Fisher

At the very tip of Pleasure Island, home to Carolina and Kure beaches, stood one of the last defenses of the Confederacy, **Fort Fisher,** which kept open supply lines for the rebel forces until the last days of the Civil War. In January 1865, a massive Federal assault by land and sea captured the fort and helped bring the war to an end. About 10 percent of the fort still stands amid the massive earthworks, all surrounded by beautiful, weathered live oaks. A National Historic Site, the grounds are home to a visitors center and the headquarters of the North Carolina Underwater Archeology division. Tourists can view a film presentation about the fort's history and the lives of those who lived and fought there (1610 Fort Fisher Blvd. South, Kure Beach, 910-458-5538, www.nchistoricsites.org).

One of three state aquariums along the North Carolina coast, Fort Fisher's **North Carolina Aquarium** (900 Loggerhead Rd., Kure Beach, 866-301-3476, www.ncaquariums.com) focuses on life in both fresh water and the sea. Its exhibits highlight habitats along the Cape Fear River and the ocean and include Luna, a rare albino alligator; sea stars; and sea turtles. The centerpiece is a two-story glass-walled tank filled with sharks, eels, fish, and exotic sea life. The aquarium offers a roster of children's activities, and in December, Santa shows up to scuba dive with the sharks.

> **i** A state-owned ferry runs between Fort Fisher and Southport more than a dozen times a day. The ferry skirts the coast and offers the only view of the crumbling 1848 Price's Creek Lighthouse, along with views of the Oak Island and Bald Head Island lights as well. The trip takes about 35 minutes one way. Fare is $5 per car.

Seagrove

Seagrove refers to the area of North Carolina south of Asheboro and northwest of Pinehurst and Southern Pines where potteries have thrived for centuries. It's also the name of a small town that is at the area's approximate center. With more than 100 pottery studios spread across about 20 square miles, a trip to Seagrove combines the relaxation of a drive in the country with the thrill of shopping and discovery. From the Triangle, take U.S. 64 west through Pittsboro to Asheboro, then head south along the Interstate 73/74 corridor and along N.C. 705. It takes between 1½ to 2 hours to get to the area from the Triangle. After that, it depends on how long you want to wander. It is a good idea to download a map of the potteries, available at www.seagrovepotteryheritage.com, before you go. But the maps are available at all area potteries, and signs throughout the region direct visitors to studios.

Seagrove pottery ranges from smiling snowman candleholders to willowy salt-fired teapots in earthy hues to the exaggerated expressions of face jugs. Pottery has been a central part of life in this area since American Indians first used the pliable clay soil for decorative and utilitarian pieces. In the late 1700s settlers of German and English descent arrived in the Seagrove area and soon established the area as a major producer of earthen vessels. These early pieces are now sought after by collectors. **The North Carolina Pottery Center,** at 233 East Ave. in Seagrove, and the **Museum of NC Traditional Pottery,** at 127 East Main St. in Seagrove, offer historical information and maps.

Dining options in the area are limited to chain restaurants along the major highways and some small country cooking establishments. It's a good idea to pack a picnic, as the potteries seldom mind if you spread a blanket and enjoy your lunch. While it's an easy daytrip, regular visitors give high marks to the **Duck Smith House** bed and breakfast at 465 North Broad St. in Seagrove.

Travel information: www.seagrovepottery heritage.com, (336) 873-7887.

Pinehurst and Southern Pines

A little more than an hour's drive from the Triangle, south on U.S. 1, is the golf mecca of Pinehurst, which has hosted the U.S. Open three times. Every golfer knows that a chance to tackle **Pinehurst No. 2** is a rare challenge, but it's certainly not the only course in town. Pinehurst, Southern Pines, and Aberdeen are home to dozens of courses, including some of the top-rated courses in the nation. Pinehurst is home to **Pine Needles Lodge & Golf Club,** owned and operated by LPGA legend Peggy Kirk Bell, and a three-time host of the Women's U.S. Open. Other acclaimed courses in the area include **National Golf Club,** a Jack Nicklaus design, **Pinewild Country Club** of Pinehurst, **Legacy Golf Links** in Aberdeen, and **Talamore Golf Resort** in Southern Pines.

The towns offer diversions for non-golfers, including spas, shopping, and sitting on verandas and porches soaking in the pine-scented air. The premiere and priciest resort is **Pinehurst,** with several accommodations including a 1901 hotel that offers up-to-the-minute luxuries in a

> # North Carolina Zoo
>
> Animals from around the world find homes that mimic their natural habitats at the state zoo's 500-acre parkland in Asheboro. Visitors can see 1,100 animals, representing more than 200 species, from African elephants and giraffes to gila monsters and polar bears. Walking trails wind through the various exhibits and a tram provides transportation as well. The zoo is open every day except Christmas. Admission is $10 for adults, $6 for ages 2 to 12. The zoo is off U.S. 64 about 75 miles from Raleigh.
>
> **North Carolina Zoo**
> 4401 Zoo Parkway, Asheboro
> (800) 488-0444
> www.nczoo.org

setting steeped in history. An on-site spa offers a full slate of treatments. Surrounding the resort is the **Village of Pinehurst,** designed in concert with the golf courses and hotels by Frederic Law Olmsted, the famed landscape architect who designed New York's Central Park. The town was modeled after a New England village, with commercial centers within easy walking distance of residences. Stroll through the pine-shaded streets and dine at **Theos Tavern,** a popular white-tablecloth Mediterranean eatery at 140 Chinquapin Rd. A short drive away are the upscale shops at **Pinehurst Place,** 905 Linden Rd., and the **Camellia Park Shoppes at Olmsted Village,** off N.C. 211, 1 mile west of the village.

Travel information: www.homeofgolf.com, (800) 346-5362.

Winston-Salem

About 1½ hours west of Raleigh, Winston-Salem makes an easy day trip, with plenty for history and art lovers to take in. Head west from the Triangle on I-40, then follow the signs from U.S. 52 to the city's most popular attraction, **Old Salem,** at 900 Old Salem Rd. Thousands come each year to see the carefully restored and maintained remains of the 1766 settlement of Salem, founded by Moravians, a Protestant sect from what is today the Czech Republic. Many of the buildings in town are original and others have been re-created in period style. Costumed interpreters perform the daily tasks that would have been typical of the life of the village, such as baking bread, forging iron instruments, and keeping a tavern, during the 18th and 19th centuries. Different days are dedicated to each period. Also in Old Salem is the **Old Salem Toy Museum,** which has one of the largest collections of toys in the world, ranging from around A.D. 225 to 1925. The **Museum of Early Southern Decorative Arts** is also in the village. Its collection includes fine art, folk art, furniture, ceramics, textiles, and metalwork from the late 17th century to the 19th century. Food and drink are available in the village at the **Old Salem Tavern,** which serves a menu of traditional Moravian food and contemporary dishes. The beloved Moravian sugar cookies, wafer thin and perfectly sweet, were first baked in Old Salem. Visitors can tour the Winkler Bakery on Main Street. Admission to Old Salem, which includes the village, museums, and gardens, is $21 for adults, $10 for ages 6 to 16.

A quick 4½-mile drive north of Old Salem next to Wake Forest University is **Reynolda House Museum of American Art** (2250 Reynolda Rd., 336-758-5150, www.reynoldahouse.org). It is the restored 1917 home of tobacco titan Richard Joshua Reynolds and his wife Katharine. The collection covers three centuries of American painting and sculpture. The museum is at the center of **Reynolda Historic District,** on land that was formerly the Reynolds' 1,067-acre estate. The district includes the formal gardens developed by the family and woodland trails. A shopping center, **Reynolda Village,** offers boutiques and casual dining options. Admission to the museum is $10.

Travel information: Old Salem, (888) 653-7253, www.oldsalem.org.

Greensboro

For residents of the western Triangle communities, a trip to Greensboro can be as short as an hour. It's a straight shot west on I-40. Greensboro's attractions include historic sites that recall the Revolutionary War era and the Civil Rights struggle.

The **Guilford Courthouse National Military Park** at 2332 New Garden Rd. (336-288-1776, www.nps.gov.guco), north of downtown, is among the most visited sites in town. It was where British forces met the American forces in a pivotal battle of the Revolutionary War in 1781. Lord Cornwallis's forces defeated the outnumbered American troops led by General Nathanael Greene, but the victory cost many British soldiers' lives and set the stage for Cornwallis's surrender to George Washington at Yorktown. Visitors to the battleground can watch a film at the visitors center on the history of the conflict, see artifacts, and examine tactical maps. The battlefield, which includes 28 monuments, can be toured by foot, bike, or automobile. Hikers can hit a trail that covers 2½ miles of the site.

Greensboro was the site of revolutionary events in the 20th century as well. On February 1, 1960, four freshmen at N.C. A&T took seats at the lunch counter at Woolworth on South Elm Street in Greensboro. Their bold defiance of Jim Crow rules helped spur a movement that eventually brought legal segregation to an end in the South. A statue of the men, **"The A&T Four,"** stands in front of Dudley Hall on the school's campus, at 1601 East Market St. The **International Civil Rights Center and Museum** opened in early 2010 in the former Woolworth where the sit-in took place. It includes the original lunch counter where the sit-ins took place, which has never been moved, as well as displays that re-create the Jim Crow era and the civil rights movement in the South. Also downtown is the **Greensboro Cultural Center** at 200 North Davie St., which houses the African American Atelier, featuring local and touring exhibits of African-American art. Dining options downtown include the **Liberty**

Oak Restaurant and Bar at 100 West Washington St., with a large, internationally inspired menu and great outdoor seating, and **Natty Greene's Pub & Brewing** at 345 South Elm St.

Travel Information: Greensboro Convention and Visitors Bureau, 2200 Pinecroft Rd. Suite 200, Greensboro, NC 27407, (336) 274-2282, www.greensboronc.org

WEEKEND GETAWAYS

Southport and Bald Head Island

South of Wilmington, and a little more than three hours from the Triangle, Southport, the beaches of Brunswick County, and Bald Head Island make for quiet weekend destinations. At the mouth of the Cape Fear River, Southport is a fishing village that dates to the Colonial era. Just off the coast, Bald Head Island is a modern luxury resort surrounded by a nature preserve. The small towns of Oak Island, Holden Beach, and Sunset Beach offer close to 30 miles of pristine beaches. You won't find as many nightlife options as in the Cape Fear beaches, but it's a perfect place to cool your heels. From the Triangle, take I-40 east to Wilmington, then follow U.S. 17 south and catch smaller state roads to Southport and the beaches. The ferry to Bald Head Island departs from Southport.

Southport

Southport's downtown is home to a number of antiques and gift shops, restaurants, and tea rooms housed in Victorian-era and turn-of-the-20th-century architecture. Visitors can start an exploration at the **N.C. Maritime Museum at Southport,** 16 North Howe St., a collection of nautical memorabilia that tells the story of Lower Cape Fear and southeastern North Carolina. Pop into the **Franklin Square Art Gallery** at 130 East West St. for a look at the offerings of a coalition of local artists. And be sure to make time for a beer or two and a basket of steamed shrimp at **Provisions,** 130 Yacht Basin Dr., where you fetch your own cold ones from the cooler and watch the pleasure crafts bob in the tide where the

Cape Fear River meets the Atlantic Ocean. More formal dining options include **Mr. P's Bistro** at 309 North Howe St. and **Live Oak Cafe** at 614 North Howe St. For lodging, choose from several B&Bs, including the small but popular **Lois Jane's Riverview Inn** at 106 West Bay St.

Travel information: (910) 457-6964, www.southport-oakisland.com.

Orton Plantation Gardens

Orton Plantation's beautiful grounds and stately, columned house are the Hollywood ideal of Southern grandeur, which is why more than 25 movies have been filmed there since the production of *Firestarter* in the early 1980s. The garden's tunnels of twisting live oaks and feathery Spanish moss have graced the big screen in productions of *Crimes of the Heart, The Divine Secrets of the Ya-Ya Sisterhood,* and *A Walk to Remember,* among many others. The land was first developed in the early 18th century, and grew to become a prominent rice plantation owned by the Moores, a powerful landholding family. Beside the Cape Fear River, the 20-acre garden is home to camellias, azaleas, flowering fruit trees, daphne, hydrangeas, crape myrtles, dogwoods, and spring and summer annuals as well as lawns, water gardens, and rice fields. Admission is $9, $3 for children ages 6 to 16. Orton Plantation is 13 miles north of Southport on N.C. 133.

Orton Plantation
9149 Orton Road Southeast, Winnabow
(910) 371-6851
www.ortongardens.com

Brunswick County Beaches

Between Southport and the South Carolina border sit the quiet beach towns of Caswell Beach, Oak Island, Holden Beach, Ocean Isle, and Sunset Beach. The main attraction here is strolling the sandy white beaches along the southernmost strip of North Carolina coastline and watching the sun rise and set. Oak Island alone offers 50 public beach access points. Visitors can also find plenty of golf, fishing, and boating. **Sea Trail Golf Resort,** (866) 368-6642, on Sunset Beach offers inclusive getaway packages with access to 54 holes of golf in the nearby Myrtle Beach area. If you need a break from the sun, you can check out the stars and laser shows at the **Ingram Planetarium,** 7625 High Market St., Sunset Beach, (910) 575-0033. With tons of rental homes and condominiums, the Brunswick beaches offer a wide variety of weekend accommodation options. One affordable beach-front option is **The Islander Inn,** 57 West First St., Ocean Isle Beach, (888) 325-4753.

Travel information: www.brunswickcounty chamber.org, (800) 426-6644.

Bald Head Island

Leave your car in Southport and hop on the ferry to Bald Head Island, where golf carts, bicycles, and your own flip-flopping feet are the only means of transportation. About 2 miles off the coast, Bald Head offers a country club atmosphere with several yacht clubs and the **Bald Head Island Club,** which includes an 18-hole golf course, croquet pitches, a pool, and tennis courts, all set amid a well-preserved semitropical island. Visitors can find a range of accommodations for a weekend getaway, from well-tended rental homes and condominiums to a bed and breakfast, the **Marsh Harbour Inn.** Visitors can climb the 108 steps to the top of **Old Baldy,** the island's 1817 lighthouse, to get an osprey's-eye view of the island. Daytime pursuits include kayaking the tidal creeks and exploring the maritime forests, treatments at the **Island Retreat Spa,** and sitting on the secluded beaches beside the Atlantic Ocean.

Travel information: www.baldheadisland .com, (800) 515-1038.

Brunswicktown

Before the Revolutionary War, Brunswicktown stood on the banks of the Cape Fear River south of Wilmington. In the early and mid-18th century, it was a shipping center and the home of royal governors but lost population to Wilmington and New Bern in the 1760s. The town's decline was sealed when British soldiers destroyed it in 1776. During the Civil War, Confederates built Fort Anderson atop the Colonial ruins. Visitors can tour the ruins of a 1750s-era chapel and those of the homes of the former royal governors. The visitors center exhibits present artifacts and an elaborate mural depicting a battle with Spanish forces at the town in the 1740s.

Brunswicktown
8884 St. Philip's Rd., Winnabow
(910) 371-6613
www.nchistoricsites.org

Outer Banks and Manteo

About four hours from most of the Triangle, Manteo is a great place to base a weekend exploration of North Carolina's Outer Banks. From there, it's an easy drive to the Wright Brothers Memorial at Kitty Hawk, the lighthouse at Corolla, and even the Cape Hatteras Seashore and Lighthouse. From the Triangle, take I-40 to U.S. 64 and go east until you cross the Croatan Sound.

Manteo and the Outer Banks

Manteo occupies the northern half of Roanoke Island, which sits between the mainland and the stretch of the Outer Banks that is home to Nag's Head and Cape Hatteras. You can spend a day on Manteo quite happily walking or biking its historic downtown and waterfront. Lighthouse lovers can see the **Roanoke Marshes Lighthouse** and historical exhibit on the Manteo waterfront, a reproduction of a cottage-style, screw-pile lighthouse that illuminated the Croatan Sound near Wanchese until 1955. At the **North Carolina Aquarium on Roanoke Island,** 374 Airport Rd., get an entertaining lesson on the aquatic life of the Outer Banks, including sharks, alligators, and river otters. **Fort Raleigh,** 1401 National Park Dr., preserves the remains of the first English settlement in the New World, the Lost Colony, and recalls the American Indian culture of the island and a freedman's colony established during the Civil War. Nearby at Waterside Theatre, 1409 National Park Dr., actors recall the events of that English settlement with summertime productions of *The Lost Colony.* First staged in 1937, it is the longest running symphonic drama in the country and draws actors from across the nation. Roanoke Island is home to a number of bed and breakfasts, including the **Roanoke Island Inn** at 305 Fernando St.

Follow U.S. 64 east across the Roanoke Sound from Manteo and you'll find yourself on the Outer Banks, a narrow stretch of land that is home to some of the most beautiful seashore in the world. It's a popular spot, especially in the summertime, so expect to deal with traffic if you go when school is out. But there's plenty to do and see any time of year. Some people find its deserted landscape most rewarding in the winter, and the deals can be great, too.

The northernmost town on this stretch of land is Corolla, famous for roaming wild horses and its brick lighthouse. The horses are the descendants of 16th-century Spanish mustangs left behind after European expeditions. You'll often see them roaming near the lighthouse. The **Corolla Wild Horse Fund,** 1126 Old Schoolhouse Lane, Old Corolla Village, was established in recent years to help protect the herd's habitat. It is illegal to feed them, but you can learn more about them at the fund's educational museum in a historic schoolhouse and through summertime programs for children. The **Currituck Beach Lighthouse,** built in 1875, is a 162-foot tower with 214 steps to the top. It is open to climb when weather permits. The surrounding grounds include the 19th-century keeper's house. Just

south of Corolla is **Duck,** home to the **Sanderling Resort and Spa,** a traveler's best bet for high-end luxury in the area. It is also home to **The Blue Point,** 1240 Duck Rd., which has an innovative menu and great views of Currituck Sound.

South of Kitty Hawk is **Nag's Head,** lined with ocean-front houses and public beach access points. It lays claim to being the state's first tourist colony. The name comes from the pirate practice of leading an old horse with a lantern around its neck back and forth across the dunes, imitating the motion of a ship bobbing at harbor. The light would lure other pirates toward the shore, where their ships would break up on the shoals, leaving them vulnerable to raids. The small historic district of **Cottage Row,** along Beach Road, offers examples of old-style beach cottages with cedar shingles and hipped roofs. Nag's Head is also home to **Jockey's Ridge State Park,** 592 Carolista Dr., which has the highest sand dunes on the East Coast. Fly a kite or take a hike and watch the hang gliders as they descend from the top.

The **Cape Hatteras National Seashore** begins at Nag's Head and stretches more than 50 miles to the Cape Hatteras Lighthouse and beyond. N.C. 12 is the main road through the seashore. The **Bodie Island Lighthouse** is 6 miles south of the northern entrance. The visitors center, in a historic keepers' quarters, provides exhibits on the history of the 156-foot lighthouse. The light is not open for climbing. Continuing south on the narrow stretch of shifting sand, no development interrupts the views of dune, sand, and ocean for miles and miles until a trio of towns, Rodanthe, Waves, and Salvo, interrupts the emptiness. Jutting out into the Atlantic, the town beaches are popular with kite boarders and wind surfers. Farther south is the town of Avon, which has the most shopping options in the area. The **Cape Hatteras Island Visitor Center and Museum of the Sea** is in nearby Buxton. The museum includes exhibits on the lighthouse and Outer Banks history. The lighthouse, which has a 248-step iron spiral staircase, is open for climbing mid-April through mid-October.

Travel information: www.outerbanks.com, (877) 629-4386.

Wright Brothers National Memorial

South of Duck are Kitty Hawk and Kill Devil Hills, made famous by Orville and Wilbur Wright and the birth of manned aircraft. North Carolina's standard license plate bears the slogan "First in Flight," despite protests from Ohio, where the brothers lived and worked. They needed the dunes and the winds of the Outer Banks to put their machine in the air. At the Wright Brothers National Memorial, visitors can climb Big Kill Devil Hill, where the Wrights performed many experiments, and stand on the spot from which the first plane took off. The visitors center includes a reproduction of the 1902 glider and the 1903 flying machine and a reproduction of the Wrights' first wind tunnel.

Wright Brothers National Memorial
Milepost 7.5 on U.S. 158, Kill Devil Hills
(252) 473-2111
www.nps.gov/wrbr

Asheville

North Carolina's mountains are full of wonderful little towns with charming scenery and friendly atmospheres, but of all the beautiful, quaint little spots, Asheville stands out. Its architecture, food, entertainment, and the laid-back vibe make it appealing to a wide variety of tourists. Between three and a half and four hours west of the Triangle on I-40, it's the perfect weekend getaway.

To get a taste of the town and its history, start in downtown Asheville. The city has created a wonderful 1.7-mile, self-guided tour through town called the **Asheville Urban Trail.** Granite markers in the sidewalk and sculptures highlight sites of historical significance during five eras of Asheville's development, from the age of the pioneers through the Gilded Age to today. The tour spotlights the city's many architectural gems, in styles including neoclassical, Romanesque Revival, Art Deco, Beaux Arts, Gothic, and Spanish Renaissance. It is a rare collection of well-preserved early 20th-century buildings that have remained intact for decades while similar structures in other cities fell to the wrecking ball of urban renewal. Asheville held onto its architectural history because it couldn't afford to knock it down. A boomtown in the late 19th and early 20th century where folks like Henry Ford and Thomas Edison came to play, Asheville was devastated by the stock market crash of 1929. Its economy remained stagnant for much of the 20th century. Today, as the town thrives again, it revels in the old gems it held onto. Among the must-sees on a tour of downtown are the domed **Basilica of St. Lawrence,** at 97 Haywood St., and the **Grove Arcade,** 1 Page Ave., a monument to several architectural styles of the early 20th century. Envisioned as a revolutionary shopping destination, today the Grove Arcade is home to shops featuring local crafts, art, and restaurants featuring local food.

On the north end of Market Street in downtown Asheville sits the yellow Victorian house where Thomas Wolfe spent his childhood (52 North Market St., 828-253-8304, www.wolfememorial.com)—the house he made famous in his time-honored novel *Look Homeward, Angel.* Giving it the pen name "Dixieland," Wolfe wrote the Old Kentucky Home Boarding House into his highly autobiographical work. During his own life, Wolfe's hometown found his descriptions of Asheville in *Look Homeward, Angel* so personal and realistic that his classic was banned for a time from the city's library. Wolfe's home was seriously damaged in a 1998 fire and about 15 percent of its artifacts were destroyed. But since it reopened in 2004, it offers guided tours and exhibits on Wolfe's life and writing and a look at how the middle class lived during Asheville's boom years in the early 20th century.

Eating is a big deal in Asheville, especially eating local. With hundreds of farms within an easy drive of the city, it boasts a thriving farm-to-table scene with restaurants in a range of prices. For an upscale taste of the cuisine created by one of the town's pioneering farm-friendly chefs, get a table at **The Market Place,** 20 Wall St. More affordable options include **Tupelo Honey Cafe** at 12 College St., where much of the produce comes from a farm the chef founded just to serve his restaurant, and **Laughing Seed Cafe** at 40 Wall St., a vegetarian's dream fulfilled. If the weather's good, sit outside, people-watch, and soak in the mountain air. Asheville is also a great beer town, with several breweries in and around the city. **Jack of the Wood** at 95 Patton Ave. is a great place to try interesting brews, including the pub's own Green Man ales, and listen to local music, including the Sunday night Irish Jam. For a look at the local literary community and a chance to see touring authors, pop into **Malaprops Bookstore and Cafe** at 55 Haywood St. For live music, check out the **Orange Peel Social Aid & Pleasure Club** at 101 Biltmore Ave., which has hosted acts including Bob Dylan and My Morning Jacket.

Thousands of visitors come to Asheville each year just for the **Biltmore Estate,** off U.S. 25 about 5 miles south of downtown, and it can keep most people busy for at least a day. The 250-room castle, modeled after a French Renaissance chateau, is the largest privately owned home in the country. Ancestors of George Washington Vanderbilt, the industrialist who opened the home in 1895, still own and operate the Biltmore Estate. A tour of the house, resplendent in period decor, takes about two hours. Surrounding the house are acres of gardens designed by renowned architect Frederick Law Olmsted, including formal areas and the country's first managed forest. At the winery, guests can tour the winemaking facility, open since 1985 in a converted dairy barn, and taste the wines. For those who want to explore the estate's 8,000 acres, Biltmore offers a litany of outdoor activities. Take a horse-drawn carriage ride, follow a guide on horseback, float the French Broad River through the estate, or spend the day shooting sporting clays. On-estate dining options include the **Deerpark Restaurant** and,

for the complete Biltmore immersion, stay on the estate at the **Inn on Biltmore Estate.**

For an Asheville experience that doesn't require a Vanderbilt's bankroll, check out **West Asheville.** From downtown Asheville, take Patton Avenue (U.S. 74) west and take a left on Clingman Road. Follow the first fork to get onto Haywood Road. This is the main street that traverses the neighborhoods that make up West Asheville. Just after the fork, Haywood Road passes through the **River Arts District,** a collection of arts and crafts studios housed in refurbished industrial buildings along the banks of the French Broad River. On the west side of the French Broad are a string of consignment shops, galleries, restaurant, and pubs that invite exploration. Have dinner at **The Admiral,** 400 Haywood Rd., where the ever-changing, inventive menu rates among the best in town but the bar scene doesn't stop for dinner, or find great sandwiches on homemade bread dressed with locally grown greens at **West End Bakery,** at 757 Haywood Rd. The mountain scenery and the brush of Birkenstocks on the sidewalk contribute to West Asheville's laid-back vibe.

About an hour southeast of Asheville on U.S. 74A, **Chimney Rock State Park,** (800) 277-9611, www.chimneyrockpark.com, is one of the Blue Ridge Mountains' most unique and visited features. A giant cylinder of stone, it juts 315 feet out of the side of a cliff, topped with a flat surface perfect for visitors. You can take a 30-second elevator ride or climb a set of stairs—whichever suits your energy level. For many years, the park was privately owned and maintained. North Carolina bought it in 2007 and created a state park. But the park still charges admission to support the amenities other parks don't offer. Along with the chimney, visitors can tour Hickory Nut Falls or walk one of several short but sometimes strenuous trails. From some high points, especially on a clear day, you can see out over Lake Lure into an endless horizon of green. Admission to the chimney is $14 for adults, $6 for ages 6 to 15, and free for ages 5 and younger.

Options for overnight stays abound in Asheville, with hotels and bed and breakfasts scat-

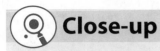

Close-up

Blue Ridge Parkway

For nearly 500 miles, the Blue Ridge Parkway presents some of the most majestic scenery in all the Appalachian Mountain chain, one meandering S-curve at a time. Built in the 1930s, much of the road was constructed by crews under President Franklin Roosevelt's New Deal programs. Drive the whole stretch through Virginia and North Carolina and you'll pass through more than a dozen tunnels hammered through the rock and climb to elevations over 6,000 feet. Most people come to enjoy the explosion of reds and yellows that breaks out every autumn and to watch the fog drop over the leafy, rounded peaks with their namesake tint of blue.

The stretches around Asheville are some of the most popular, both to the north and south. You can admire **Linville Falls** after a short walk from milepost 316. **Grandfather Mountain** stands off milepost 305, near the famous **Linn Cove Viaduct** that curves around the peak without carving into it. And at milepost 355, you can reach the top of **Mt. Mitchell,** the tallest peak east of the Mississippi River. The parkway is not a road to drive quickly, and when the leaves change in the fall, you'll likely find yourself behind a slow-moving chain of camper trucks and Winnebagos, rarely breaking 30 mph.

See www.blueridgeparkway.org for details and downloadable maps.

---

tered throughout the city. Across I-240 from downtown is the **Montford** neighborhood, a wooded, hilly residential area home to a dozen beautifully restored Victorian homes that are now B&Bs. A few miles from downtown, the historic **Grove Park Inn Resort and Spa,** 209 Macon Ave., overlooks the city and offers an 18-hole golf course, a cavern-like spa with waterfall pools, and several restaurants.

Travel information: www.exploreasheville .com, (828) 258-6101.

Charlotte

North Carolina's largest city, with 1.7 million people in its greater metropolitan area, Charlotte is a gleaming citadel of the New South. It's a 2½ to 3-hour drive from the Triangle, taking I-40/I-85 west to Greensboro, then heading south on I-85 where the roads diverge. Charlotte's downtown, called Uptown, is home to shiny skyscrapers, many occupied by the banks that have found a new Southern hub in the Queen City in recent decades. It boasts two professional sports teams, the NFL's Carolina Panthers and the NBA's Charlotte Bobcats, and the area is ground zero for NASCAR fans. Charlotte also supports a thriving arts scene and offers some of the best shopping in the state.

Uptown

A walking tour of Uptown starts at the intersection of Trade Street and North Tryon Street, where Charlotte's signature public art statues tower at each corner. The **Raymond Kaskey sculptures** are giant human figures with the titles "Transportation," "Commerce," "Industry," and "Future." At that corner, inside the **Bank of America Corporate Center** at 100 North Tryon St., three frescos by renowned North Carolina painter Ben Long cover the walls. The evocative works depict the construction of the building, the chaos of daily life, and the artist's hope for the future. More public art dots the surrounding blocks, including another Ben Long fresco on the domed ceiling of the **Transamerica Square**'s arcade at 401 North Tryon St.

Several museums are within easy walking distance of Uptown's center. **Discovery Place** at 301 North Tryon St. is a hands-on science and technology museum for children. Kids can explore the laws of physics with interactive exhibits, build miniature eco-friendly dwellings, and perform tests with solar energy. Exhibits change frequently. Admission is $10 for adults, $8 for children ages 2 to 13. The museum also houses an IMAX theater. At **ImaginOn,** 300 East Seventh St., kids get similar hands-on opportunities to experience stories and literature through a combination of library and theater programs. At 721 North Tryon St., the **McColl Center for Visual Art** focuses on the contemporary works of national and regional artists and sponsors frequent interactive programs for children and adults. The new Mint Museum Uptown, which combines the collections of the Mint Museum of Craft + Design and the American, contemporary and European collections of the Mint, is scheduled to open at 500 South Tryon St., in late 2010.

A little more than 5 miles from Charlotte's city center is the **Billy Graham Library** at 4330 Westmont Rd., which commemorates the story of one of the city's most famous sons. An evangelical pastor who has preached to millions around the globe and counseled presidents, grew up the son of a dairy farmer on the outskirts of Charlotte. The library site includes his childhood home, moved and rebuilt from its original site nearby, and multimedia displays that look back at Graham's career of more than 50 years as a spiritual leader. Admission is free. The library is off the Billy Graham Parkway, accessible via I-77 and Tryon Road.

With the opening of the **NASCAR Hall of Fame** in Uptown Charlotte, the area secures its status as the country's top destination for racing fans. Several other sites in the area celebrate racing's legends and history. In Kannapolis, a small town about 30 miles north of Charlotte on I-85, fans of Dale Earnhardt Sr. can drive the **Dale Trail,** a tour of Earnhardt's hometown commemorating the life of the fallen champion driver. For a downloadable map, go to www.daletrail.com. In Mooresville, about 30 miles north of Charlotte on I-77, is the **North Carolina Auto Racing Hall of Fame** at 119 Knob Hill Rd. The museum features more than 35 automobiles, an art gallery, and a cinematic celebration of great moments in racing history. Admission is $6. In Concord, about 30 miles west of Charlotte on U.S. 29, is the famous **Lowes Motor Speedway.** When drivers aren't

racing around the 1½- mile track, the facility is open for tours. The track also hosts car shows and runs a stock car driving school. Go to www.lowesmotorspeedway.com for details.

For a deeper understanding of Charlotte and the surrounding region, visit the **Levine Museum of the New South** at 200 East Seventh St. The focus is on the history of the South since the Civil War, telling the region's stories from all perspectives—men and women, black and white—through interactive exhibits. Admission is $6, $5 for children. At the **Harvey B. Gantt Center for African-American Arts and Culture** at 551 South Tryon St., explore the cultural contributions and achievements of the African-American community in a spectacularly designed new building that weaves historical themes into its modern design. Admission is $8. The **NASCAR Hall of Fame** at 501 South College St. is a three-story, 150,000-square-foot temple to the brand of racing born in the Carolinas. Visitors can experience racing through the hall's collection of artifacts, interactive exhibits, and simulator rides and through presentations at the High Octane Theater. Admission is $19.95 for adults, $12.95 for children.

On the western edge of Uptown is a Victorian reminder of Charlotte's past, the **Fourth Ward.** Between West Fifth Street and West Tenth Street, the ward is home to blocks of restored late 19th-century and early 20th-century homes; the Old Settler's Cemetery, which was the city's first burial ground; and a charming city park. A map of the neighborhood with architectural details is available online at www.athomecharlotte.com/fourthward and at the INFO!Charlotte visitors center at 330 South Tryon St.

For lunch or brunch Uptown, duck into **Mert's Heart and Soul** at 214 North College St. for comfort food with a New South flair. The setting is casual and the food is well made, especially the sweet potato pancakes. For a more dramatic dining experience, you can go to **Bentley's on 27** at 201 South College St. at the top of the Charlotte Plaza Building, where the views of the city compete with the elegance of the French cuisine.

Uptown has a good collection of high rise hotels, including three with stops on the city's LYNX light rail: the **Westin** at 601 South College St., the **Hilton Charlotte City Center** at 222 East Third St., and the **Holiday Inn Center City** at 230 North College St.

U.S. National Whitewater Center

A dozen miles west of Uptown on the banks of the Catawba River is the **U.S. National Whitewater Center,** a training site for U.S. Olympic canoeists and kayakers. It is open to the public for kayaking and other sports. The facility has the world's largest re-circulating river, where kayakers can run class II, III, and IV rapids, then be returned with their boats to the top of the falls again via a conveyor belt. Canoeists can float the flat water of the Catawba River. Bikers can explore 14 miles of single-track trails on the center's 307 wooded acres. Climbers can tackle 40 roped climbs and a 46-foot spire at the outdoor climbing walls. The center also offers eco-trekking hunts for geo-cachers. Day passes to the center range from $29 to $49, depending on the sports. The center is off Moore's Chapel Road, accessible via I-485 exit 12.

Beyond Uptown

Charlotte is a sprawling metropolitan area with plenty to offer beyond the city center. The **Mint Randolph (Mint Museum of Art),** about 2 miles south of Uptown at 2730 Randolph Rd., has collections of ancient, Asian, African and American Indian art and historic costumes, and hosts frequent touring exhibitions. It is housed in the original U.S. Mint, a Federal style building that printed U.S. currency from 1836 until the Civil War. Admission is $10. The **North Davidson Arts District,** about 2 miles north of Uptown a block off North Tryon Street, offers a funky alternative to the polish of the city center. Centered around North Davidson Street and 36th Street, the community has art galleries, coffeehouses, boutiques, and eateries offering a range of cuisine from Tex-Mex to French bakeries. **Revolution,** at 3228 North Davidson St., is a popular stop for handmade pizza, and **Dog Bar** is a favorite watering hole of pooch lovers as it welcomes canines year-round. Also a favorite with pet lovers is **Meow and Fetch** boutique at 453 East 36th St. The **Evening Muse** at 3227 North Davidson St. is a great place to see local and national acts.

Shoppers flock to **Concord Mills** in Concord, about 3 miles from Lowes Motor Speedway, for deals at outlet stores including T.J. Maxx, BCBG Max Azria, and Saks Fifth Avenue Off 5th. The center, at 8111 Concord Mills Blvd. off I-85, is also home to a Bass Pro Shops Outdoor World and Dave and Busters.

Appendix

LIVING HERE

In this section we feature specific information for residents or those planning to relocate here. Topics include real estate, education, health care, and much more.

RELOCATION

Recent transplants to the Triangle list myriad reasons for their choice. If you close your eyes and listen to them, you see the list of pros they made when assessing the area. It's much longer than the list of cons. Temperate climate? Check. Relatively stable job market? Check. Good schools? Check. Well-run towns and cities that provide reliable and, in some cases, outstanding services? Check. Fairly manageable traffic compared to areas with similar amenities? Check. Easy access to international airport and interstates? Check. The Triangle looks as good on paper as it does in real life, which makes the decision to move here easy.

The trickier question is where in the Triangle is the best place for you? Job location and commute certainly factor heavily in the choice. School systems are an important part of the equation for parents. Leisure activities such as golf and swimming could be crucial as well. The Triangle has neighborhoods that suit all of these concerns.

THE MARKET

Real estate sales and home prices in the Triangle slumped along with those nationwide in response to the economic recession and credit crunch that began in 2007, but not on the same scale as more volatile markets in California, Nevada, and Florida. The Triangle did not experience the massive price appreciations that preceded the bubble, so it didn't feel the same shockwaves when the bubble burst. According to the Federal Housing Finance Agency, in late 2009 Raleigh-Cary ranked 158th and Durham–Chapel Hill ranked 86th in home price appreciation, compared to 297 other metro areas. In early 2010, California research firm Hanley Wood Market Intelligence ranked the Raleigh-Cary market the healthiest in the nation and the Durham–Chapel Hill market the sixth healthiest among the top 100 U.S. housing markets. The firm considers home prices, employment conditions and income growth potential when compiling the rankings.

Prices and appreciation rates vary widely from neighborhood to neighborhood, of course. In general, Chapel Hill has the most expensive home prices in the Triangle, with Cary and Raleigh in the middle, and Durham being the most affordable. Many factors affect home prices within these areas as well.

Cary

Originally popular for its location near RTP, Cary has developed a multitude of amenities that make its homes sought after. In 2008, the town ranked 16th on *Money* magazine's list of America's best small cities. Its parks and recreational facilities and its greenway system are top-notch, and the town runs its own beautiful amphitheater that is home to the N.C. Symphony's summer performance series. Getting into a house in Cary could be pricier than some other areas, but the town has a wide range of options, including town home communities. Among the most popular upscale neighborhoods are MacGregor Downs Country Club and Regency Park.

Chapel Hill

From the beautiful old neighborhoods around the UNC campus of Franklin-Rosemary, Gimghoul, and McCauley-Cameron to the new amenities-laden developments of Southern Village and Meadowmont, Chapel Hill has a lot to offer. Southern Village is among the most popular for buyers looking for modern conveniences and recently built homes. South of downtown, the neighborhood includes restaurants, a movie theater, an elementary school, and a day care and is served by a weekly farmers' market. Another popular choice is Meadowmont, which also has dedicated retail establishments in Meadowmont Village.

Durham

Durham is home to many historic neighborhoods where buyers can often find charming properties that would cost much more in other Triangle cities. The city's density is a draw, especially for those who work in town. But it's fairly easy to get to RTP from just about anywhere in the Bull City. Morehead Hill, where Colonial Revival and bungalow architecture prevails, is a National Historic District, as is Watts-Hillandale, the leafy enclave of bungalows that surrounds the N.C. School of Math and Science. Old North Durham, one of the city's original streetcar suburbs, is experiencing a revitalization, and Forest Hills and Hope Valley have long been among the city's most popular neighborhoods. Downtown, the transformation of warehouses into lofts continues to make this section of the city an attractive home for singles. Plenty of new developments outside the city core provide easier access to the rest of the Triangle as well, including Audubon Park, Hope Valley Downs, and Woodcroft.

Raleigh

In Raleigh, many neighborhoods inside the I-440 beltline (ITB) attract families with children, historic architecture buffs, and singles. If you live and work ITB you can often avoid the heavy traffic of long commutes. Some people are drawn by the idea of being close to the action of downtown. With downtown's continued revitalization, proximity to the area means easier access to dining, shopping, and community events. Homes are generally older and neighborhoods are leafy, shaded by hardwoods that have stood for a century or more. Five Points, Hayes-Barton, Cameron Park, Bloomsbury, Oakwood, and University Park fall into this category. A growing number of downtown condominiums are pulling young people into the city center as well.

Outside the Beltline, North Raleigh is the most attractive area, and in general allows buyers to get more house for their money than ITB. Easy access to shopping centers, malls, athletic clubs, and recreation activities make this area a draw for families. Some of these neighborhoods, especially the older ones, enjoy the same leafy surroundings as older ITB neighborhoods. Popular subdivisions here include Stonebridge, Stone Creek, Stonehenge, Wood Valley, Bent Tree, CrossGate, Durant Trails, Falls Village, and Alyson Pond.

In far North Raleigh, the number of subdivisions increases. Among the largest developments is Wakefield Plantation near Wake Forest, which is divided into several different communities. Daltons Ridge, Norwood Crest, and Forrest Ridge are also popular.

REALTORS

More than 8,000 Realtors and hundreds of real estate firms serve the Triangle, according to the listing service Triangle MLS, so there's no shortage of property experts to help relocators. This list accounts for some of the bigger, better-known firms in the area.

ALLEN TATE COMPANY
3201 Glenwood Ave., Suite 301, Raleigh
(919) 719-2929

AMMONS PITTMAN GMAC REAL ESTATE
307 S. Salem St., Apex
(919) 362-6848

CAROLINA REALTYMAX, INC.
Glenwood Executive Suites, 3301 Woman's Club Dr., Suite 110, Raleigh
(919) 791-0570

CENTURY 21 HAYWOOD DAVIS REALTORS INC.
1011 Broad St., Durham
(919) 286-2121

COLDWELL BANKER ADVANTAGE
6020 Creedmoor Rd., Raleigh
(919) 783-6066

COLDWELL BANKER HOWARD PERRY AND WALSTON
5509 Creedmoor Rd., Suite 100, Raleigh
(919) 781-5556
2705 N. Duke St. • Durham, NC 27704
(919) 317-4200

COLDWELL BANKER WARD & MISENHEIMER
6224 Fayetteville Rd., Suite 1, Durham
(919) 544-7171

ERA UNITED HOME REALTY
117 Edinburgh S. Dr., Suite 112, Cary
(919) 467-1500

FONVILLE MORISEY REALTY
1000 Saint Albans Dr., Suite 400, Raleigh
(919) 785-4384

FRANKLIN STREET REALTY
1525 E. Franklin St., Chapel Hill
(919) 929-7174

HODGE & KITTRELL, INC.
3200 Wake Forest Rd. Suite 101, Raleigh
(919) 876-7411

HOMETOWNE REALTY
328 E. Main St., Clayton
(919) 550-7355

KELLER WILLIAMS
115 Crescent Commons Dr., Suite 100, Cary
(919) 882-3200

LINDA CRAFT AND TEAM REALTORS
7300 Six Forks Rd., Raleigh
(919) 235-0007

THE PREISS COMPANY
1700 Hillsborough St., Raleigh
(800) 598-1293

PRUDENTIAL–YORK SIMPSON UNDERWOOD
N. Hills Office
3700 Computer Dr., Raleigh
(919) 782-6641

PREMIER PROPERTIES OF THE TRIANGLE
1 Gardenview Place, Durham
(919) 405-3888

REALTY WORLD PARTNERS
2891 Jones Franklin Rd., Raleigh
(919) 342-6903

RE/MAX CITY CENTRE
207 Fayetteville St., Raleigh
(919) 782-1110

RE/MAX PREFERRED ASSOCIATES
7101 Creedmoor Rd., Suite 113, Raleigh
(919) 845-2197

WEICHERT REALTORS–TRIANGLE HOMES
1408 Boulderstone Way, Cary
(919) 468-7076

WEICHERT REALTORS–MARK THOMAS PROPERTIES
3901 University Dr., Durham
(919) 403-5315

REAL ESTATE GUIDES

APARTMENT FINDER
www.aptbook.com
The free guide catalogs 220 rental communities in Raleigh and 60 more in other parts of the Triangle. Order it for free online.

HOMES & LAND OF DURHAM, CHAPEL HILL, AND BURLINGTON
www.homesandlandofdurhamchapelhill.com
Catalogs real estate offerings and rentals in the western Triangle.

HOMES & LAND OF RALEIGH
www.homesandlandofraleigh.com
Catalogs real estate offerings and rentals in Raleigh and Wake County.

NEW HOME GUIDE
www.pdatagroup.net/nhg

You can order this guide to the Triangle real estate market, which covers everything from town homes to mansions, online for a $5 shipping fee.

THE ORIGINAL RELOCATION GUIDE
www.relocationguide.biz
This regional publishing company publishes glossy magazine guides to the Triangle and one for Johnston County.

MEDIA

Newspapers

THE CAROLINIAN
www.raleighcarolinian.info
This twice weekly publication serves Raleigh's African-American community.

THE HERALD-SUN
www.heraldsun.com
The paper of record for Durham, the *Herald-Sun* also covers Chapel Hill and Hillsborough.

THE INDEPENDENT WEEKLY
www.indyweek.com
An alternative local publication with offices in Durham covers Raleigh, Durham, Chapel Hill, and Orange County.

THE NEWS & OBSERVER
www.newsobserver.com
A longtime presence in Raleigh and throughout eastern North Carolina, the *News & Observer* is currently owned by the McClatchy Corporation, based in Sacramento, California. The *N&O* is the parent company of several smaller local papers and sections dedicated to communities within the Triangle, listed below.

THE CARY NEWS
www.carynews.com

THE CHAPEL HILL NEWS
www.chapelhillnews.com

THE DURHAM NEWS
www.thedurhamnews.com

THE EASTERN WAKE NEWS
www.easternwakenews.com

THE GARNER CLAYTON RECORD
www.garnerclayton.com

THE MIDTOWN RALEIGH NEWS
www.midtownraleighnews.com

THE NORTH RALEIGH NEWS
www.northraleighnews.com

SOUTHWEST WAKE NEWS
www.southwestwakenews.com

TRIANGLE BUSINESS JOURNAL
www.triangle.bizjournals.com
Part of the American City Business Journals chain, the weekly paper covers business in the Triangle.

Magazines

CAROLINA PARENT
www.carolinaparent.com
Carolina Parent publishes a monthly magazine aimed at Triangle parents of children high school age and younger. The magazine puts out three special guides per year, the *Baby Guide, Ultimate Family Resource Guide* and the *Parents' Guide to North Carolina Colleges*. The magazine's circulation is 58,000, and its audited readership totals more than 120,000.

CHAPEL HILL MAGAZINE
www.chapelhillmagazine.com
Chapel Hill Magazine is a bi-monthly publication that focuses on lifestyle issues, covering dining, literature, fashion, and the arts. The magazine is mailed to 11,250 households in Chapel Hill, Carrboro, Hillsborough, and northern Chatham County, and more than 1,300 businesses.

DURHAM MAGAZINE
www.durhammag.com
Durham Magazine publishes bi-monthly. Dining, the arts and community issues are its main subjects. The magazine goes to 15,000 households in the Durham community.

EDIBLE PIEDMONT
www.ediblepiedmont.com
Edible Piedmont, which publishes quarterly, focuses on issues of local food and farming. Its coverage area ranges from Charlotte and Winston-Salem-Greensboro in the east to the coast and focuses heavily on the Triangle, where it is based. The publication is an Edible Communities franchise, which has similar magazines across the country.

FIFTEEN-501
www.fifteen501.com
Fifteen501 aims for residents making more than $250,000 annually who live in Durham, Orange, and Chatham counties along the U.S. 15-501 corridor. It publishes quarterly and focuses on fashion, food, home decor, environmental issues and travel. It delivers to 25,000 households.

METRO MAGAZINE
www.metronc.com
Food, wine, social issues, architecture, and conservative commentary are the mainstays of *Metro Magazine*, which publishes monthly. The magazine covers a 22-county area that ranges from the Triangle to the coast. The circulation is reported at 40,000.

MIDTOWN MAGAZINE
www.midtownmag.com
Midtown Magazine focuses on the North Hills area of Raleigh and the surrounding neighborhoods, covering fashion, food, and home decor. It publishes bi-monthly.

TRIANGLE EAST MAGAZINE
www.triangleeastmagazine.com
Triangle East covers life in the eastern Wake county communities of Garner, Knightdale, Wendell, Wake Forest, Willow Springs, and Zebulon, and parts of Raleigh and Clayton. The magazine focuses on dining, shopping, fashion, and issues of concern to parents with children high school age and younger. It publishes monthly and claims a readership of 64,000.

WAKE LIVING
www.wakeliving.com
Wake Living publishes quartlery with focuses on food, education issues, home and garden decor, travel, health and the environment. The magazine targets households with more than $375,000 in annual income and deliver to 35,000.

Radio Stations

CHRISTIAN

WRTG	1000 AM
WTIK	1310 AM
WCBQ	1340 AM
WSRC	1410 AM
WDUR	1490 AM
WARR	1520 AM
WRTP	1530 AM
WCLY	1550 AM
WHPY	1590 AM

CLASSICAL

WCPE	89.7 FM
WNCU	90.7 FM

COLLEGE/ALTERNATIVE

WKNC	88.1 FM
WXDU	88.7 FM
WXYC	89.3 FM

COLLEGE/JAZZ

WSHA	88.9 FM
WNCU	90.7 FM

COUNTRY

WQDR	94.7 FM
WBBB	96.1 FM
WKRX	96.7 FM
WMPM	1270 AM

GOSPEL

WNNL	103.9 FM
WAUG	750 AM

NEWS/TALK

WDNZ	570 AM
WDNC	620 AM

WPTF	680 AM
WTSB	1090 AM
WCHL	1360 AM

NPR AFFILIATE

| WUNC | 91.5 FM |

POP

| WDCG | 105.1 FM |

R&B

| WFXC | 107.1 FM |

ROCK

| WWMY | 102.9 FM |
| WRDU | 106.1 FM |

SOFT ROCK

| WRSN | 93.9 FM |
| WRAL | 101.5 FM |

SPANISH

| WETC | 540 AM |
| WFTK | 1030 AM |

SPORTS

| WRBZ | 850 AM |

VOLUNTEER-OPERATED TALK AND MUSIC

| WCOM | 103.5 FM |

TV Stations

TRIANGLE AREA NETWORK AFFILIATES
WRAL-TV CBS
WTVD ABC
WNCN NBC-17
WRAZ Fox 50
WLFL CW 22

Time Warner Cable

www.timewarnercable.com/carolinas
The Triangle's only 24-hour news station is News 14 Carolina, owned by Time Warner Cable. The company provides cable television service to the Triangle and much of eastern North Carolina.

RELIGION AND WORSHIP

A wide range of believers can find faith communities in the Triangle, from mammoth Christian churches that serve congregations numbering in the thousands to small B'hai groups to a striking Hindu temple. The area is overwhelmingly Christian, with Baptist, Presbyterian, Methodist, Episcopal, and AME Zion and other denominations with strong Southern allegiances dominating in terms of membership numbers.

The Catholic Church has a historic presence in the community and parishes in all corners of the Triangle. Catholic churches in the Triangle are part of the Diocese of Raleigh, which runs from Burlington to the coast. The area's growing Hispanic population has given rise to many Spanish-speaking congregations, and Korean churches of Presbyterian, Methodist, and Baptist denominations can be found throughout the Triangle.

The Jewish community in the Triangle stretches back as far as the early 19th century, when prominent landowner Moses Mordecai held an enduring homestead in what is today Raleigh. Jewish merchants moved to Durham and Chapel Hill in more significant numbers in the early 1900s, and in the 1950s and '60s E. J. "Mutt" Evans served as mayor of Durham for six terms. Today, the Triangle is home to several Jewish congregations and schools. The area has no kosher groceries, though some groceries carry kosher foods and purveyors from larger cities make frequent deliveries to the Triangle.

The growing number of Triangle residents of Indian descent contributes to a thriving Hindu community. In 2009, the community celebrated the opening of a $3.4 million temple in Cary. Built to worship the Hindu god Venkateswara, it is a stunning, ornately carved building modeled after a temple in India.

The Triangle has been home to several small, established Islamic communities since the 1980s. Congregations are centered in Raleigh, Morrisville, Durham, and Apex. A handful of Buddhist organizations offer instruction in meditation and life practices in Raleigh, Durham, and Chapel Hill.

EDUCATION

With its many colleges and universities and large number of research-oriented jobs, the Triangle attracts a highly educated population. The area has one of the highest concentrations of PhDs in the country. This education level helps fuel further education of the next generation by parents who demand performance from schools and offer support to help students and teachers achieve. Myriad opportunities to learn in a formal setting present themselves to Triangle residents. Strong community colleges go beyond basic education to offer skills for mid-life students, and the universities welcome returning scholars with outreach education programs as well. Beyond the classroom, the many institutions of higher learning offer cultural and intellectual programs for the general public, contributing to the quality of life. This chapter aims to present an overview of the institutions that educate Triangle residents of all ages.

CHILD CARE

Because the Triangle has a national reputation for being one of the best places in the country to raise a child, a great many families with children and couples contemplating parenthood settle here. Child-care options are plentiful, though competition can be stiff for the most sought-after spots. It is not unheard of for parents to begin shopping for preschool options before their child is even born. Waiting lists for some day cares and preschools can be many months long, so if you find out you are pregnant, start thinking about signing up for infant care as soon as possible.

Options include private all-day care centers, church-run centers, Montessori schools, and some publicly funded centers. In-home care options abound as well, including personal nannies, nanny-share arrangements, and stay-at-home mothers and grandmothers who keep children in addition to their own. The state's Department of Health and Human Services' Division of Child Development regulates child-care centers and in-home family caregivers who care for three or more preschoolers.

The state also operates a directory of day care providers that includes a star rating for quality. A caregiver or center can earn between one and five stars based on the level of education staff members have and the quality of the programs the center administers. Parents can search for state-rated agencies at http://ncchildcaresearch .dhhs.state.nc.us.

Another resource for parents seeking child-care is the **Child Care Services Association,** online at www.childcareservices.org. Based in Chapel Hill, it is a non-profit support group for parents funded by the United Way, Smart Start, and various other local and state government agencies. It provides an online tutorial that walks parents through the steps to take when evaluating a caregiver or childcare center and offers free care giver listings with star-ratings. In addition to the free referral services, Child Care Services Association offers technical assistance to child care businesses, and educational scholarships and salary supplements to child care professionals.

Parents new to the area can also find information about child care and other resources for their children by joining parent groups. Most of these Triangle groups are best found online, where you can view the chat activity and determine if the group is a good fit for you. This is a partial list of the Triangle's parenting groups:

CAPITAL AREA PARENTS WITHOUT PARTNERS
www.capitalareapwp.org/

CHAPEL HILL–CARRBORO MOTHERS CLUB
www.chapelhillmothersclub.org

DURHAM MOTHERS CLUB
http://dmc.findsmithgroups.com/signin.do

JOHNSTON MOMMIES
www.johnstonmommies.com

MAMAS LATINAS DEL TRIANGULO
mamaslatinasdeltriangulo@yahoo.com

MOCHA MOMS OF DURHAM
http://durhammochamoms.tripod.com/

MOCHA MOMS OF RALEIGH
http://raleigh-mochamoms.tripod.com/index.html

MOMS CLUB OF APEX
www.momsclub.org/links.html

MOMS CLUB OF GARNER
www.momsclub.org/links.html

MOMS CLUB OF WAKE FOREST
www.momsclub.org/links.html

MOMS CLUB OF CLAYTON
www.momsclub.org/links.html

MOMS CLUB OF CHAPEL HILL
www.momsclub.org/links.html

MOMS CLUB OF CARY-MORRISVILLE
http://carynmorrisvillemomsclub.bravehost.com/

MOMS CLUB OF CARY-SOUTH
www.momsclub.org/links.html

MOMS OF BOYS
www.momsofboys.org

MOMS WITH DOCTORATES OF EAST WAKE/ NORTH RALEIGH
www.meetup.com/Moms-with-Doctorates-of-East-Wake-North-Raleigh

MOTHERS UNLIMITED
www.mothersunlimited.com

NURSING MOTHERS OF RALEIGH
http://nursingmothersofraleigh.org/

TRIANGLE DADS
www.triangledads.com/

TRIANGLE MOMMIES
www.trianglemommies.com

SCHOOL DISTRICTS

The Triangle's public school systems are some of the best in the state, and in some cases, the country. School districts are organized by county except in the case of Chapel Hill–Carrboro, which has its own district distinct from Orange County.

Wake County is the largest system in the state and has been praised for its commitment to economic diversity and its many magnet schools, including Enloe High School, which consistently rates among the country's top schools. The 2009 school board election saw a backlash against these policies, though, as parents voted in members who vowed to end lengthy bus rides caused by districting policies. How Wake County will deal with the continued growth of its school system and maintain its vaunted reputation is a matter that will hold the attentions of policy makers and politicians for the next decade. Chapel Hill–Carrboro has some of the best schools in the state as well and the highest district-wide SAT scores in the state. Others systems that serve the Triangle are Orange County, which includes Hillsborough; Durham County; and Johnston County, which includes Clayton.

HIGHER EDUCATION

CAMPBELL UNIVERSITY NORMAN ADRIAN WIGGINS SCHOOL OF LAW
225 Hillsborough St., Suite 401, Raleigh
(919) 865-4650
www.campbell.edu
Campbell University is a Christian college whose main campus is in Buies Creek, about an hour south of Raleigh in Harnett County. The school relocated its law school to a new building in

downtown Raleigh in 2009, to give students more access to working courts and the state legislature. About 400 students attend Campbell's law school. The Raleigh division of the North Carolina Business Court is located in the school's building.

DUKE UNIVERSITY
2301 Erwin Rd., Durham
(919) 684-3214
www.duke.edu

Consistently ranked among the best institutions of higher learning in the country, Duke University enrolls about 6,500 undergraduates and 7,000 graduate students. Previously Trinity College, the school took the Duke name in 1924 when industrialist James Buchanan Duke endowed the school with millions and set off a building campaign that included the landmark Duke Chapel. The private school's graduate programs in law, divinity, medicine, nursing, and business are acclaimed. Duke scholars and scientists undertake ambitious research that ranks its medical facilities among the best in the world. Its beautiful campus was built in neo-Gothic and Georgian style and sprawls across much of Durham. The school is known as well for its excellent men's basketball program as for its academics, and the town's most famous resident is probably Coach Mike Krzyzewski, Coach K for short.

MEREDITH COLLEGE
800 Hillsborough St., Raleigh
(919) 760-8600
www.meredith.edu

Meredith is a private women's college that offers undergraduate degrees in liberal arts and co-educational graduate programs in business, nutrition, and education. Students number 2,000 undergraduates and 250 graduate students. The school was chartered in 1891. The pretty, green 225-acre campus is located in west Raleigh on Hillsborough Street, close to the North Carolina Museum of Art. Meredith students participate in six division III sports—basketball, soccer, volleyball, tennis, softball, and cross-country—but not football, as suggested by the popular "Meredith Football" T-shirts that some wear in jest.

NORTH CAROLINA CENTRAL UNIVERSITY
302 E. Lawson St., Durham
(919) 560-6100
www.nccu.edu

Established in 1910 as the National Religious Training School and Chautauqua for African-American students, N.C. Central is today part of the University of North Carolina's 16-school system. It enrolls about 9,000 students. The school offers bachelor's degrees in more than 100 fields and graduate degrees in 40 disciplines, including law, business, education, and library and information sciences. Its biotechnology research department works in concert with companies in the Research Triangle Park. N.C. Central is a NCAA division I school and a member of the Mid-Eastern Athletic Conference. Among its most successful extracurricular organizations is its marching band, the NCCU Marching Sound Machine, which is scheduled to march in the 2011 Rose Bowl Parade.

NORTH CAROLINA STATE UNIVERSITY
203 Peele Hall
(919) 515-2011
www.ncsu.edu

North Carolina State University was established in 1887 to offer instruction in the practical matters of agriculture and mechanics. Today, the university enrolls more than 31,000 students who concentrate in a variety of academic and research disciplines. The university's leading colleges offer instruction and research in the fields of agriculture, design, education, engineering, textiles, and veterinary medicine. The school's Centennial Campus brings industry and academics together and is home to 130 corporate and government research partnerships. The student population long ago outgrew the sprawling campus, so many of N.C. State's students live off-campus and take advantage of the school's extensive Wolfline bus system. This means that pockets of campus life sprout throughout the city, in central Raleigh along Hillsborough Street, and in west Raleigh as well. Wolfpack football brings huge crowds to Carter-Finley Stadium, adjacent to the RBC Center, where the N.C. State's men's basketball team plays.

PEACE COLLEGE
15 E. Peace St., Raleigh
(919) 508-2000
www.peace.edu

A liberal arts college for women, Peace College enrolls about 700 undergraduate students. It was founded by the Presbyterian Church in 1857 but is private today. It has been a four-year baccalaureate college since 1997. The school offers degrees in 16 academic areas, including musical performance, teacher education, biology, and anthropology. The quiet, stately campus is surrounded by a grove of towering oaks in downtown Raleigh a few blocks from the Legislative Building.

SAINT AUGUSTINE'S COLLEGE
1315 Oakwood Ave., Raleigh
(919) 516-4042
www.st-aug.edu

A private, historically black college founded in 1867 by Episcopal clergy, St. Augustine's enrolls about 1,500 students. Among its degrees programs are liberal arts, business administration, computer science, music, visual arts, and education. Its campus borders the historic neighborhoods of Idlewild and College Park in southeast Raleigh, and sits about 10 blocks from the downtown legislative district. The most striking building on the campus is the shell of Saint Agnes Hospital, which served during the first half of the 20th century as the pre-eminent teaching hospital for African Americans between Atlanta and Washington, D.C. The building is undergoing a $13 million renovation.

SHAW UNIVERSITY
118 E. S. St., Raleigh
(919) 546-8200
www.shawuniversity.edu

Shaw is a private, historically African-American liberal arts university founded in 1865. It is affiliated with the National Baptist Convention. Enrollment stands at close to 3,000. The school began as the Raleigh Institute, a Baptist school for freed African-Americans. Shaw played a founding role in the civil rights movement when the Student Nonviolent Coordinating Committee began at a conference held at the school in 1960. The school offers degrees in liberal studies, sociology, public administration, computer information systems, elementary education, and divinity. Shaw partners with N.C. State University and N.C. A&T University in Greensboro to offer dual degree programs in dentistry, pharmacology, and engineering. The Shaw Bears play in the NCAA division I Central Intercollegiate Athletic Association. The school sits at the southern edge of downtown Raleigh, its historic buildings across the street from the Progress Energy Center.

UNIVERSITY OF NORTH CAROLINA AT CHAPEL HILL
Campus Box 3110, Chapel Hill
(919) 962-2211
www.unc.edu

The oldest state university in the country, the school enrolled its first student, Hinton James, in 1795. Its mission was to offer a classical education to residents of North Carolina. Today the university enrolls about 18,000 undergraduates and more than 10,000 graduate students. Its post-graduate programs include law, business, medicine, dentistry, and social work among many others. Research initiatives include groundbreaking work in medicine, pharmacy, and public health, and the research faculty includes a Nobel Prize winner. The affiliated UNC Hospital system serves the state and focuses on pediatrics, women's health, and cancer treatment. From its oldest buildings set under towering oak and poplar trees near Franklin Street to its newest areas of growth, the Carolina campus offers visitors and students beautiful open spaces and quiet retreats. The football arena, Kenan Stadium, is one of the most beautiful gridirons in the country, set in a bowl of pines and hardwoods. Franklin Street, adjacent to the campus, is the hub of student life and where fans throng to celebrate when UNC wins a national men's basketball championship or a regular season game against arch-rival Duke.

TECHNICAL SCHOOLS

CENTRAL CAROLINA COMMUNITY COLLEGE
764 W. St., Pittsboro
www.cccc.edu
(800) 682-8353

Central Carolina Community College has sites in three counties, including Chatham. The Pittsboro campus has a focus on sustainability education and offers coursework in the fields of sustainable agriculture and alternative fuel technology. A culinary arts program is planned for the campus. Chatham County Small Business Center is located at the campus.

DURHAM TECHNICAL COMMUNITY COLLEGE
1637 Lawson St., Durham
(919) 536-7200
www.durhamtech.edu

Durham Tech enrolls about 25,000 students annually. The bulk of the school's students are in continuing education classes. Other coursework includes health technology, nursing assistant programs, business technology, and industrial and information technology. Durham Tech awards associate degrees in nursing, medical assisting, basic law enforcement, opticianry, and several other health-related fields. The school has two campuses outside its main site in central Durham, one in northern Durham and one in Orange County.

WAKE TECHNICAL COMMUNITY COLLEGE
9101 Fayetteville Rd., Raleigh
(919) 866-5000
www.waketech.edu

Part of the North Carolina Community College System, Wake Tech is the second largest community college in the state. About 65,000 students attend Wake Tech classes every year. The main campus is in far south Raleigh, and the school has six other sites around the county. The school offers courses in high school equivalency education, English as a second language, law enforcement, small business, and health sciences. Degrees include two-year associate degrees in science, applied science, and general education. The main campus is also home to a cooking school that operates a student-run restaurant during some parts of the semester.

PRIVATE SCHOOLS

CARDINAL GIBBONS HIGH SCHOOL
1401 Edwards Mill Rd., Raleigh
(919) 834-1625
www.cghsnc.org

A century old in 2009, Cardinal Gibbons was founded to serve Raleigh's small but growing Catholic community. In its early years, only about 50 students attended, and its first graduating class had three members. Raleigh's Catholic school was the first in North Carolina to desegregate, beating the Supreme Court's 1954 decision by a year. Private and co-educational, Cardinal Gibbons is the only diocesan Roman Catholic high school in the Raleigh diocese. Nearly all of its roughly 1,100 students go on to college. Its sports teams have won numerous state championships, as have its cheerleaders.

CAROLINA FRIENDS SCHOOL
4809 Friends School Rd., Durham
(919) 383-6602
www.cfsnc.org

With 480 students, this Quaker school offers courses for students aged 3 to 18, including a pair of early schools in Durham and Chapel Hill off the main campus. Founded in 1962 by the Religious Society of Friends, the school prides itself on racial and socioeconomic diversity. The school has both a committee to see that a multicultural balance is kept and an endowment offering tuition aid to make sure all ethic groups are represented. Here, more than 95 percent of the student body goes on to college. As part of their studies, all students take dance, art, music, fitness, and foreign language classes. The student-to-teacher ratio stands at a remarkable 9 to 1. Tuition costs as much as many colleges, but 20 percent of the student body receives some assistance. In keeping with Quaker practice, students also experience times of shared silence.

CARY ACADEMY
1500 N. Harrison Ave., Cary
(919) 677-3873
www.caryacademy.org
Set in the booming suburb of Cary, this academy for middle- and high-schoolers boasts 100 percent of its graduates accepted to four-year colleges. There are no grade-point averages calculated at Cary Academy, and students are not ranked. But middle-school students can expect as much as two hours of homework a night; three for grades 9 to 12. The academy reports giving out more than $1 million in annual aid. Fees are more for 10th graders, who can participate in an international exchange program. But all students, who operate on a trimester, will see fewer than 18 students per class.

DUKE SCHOOL
3716 Old Erwin Rd., Durham
(919) 493-1827
www.dukeschool.org
Set on a 40-acre campus with access to wetlands, the school was founded in 1947 as a lab for Duke University students studying education and psychology. It has been independent of the university since 1984 and now caters to children from preschool through eighth grade. Students here enjoy a teacher-student ratio of 1 to 12, and the curriculum is integrated so that technology, art, and music become part of everyday studies rather than a separate course. Students learn through sets of longer-term projects. For example, they might track a hurricane's path or program a wheelchair made of LEGOs.

DURHAM ACADEMY
3601 Ridge Rd., Durham
(919) 493-5787
www.da.org
With three schools offering classes from pre-kindergarten to 12th grade, Durham Academy offers a unique selection of courses for its roughly 1,100 students. Middle-schoolers can take Latin. High-schoolers can select bioethics, film, and advanced placement statistics. Nearly three-quarters of the faculty have earned advanced degrees and recent senior courses average SAT scores of 1,320. Spread over three campuses and 75 acres, Durham Academy provides more than 400 computers, 15 science labs, three performing arts centers and nine athletic fields. And through an extended program, students can choose activities such as chess, violin, and fencing.

EMERSON WALDORF SCHOOL
6211 New Jericho Rd., Chapel Hill
(919) 967-1858
www.emersonwaldorf.org
Toddlers to high-schoolers at this Waldorf school study music and art every day. They begin German and Spanish courses in the first grade. By the time they reach high school, their math, science, and literature studies are augmented by special classes in copper working and blacksmithing. The school boasts that kids can be kids at Emerson without having to face hours of homework or stressful tests until they are ready. Set on a wooded 54-acre campus outside Chapel Hill, Emerson had its first high-school graduation in 2006 with 15 students.

THE FLETCHER ACADEMY
400 Cedarview Court, Raleigh
(919) 782-5082
www.thefletcheracademy.com
Founded in 1981, Fletcher is the first school in North Carolina dedicated to children with learning disabilities. With 12 grades, full-day classes, and no more than five students to a teacher, children here can move from severe dyslexia that hampers progress in public school to become college graduates.

THE HILL CENTER
3200 Pickett Rd., Durham
(919) 489-7464
www.hillcenter.org
The Hill Center offers a half-day program to children with learning disabilities or attention deficit disorders who are enrolled part-time in another public or private school. More than 90 percent of its high-school students go on to college.

IMMACULATA CATHOLIC SCHOOL
721 Burch Ave., Durham
(919) 682-5847
www.immaculataschool.org

With about 400 students, Immaculata offers a Catholic school education to children from pre-kindergarten through eighth grade. Students taking the Iowa Test of Basic Skills consistently rank in the top third, often the top quarter, of all students who participate. Students are grouped in classes of 18 to 24, and all wear simple uniforms. Set in downtown Durham, Immaculata turned 100 years old in 2009.

THE LERNER JEWISH COMMUNITY DAY SCHOOL
1935 W. Cornwallis Rd., Durham
(919) 286-5517
www.lernerschool.org

About 150 students attend this Jewish school, two-thirds of them in kindergarten through fifth grade and the rest three- and four-year-olds. Curriculum covers traditional coursework, art, music, physical education, Judaic studies, and Hebrew language. After school, students can take piano, guitar, drama, sports, and Hebrew games. Congregational affiliation is mixed and about 15 percent of the students follow strictly kosher diets. Here, the students work on an eight-acre wooded campus and scores average in the 93rd percentile on standardized tests.

THE MONTESSORI SCHOOL OF RALEIGH
7005 Lead Mine Rd., Raleigh
(919) 848-1545
www.msr.org

Children can start at Raleigh Montessori at only 18 months of age and follow their studies through middle school. Many leave for competitive college preparatory schools. Students learn in small groups according to age—six to nine, for example. Students follow the "learn by doing" credo of Montessori schools nationwide. As young as age three, they study art, music, and movement. By their final year, they plan and take a trip to Europe. For the last seven years, scores on the Secondary School Admissions Test averaged in the 92nd percentile nationwide.

NORTH RALEIGH CHRISTIAN ACADEMY
7300 Perry Creek Rd., Raleigh
(919) 573-7900
www.nrcaknights.com

North Raleigh Christian Academy opened in 1996 with 450 students, and within six years, attendance had more than doubled as the school added new campuses in the fast-growing north end of the city. Enrolling students in kindergarten through 12th grade, the school offers a dozen AP courses and an elective Bible unit for all high-school grades.

THE RALEIGH SCHOOL
1141 Raleigh School Dr., Raleigh
(919) 546-0788
www.raleighschool.org

The Raleigh School has about 260 students in kindergarten through fifth grade, and another 180 toddlers in its preschool program. Set on 14 acres of woods in West Raleigh, it was founded in 1952 as a co-educational day school. Students here take courses inside and outdoors, and the classrooms are designed for hands-on learning and collaboration. It avoids grades or prizes for good work as artificial rewards, and instead stresses that the challenges and fun of learning are their own rewards.

RAVENSCROFT SCHOOL
7409 Falls of Neuse Rd., Raleigh
(919) 847-0900
www.ravenscroft.org

Founded in 1862, Ravenscroft spent its first century as an Episcopalian school until becoming non-sectarian in 1966. Today, all of its graduates typically go on to college. Its mean score on the Scholastic Aptitude Test is better than 1,200, and in 2008, 87 percent of those students that took advanced-placement exams scored a 3 or better. More than 1,200 students attend between pre-kindergarten and 12th grade. Set in North Raleigh, the school aims to rank among the best academic programs in the Southeast.

ST. DAVID'S SCHOOL
3400 White Oak Rd., Raleigh
(919) 782-3331
www.sdsw.org

An independent Episcopal school, St. David's offers instruction to students in kindergarten through 12th grade, guided by twin goals of providing academic challenge and character education. More than 40 percent of the faculty holds advanced degrees, and the average class size is 14 students. St. David's offers 19 advanced-placement courses, and 90 percent of students score a 3 or higher on AP tests. Students attend daily chapel services and can participate in athletic teams, band, chorus, drama, and visual arts programs.

ST. MARY'S SCHOOL
900 Hillsborough St., Raleigh
(919) 424-4100
www.sms.edu

Set on a 23-acre campus just outside downtown Raleigh, St. Mary's is the nation's seventh-largest boarding and day school for girls. Female students in grades nine to 12 can take 16 advanced-placement courses and compete in 11 sports. Founded in 1842, the historic school has 39 nationally recruited faculty and staff living on campus, and 75 percent of the faculty hold graduate degrees. The school's roughly 300 students come from 12 states and eight different countries.

ST. TIMOTHY'S SCHOOL
4523 Six Forks Rd., Raleigh
(919) 787-3011
www.sttimothys.org

Since 1958, St. Timothy's has emphasized small class sizes at its Episcopal school for kindergarten through the eighth grade. About half the faculty members have or are pursuing advanced degrees. Set in the Midtown section of Raleigh, the school starts an honors reading program in the third grade. By the eighth grade, St. Timothy's students are taking geometry classes. At St. David's, officials boast that the shyest kindergartner can eventually run for student council president.

TRIANGLE DAY SCHOOL
4911 Neal Rd., Durham
(919) 383-8800
www.triangledayschool.org

At Triangle Day School, students enjoy Internet access in every classroom. They take music, drama, and art history starting in kindergarten, and can begin foreign language classes at that age. With 150 students from kindergarten up to the eighth grade, it's an intimate atmosphere. Independent and non-sectarian, more than half the school's teachers have advanced degrees. Founded in 1991, the students can walk over a 15-acre site in Durham near a Civil War landmark. Many Triangle Day students go on to the region's best high schools.

TRINITY ACADEMY OF RALEIGH
10224 Baileywick Rd., Raleigh
www.trinityacedemy.com

Trinity's goal is to create thinking Christians. While faith is central to the curriculum, the school prides itself on providing each student with a liberal arts education and challenging them to understand and defend their beliefs. Trinity hopes its students will become eloquent both in speech and on paper. All take logic and rhetoric courses and are encouraged to write frequently. Set in North Raleigh, Trinity takes students from kindergarten to 12th grade. In recent years, 100 percent of its graduates were accepted to college.

TRINITY SCHOOL OF DURHAM AND CHAPEL HILL
4011 Pickett Rd., Durham
(919) 402-8262
www.trinityschoolnc.org

An independent Christian school, Trinity has 60 different congregations represented in its student body. Set on the Orange County line on a 22-acre campus, the school was formed in 1995 by a group of Durham-area churches seeking to combine academic excellence with Christian commitment. By 2000, the school had a permanent building with 160 students, a total that has since risen beyond 400 from kindergarten to 12th grade.

HEALTH CARE

With two medical schools sitting within a dozen miles of each other—Duke in Durham and UNC in Chapel Hill—the bar for health care in the Triangle is high. Both schools operate teaching hospitals and research laboratories that consistently lead to health care breakthroughs, and Duke has been named among the top medical schools and hospitals in the country. Duke and UNC both operate extensive networks of clinics and offsite treatment facilities that extend the reach of their expertise beyond their campuses. A third health network, WakeMed, operates a similarly wide-ranging network. Between these three operations, specialized care for just about any need is available in the Triangle, from neonatal surgery to cancer treatment to rehabilitation centers to geriatrics. Duke is also home to some of the best-known diet and weight loss centers in the country.

HOSPITALS

CHATHAM HOSPITAL
475 Progress Blvd., Siler City
(919) 799-4000
www.chathamhospital.org
Chatham Hospital has served central Chatham County for seven decades. Since 2008, it has been part of UNC Health Care, the state-owned non-profit health care system affiliated with the University of North Carolina School of Medicine. UNC has since opened a new 25-bed hospital 15 miles west of Pittsboro Hospital in Siler City. The hospital has a 24-hour emergency room and offers services including cardiac rehabilitation, diabetes education, physical therapy, surgery, and a sleep lab. A critical care unit, a medical-surgical floor, and a day-surgery department are on site.

More than 70 doctors serve Chatham Hospital, and the staff is strongest in emergency and family medicine and radiology. The facility's radiological capabilities include mammography, ultrasound, and bone densitometry. A 31,000-square-foot expansion to dedicate more room to specialists, physical therapy, and diabetes treatment is underway.

DUKE HEALTH RALEIGH HOSPITAL
3400 Wake Forest Rd., Raleigh
(919) 954-3000
www.dukeraleighhospital.org

Duke Raleigh began its life as Mary Elizabeth Hospital in 1914 and later became Raleigh Community Hospital. Duke University Health System bought the hospital in 1998. Duke Raleigh sits just outside the I-440 Beltline in North Raleigh. It has 186 beds and a 24-hour emergency room.

More than 500 doctors are on staff. Services include treatment in cancer, cardiovascular disease, orthopaedics, wound healing, radiation-oncology, intensive and critical care, same-day surgery, and diabetes center. Surgical specialties available at Duke Raleigh include laser and laparoscopic surgery, cochlear implantation, acoustic neuromas, and newborn hearing screening.

DUKE UNIVERSITY HOSPITAL
2301 Erwin Rd., Durham
(919) 684-8111
Duke University Hospital is the flagship hospital for the Duke University Health System, where the efforts of Duke University's medical and nursing schools as well as its research and teaching expertise combine. Duke University Hospital has about 950 beds and is served by hundreds of physicians who work under the umbrella of Duke University Health System, one of the highest ranked academic hospitals in the country. At Duke Hospital, patients are availed of the wide range of medical specialties taught and researched at Duke University Medical School

and the affiliate hospitals and clinics. Among the specialties at which Duke University Hospital excels are cancer treatment, endocrinology, gastroenterology, gynecology, heart surgery, neurology and neurosurgery, psychiatry, respiratory disease, and urology.

Duke has been a leader in medical research since its inception in the 1920s after a $4 million gift from James Buchanan Duke endowed the hospital, nursing school, and medical school. Today, Duke University Health System employees number more than 14,000. Close to 900 physicians work as residents and fellows, and there are more than 1,500 faculty members. Patients come from around the world and across the country to seek treatment at Duke.

Duke University Health System has more than 200 clinics and treatment facilities in North Carolina and southern Virginia. Most of these are concentrated in the Triangle. They include the Adult Bone Marrow Transplant Outpatient Clinic, the Duke Birthing Center, the Duke Cardiology Clinic and several satellite clinics, Duke Children's Hospital, the Duke Oncology Center, and Duke Radiation Oncology.

Duke is a long-time leader in weight loss practice. The Duke Center for Living is home to the Duke Diet and Fitness Center, one of the oldest residential weight loss centers in the country. Other weight-loss services include the Duke Center for Metabolic and Weight Loss Surgery and the Duke Eating Disorders clinic.

DURHAM REGIONAL HOSPITAL
3643 Roxboro Rd., Durham
(919) 470-4000
Durham Regional Hospital is part of the Duke University Health System. It was formerly Durham County General Hospital and has a long tradition of community service. Duke entered into a long-term partnership with the hospital in 1998. Durham Regional has 369 beds, including a special care nursery, a critical care unit, and a psychiatric unit. Durham Regional also has the inpatient Durham Rehabilitation Institute, Davis Ambulatory Surgical Center, and the only select specialty long-term acute care center in the Triangle. Other

services include gastroenterology, cardiac care, orthopaedic surgery, radiology, urology, and a birthing center.

DURHAM VA MEDICAL CENTER
508 Fulton St., Durham
(919) 286-0411
www.durham.va.gov
The Durham Veteran's Administration hospital serves veterans in 26 surrounding counties. Hospital services include rehabilitation, mental health, counseling on transition to civilian life, primary care, and specialties including neurology, radiation, oncology, audiology, and women's care. A pharmacy is on site. The Durham VA operates outpatient clinics in Durham, Raleigh, Greenville, and Morehead City.

REX
4420 Lake Boone Trail, Raleigh
(919) 784-3100
Rex sits just inside the I-440 Beltline in northwest Raleigh. It is part of UNC Health Care, the state-owned non-profit health care system affiliated with the University of North Carolina at Chapel Hill's School of Medicine. Founded in 1894, it opened in the former home of Governor Charles Manly after a Raleigh tanner named John Rex left money and instructions for its establishment in his will. Today Rex has 665 beds and more than 950 doctors and an emergency room.

On the main Rex campus, services include heart care, surgery, oncology, orthopedic and spine care, and a birthing center. The hospital is also home to a wound healing center, a rehabilitation and nursing care center, a sleep disorders center, a women's services center, and a cancer center. Rex operates more than 20 satellite clinics and centers in Wake County, including wellness centers, cancer centers, and express care clinics.

WAKEMED CARY HOSPITAL
1900 Kildaire Farm Rd., Cary
(919) 350-2300
www.wakemed.org
The non-profit WakeMed health care system opened WakeMed Cary in 1991 to serve Cary

and western Wake County. It has 156 beds and an emergency room. Services offered include women's pavilion and birthing center, an outpatient laboratory, cardiopulmonary and neurodiagnostic services, a sleep center, day surgery, endoscopy, and radiology work.

WAKEMED RALEIGH HOSPITAL
3000 New Bern Ave., Raleigh
(919) 350-8000
www.wakemed.org
WakeMed Raleigh is the flagship hospital of the non-profit WakeMed health care system. Located in southeast Raleigh, WakeMed has 870 beds and almost 1,000 physicians on staff. Its services include cardiac care, critical care, and children's care. It has a freestanding emergency department dedicated solely to children that serves more than 40,000 patients annually. Other services for children at WakeMed include intensive care units for infants and children, children's diabetes and asthma programs, and pediatrics specialists in surgery, neurology, endocrinology, orthopaedics, neonatology, and child development. WakeMed also offers a stroke center, an intensive care unit for neuro patients, a trauma center, and physical rehabilitation care program. WakeMed operates nine satellite campuses in Wake and Johnston counties that provide emergency care, radiology, speech therapy, rehabilitation, and laboratory testing.

REFERRAL SERVICES

New residents looking for primary care physicians or specialists can find referrals via the large health care systems.
- **WakeMed's Doctor Choice** helps Wake County residents find primary care physicians and specialists within their insurance provider networks. Call (919) 350-8900 or search online at www.wakemed.org.
- **Duke Raleigh's online physician directory** is at www.dukeraleighhospital.org/physicians.
- **UNC HealthLink** provides physician referrals at (919) 966-7890 and at http://findadoc.unc healthcare.org.

- To find a doctor in the **Duke University network,** call (888) 275-3853 or go to www .dukehealth.org/physicians.

HEALTH HOTLINES

- **AIDS:** CDC information (800) 232-4636
- **Alzheimer's:** Helpline (800) 228-8738
- **Cancer:** Hotline (800) 422-6237
- **Careline:** Information on public health in NC (800) 662-7030
- **HopeLine of North Carolina:** Crisis hotline for individuals who need someone to listen and offer referrals for issues of suicide, child abuse, domestic violence, sexual assault, mental health, interpersonal relationships, sexual issues, and substance abuse; (919) 231-4525 or (877) 235-4525 (toll free).
- **Interact:** Offers listening and referral services for victims and survivors of domestic violence; (919-828-7740 or 866-291-0855) and sexual assault (919-828-3005 or 866-291-0853).
- **National Child Abuse Hotline:** (800) 422-4453

WALK-IN CLINICS

The area's major area health systems operate clinics for walk-in patients throughout the Triangle. If you have any questions, call the clinic to determine if your health situation is appropriate for the facility.

DUKE URGENT CARE BRIER CREEK
10211 Alm St., Raleigh
(919) 206-4889

DUKE URGENT CARE HILLANDALE
1901 Hillandale Rd. Suite D, Durham
(919) 383-4355

DUKE URGENT CARE KNIGHTDALE
162 Legacy Oaks Dr., Hwy 64 and I-540, Knightdale
(919) 373-1800

DUKE URGENT CARE MORRISVILLE
10950 Chapel Hill Rd., Morrisville
(919) 327-1630

DUKE URGENT CARE SOUTH
5716 Fayetteville Rd., Durham
(919) 572-1868

REX EXPRESS CARE OF CARY
1515 Southwest Cary Parkway, Suite 130,
Cary
(919) 387-3180

REX EXPRESS CARE OF KNIGHTDALE
6602 Knightdale Blvd., Suite 102, Knightdale
(919) 747-5210

REX EXPRESS CARE OF WAKEFIELD
11200 Governor Manly Way, Suite 114,
Raleigh
(919) 570-7660

WAKEMED APEX HEALTHPLEX
120 Healthplex Way, Apex
(919) 350-4300

WAKEMED NORTH HEALTHPLEX
10000 Falls of Neuse Rd., Raleigh
(919) 350-1300

INDEX